Technology
Valuation
Solutions

Technology
Valuation
Solutions

F. PETER BOER

WILEY

John Wiley & Sons, Inc.

Published by John Wiley & Sons, Inc., Hoboken, New Jersey.
Published simultaneously in Canada.

For general information on our other products and services, or technical support, please
contact our Customer Care Department within the United States at 800-762-2974, outside
the United States at 317-572-3993 or fax 317-572-4002.

Wiley also publishes its books in a variety of electronic formats. Some content that appears
in print may not be available in electronic books.

For more information about Wiley products, visit our web site at www.wiley.com.

Designations used by companies to distinguish their products are often claimed by
trademarks. In all instances where the author or publisher is aware of a claim, the product
names appear in Initial Capital letters. Readers, however, should contact the appropriate
companies for more complete information regarding trademarks and registration.

Library of Congress Cataloging-in-Publication Data:
Boer, F. Peter, 1940–
   Technology valuation solutions / F. Peter Boer.
      p. cm.—(Wiley finance series)
   ISBN 0-471-65467-1 (cloth/cd-rom)
   1. Research, Industrial—Evaluation. 2. Research, Industrial—Cost
effectiveness.
   3. Technological innovations. I. Title. II. Series.
T175.B55 2004
658.5'7—dc22   2004005533

Printed in the United States of America.

10 9 8 7 6 5 4 3 2 1

Contents

Preface

Millions of spectators thrill to sports featuring extreme risk. But few understand that the continuous innovation on which our economy is built also depends on managing extreme risk. Competition is fierce, failure is rife, and the value created for the winners (and often the spectators) can be glorious. Relatively few people have played in this arena, and few of those have analyzed their experience in depth.[1] This is stuff worthy of more attention.

The purpose of this book is to share concepts, case histories, and software that I have developed in more than 30 years of direct experience in managing technology and technology-based businesses, as a director of seven firms, and as a consultant and an educator. Most of my students, both in business school and in industrial short courses, have found the combination of a financial perspective, sensible management methods, and real-world experience in technology management to be valuable, if not unique. This book unifies these themes, and shows the way toward practical, value-based research and development (R&D) management.

WHY IS TECHNOLOGY VALUATION IMPORTANT?

No economic phenomenon is more important to the modern world than the creation of wealth through technological innovation. About a half-trillion dollars are spent on R&D globally to ensure this phenomenon continues. The majority of it occurs in private-sector companies, large and small. In their laboratories, scientists and engineers are tasked to invent, improve, develop, and commercialize new or improved products and processes. Over half of the world's economic growth is produced through this mechanism.[2] But technological innovation is a notoriously risky and competitive business. The value of an idea is diminished not only by the risk of technical or commercial failure, but also by the time value of money and the costs of the R&D effort itself. These three dark factors cannot be ignored. Only a small minority of proposed innovations overcome the obstacles and achieve commercial success.[3] It is the flow of these technological gems that propels the world's economy.

Fortunately, there is a real possibility that an innovation will prove far more valuable than its creators dared imagine—a result that has occurred time and time again. The steam engine was first conceived for the limited objective of pumping water from mines; the options it created for innovation in transportation and manufacturing had yet to be envisioned. The applications of the transistor and the laser, major innovations of our own time, were likewise barely imagined by their discoverers.

Balancing the upsides against the downsides in an uncertain world is complex and nonobvious. There is a school of thought that proclaims the effort is not even worth attempting on a quantitative basis; that fundamental technical competence, attention to the right situational factors (attributes), and good judgment will win through. Indeed a leading book on the link between R&D and corporate strategy argues that "the rigor implied by NPV [net present value] or DCF [discounted cash flow] considerations becomes not only meaningless but potentially harmful."[4] That potential for harm must be acknowledged. Its source is found in low-quality, or very narrow, assumptions that make their way into spreadsheet analysis. However, I do not share this view, and believe that powerful modern planning tools such as cash flow analysis, the electronic spreadsheet, decision analysis, and real options can illuminate the issues in ways that no scoring system based on attributes can. If you have a cannon, shoot it! And be aware that some of your competitors are arming themselves with similar weapons to hone their own battle plans.

AIM OF THIS BOOK

My specific aim is to present a method by which those charged with planning innovation can easily and rapidly calculate the value of a project or project proposal, and a method that takes full account of its risks. I call this financial model *risk-adjusted valuation*. Understanding the method will be fostered by working through detailed examples, each based on a real-world business scenario.

It is a practical imperative that such a calculation be based on a limited set of input parameters, and that these parameters be readily available to the practitioners. The world changes rapidly and abounds with uncertainty, so in this sphere ease of use often outweighs accuracy. My experience is that in a real company any methods that require detailed consultation and verification with a host of internal experts will die of their own weight. By contrast, analyses that are based on numbers from budgets, five-year forecasts, and historical financial ratios, all readily available business documents, will win through.

It is vital that the software be simple and transparent, even though some of the algorithms themselves, such as the Black-Scholes formula, the Markowitz portfolio optimization algorithm, and the growth-in-perpetuity equation, may be mathematically challenging. A "black box" approach will not earn trust. A practical test that these conditions are met is that the software produces the obvious answer for simple cases. Complexity can then be added as desired, while confidence is maintained. For example, I have shown that the Black-Scholes options value converges exactly to a simple decision tree (as it should) when the volatility parameter is set to zero, and the growth-in-perpetuity formula gives a result that is invariant to the choice of horizon year.

Once these technical issues are mastered, the rewards come quickly. The immediate benefit is the ability to see the value of a project at each of its stages (outputs) on the same screen as perhaps two dozen input parameters. A host of what-if questions can be answered in a few keystrokes.

Most research managers will immediately understand the usefulness of a transparent one-step process for comparing the risk-reward profiles of the projects in their R&D portfolio. It is invaluable for distributing scarce resources. However, risk-adjusted valuation has implications beyond research—for transaction support and for corporate strategy.

As an example of a transaction, a company may wish to weigh commercializing the fruits of its research directly, doing so in concert with a strategic partner, evaluating licensing its technology to a third party, or, in our global economy, some combination of these strategies. A valuation can be performed for each alternative course to find the solution that maximizes value. The analysis will inevitably guide the negotiating positions taken by those charged to reach a deal.

Another type of transaction is to spin off technology into a start-up, consisting of inventors, entrepreneurs, and financial backers. Valuation will be at the heart of this exercise. By calculating the buildup in value of the start-up company as it reaches each of a series of R&D milestones, it is possible to estimate the ownership at each stage for the founders and employees, and for the investors in each financing round. Will these be reasonable for all concerned?

A broader consequence is that these methods can be applied to an entire R&D portfolio to estimate the value that a company may have in its research pipeline. This value may be more than the sum of individual projects, for value may be added by diversification and economy of scale. From the point of view of a venture capital fund, the risk-adjusted valuation method will similarly track the buildup value of an investment portfolio. It will also make apparent how much further investment is needed to realize that value.

WHO SHOULD READ THIS BOOK

An important user community consists of those R&D executives and planners, at all levels, with a need to justify their recommendations regarding the investment of R&D resources. This task is an inevitable part of both the annual budget and various long-term planning exercises. Part of their audience will be persons with financial training who lack familiarity with R&D. In my experience, such people appreciate an effort to change the dialogue from a qualitative to a quantitative assessment of the financial impact of new technology, and from a "trust me" or "trust my instincts and experience" approach to a quantitative estimate of the risk elements.

A second user community will be R&D practitioners with a need or desire to upgrade their financial savvy. They may engage for a positive reason—they are high performers slated for increased responsibility—or for a negative reason—their ideas have too often failed to convince management and they need to improve their understanding of the business environment. For example, a newly minted PhD biologist may not understand why a project that earns a profit may still destroy value. But she will need to understand this paradox on her path to becoming vice president of R&D!

A third user community will be students enrolled in business courses that deal with technology investment and management. I have used variations of the case studies in this book in my courses at the Yale University School of Management, and believe there is ample material herein to support a half semester or more of such a course. Other material has been added to round out this book.

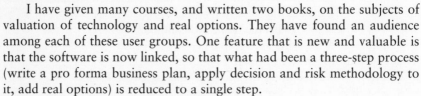

I have given many courses, and written two books, on the subjects of valuation of technology and real options. They have found an audience among each of these user groups. One feature that is new and valuable is that the software is now linked, so that what had been a three-step process (write a pro forma business plan, apply decision and risk methodology to it, add real options) is reduced to a single step.

STRUCTURE OF THIS BOOK

This book is structured as a series of situations or cases requiring analysis. A problem is posed, and the solution is outlined. In the process the methodology is illustrated and its features discussed. Some of the cases are designed primarily to illustrate methods. Other cases provide an R&D practitioner's perspective of what the issues feel like at each stage of an

R&D project. The book lends itself to self-study by a scientist, engineer, or manager who wishes to become literate in the tools of technology valuation. The Microsoft Excel templates on the accompanying CD-ROM, contain extensive comments as well as depict the solution (references to the CD-ROM are indicated by the CD icon in the margins). Readers can readily substitute their own numbers into any of my spreadsheets. If they feel the template misses important features of their business models, they can make fundamental modifications in the models to capture them.

The pedagogical philosophy I have chosen is not unlike the choices one has for learning a new computer program. There are two well-recognized alternatives: read the manual, or jump right in. Even though the latter approach usually implies resorting to the manual when one is stymied, in practice, many of us find it to be more efficient. Reading the manual is more meaningful after one encounters some of the pitfalls.

In my earlier book *The Valuation of Technology*,[5] it took eight chapters to prepare the groundwork for a pro forma business plan. In this book, we will "jump right in" in Chapter 4. This condensed approach has been tested in a new format I have developed for fast-paced one-day workshops, which now seem to be preferred by industrial customers to more comprehensive three-day courses. However, in this more concise format, some of the fundamentals must inevitably be glossed over. Readers are advised to fill any gaps in their understanding, since a credible answer will invariably depend on credible assumptions. These gaps can be filled in two ways: (1) through discussion sections in this book that address alternative approaches and pitfalls and (2) by reading the material referenced in endnotes, including sections of *The Valuation of Technology* that address these subjects in more detail.

Chapter 1 reviews the concepts of discounted cash flow analysis and the cost of capital using a biotechnology licensing case that requires a decision between a smaller cash payment now and larger payments later.

Chapter 2 deals with horizon value, an important, if somewhat complex, calculation. An example from the plastics industry is used to illustrate five methods for calculating this key parameter. Two are based on liquidation scenarios, two are based on comparisons with other ongoing businesses, and the last is based on an estimate of future cash flows.

Chapter 3 addresses risk. As noted earlier, R&D management is very much the art of creating value by managing an extraordinary degree of risk. The quantitative tools needed to transform R&D practice from what many considered an art to an analytical science have evolved rapidly in the past two decades.[6] The decision tree method for evaluating unique risk and the real options method for evaluating market risk are introduced with examples based on a bioremediation project and an investment in a new line of computers, respectively. Then a major step forward is outlined: integrating decision and risk analysis, real options, and stage-gate methodologies, using the bioremediation case again. Subsequent chapters will incorporate all of these tools, which had hitherto been introduced separately, in combination. And they will be applied to quite different cases.

Chapter 4 discusses a medical device, which is both a new-to-the-world invention and a new application. This circumstance is the most challenging and uncertain in both execution and planning. The case is illustrative of the thought processes and data required to make an initial decision as to whether to fund a big idea.

Chapter 5 discusses a new-to-the-world packaging material for which applications already exist. In this chapter, all the techniques introduced earlier (financial statements, decision trees, and real options) are integrated into a powerful model, allowing the planner to answer all the what-if questions, whether they regard timing, R&D risk, pricing uncertainty, capital investment, or an array of other business and financial parameters.

Chapter 6 explores another realm of technology valuation—the start-up company whose only asset is its R&D portfolio. How should such a company be valued? I show how the template used for valuing a project inside an established company can be transposed to estimate shareholder value at each milestone in the life of a start-up. If equity must be sold to finance subsequent research, the amount that remains for founders and earlier-round investors can be calculated based on the perceived value of the technology and the costs of proceeding forward. The case studies feature a biomed start-up and an instrument company.

Chapter 7 deals with a genuine technology breakthrough in the petrochemical industry. Process breakthroughs often have the economic effect of stealing most future growth from older processes, as well as replacing aging plants as they become uneconomic.

Chapter 8 addresses product improvements (in a textile application). Product improvement is for most operating firms the single largest category of R&D activity. This case involves the concept of how the value created is shared between supplier and customer, and offers a broad discussion of value in use.

The next two chapters deal with portfolios. Chapter 9 explores the concept of a balanced R&D portfolio, and the structural considerations that make balance an imperative. In this chapter, I relate my personal experiences in inheriting and transforming such a portfolio at W. R. Grace & Company, with an analysis of the outcomes of five key projects and the forces that drove these outcomes. This chapter also contains a discussion of the pros and cons of financial modeling.

Finally, Chapter 10 looks at the question of whether a portfolio can be worth more than the sum of its component projects, via diversification of risk and economies of scale. The answer is clearly yes. It presents a detailed case that applies financial portfolio theory to the R&D situation, followed by a critique of the strengths and weaknesses of this approach.

ORIGINS OF THIS BOOK

This book builds on what I have presented before (in two books and half a dozen articles) with new insights and expanded case material. Most of the cases derive from my personal business experience, but I have generally simplified detail, altered actual numbers, and in some cases combined aspects of two or more real situations into a single case. These changes were made for pedagogical reasons, to disguise actual firms, and to avoid disclosing sensitive data. More importantly, the cases encapsulate the spirit and feel of real problems.

My first book, *The Valuation of Technology: Business and Financial Issues in R&D*, was aimed at an audience similar to this one. It illustrated advanced techniques for assessing R&D risk (such as decision trees, real options, and Monte Carlo calculations) but in hindsight dealt with these subjects too briefly, all within a single chapter. This is a rich area and there is a need for an expanded and integrated treatment.

My second book, *The Real Options Solution: Finding Total Value in a High-Risk World* (John Wiley & Sons, 2002), explored the inferences of a key insight: that *plans are options*. This statement has important consequences for the methods by which opportunities, and hence companies that possess opportunities, should be valued. Its implications are still poorly recognized. However, in that book, I chose to make my case at a level aimed at the general business reader, rather than the planning professional. It led one reviewer to comment that he enjoyed the insights about value creation, but was looking forward to a second book containing detailed examples. Fair enough—here it is.

The decisive impetus for this book was the realization that I could seamlessly link decision trees to real options. R&D executives have increasingly relied on stage-gate methods for managing R&D processes,[7] and these models lent themselves readily to decision tree analysis. But in options terms, each successfully completed stage of a project could be considered as the purchase of an option to enter the next stage. Were these two viewpoints separate formulations of the risk equation or could they be integrated? When I realized[8] they were equivalent, a one-step analysis came into view and the backbone of a new book was before me.

In writing books, one needs to make editorial choices, and one of mine is not to offer another book about real options methods. A host of recent books cover this area more than adequately,[9] and I see my focus, based on my background as an R&D practitioner, as linking the existing methodology and software to the technology community and the R&D process, rather than in refinements in real options methodology. One of my biases is that the closed-form, "plug and chug," Black-Scholes equation is user-friendly and transparent, and allows the practitioner to focus on the other large uncertainties inherent in valuing R&D projects.

I also admit to being not particularly concerned by accounting arcana. For example, different classes of assets required by a project must be depreciated at different rates. Tax laws allow accelerated depreciation, which accelerates cash flow, an economic incentive, and in the process creates liabilities called deferred taxes. The application of tax strategies is highly situational and may have more to do with the firm than with the project. I believe good enough results for *decision support* can be obtained using average asset life and average effective tax rates, which can largely balance errors introduced by lack of accounting precision. However, when *transaction support* is the objective and legalities are in play, one must get the accountants involved, which in practice means to invite them to rework the pro forma business plan.

The R&D environment is in any case highly dynamic, since *every new data point affects valuation*. The data may be technical, or it may relate to customers or competition. If the new data is adverse, valuation goes down (costs are increased while rewards are reduced); if it is favorable, valuation correspondingly increases. Less obviously, when the data comes in about as expected, valuation also goes up, because risk has been reduced. Given this intrinsic variability in value along the time dimension, precision in methodology or accounting at any instant is of marginal worth from a strategic viewpoint.

ACKNOWLEDGMENTS

The true sources of the ideas in this book are my many colleagues in industry, academia, and government with whom I have shared experiences over four decades. They are too many to mention by name, but should they be reading this volume, my appreciation for the fun of working together on exciting business problems and novel technologies is deeply felt. My wife, Ellen, has been a wonderful source of inspiration for my writing activities, and her unstinting support is very much appreciated.

In producing the manuscript itself, I wish to thank Jessica Colvin Boer (Harvard MBA, 1998) and Louis Hegedus for their time and care in offering detailed critiques of some chapters and sections. My assistant, May Adams, as always, has provided me with terrific administrative help. The continuing support of John Wiley & Sons, and especially Jeanne Glasser, is gratefully acknowledged.

F. PETER BOER

Boynton Beach, Florida
July 2004

Technology
Valuation
Solutions

"I'll Teach You
the Value of Money"

The purpose of this chapter is to present two building blocks that are essential for calculating the value of a technology proposal—discounted cash flow (DCF) and the cost of capital. Each of these tools is individually powerful and can be used to analyze real-world problems.

DISCOUNTED CASH FLOW

Case 1: The Licensing Manager's Dilemma: Cash Now
or More Cash Later?

MabPharma is a fictitious research-based company specializing in the discovery of monoclonal antibodies that inhibit metastatic cancer. One of their candidate drugs is in late-stage clinical trials and the results appear at least as promising as several other monoclonal products that have already received Food and Drug Administration (FDA) approval. A New Drug Application (NDA) has been filed, and all indications are that approval is imminent. However, MabPharma does not wish to invest in the assets required to manufacture and market this product, and would prefer instead to invest further resources in exploiting the company's strong technology lead in monoclonal drug development.

Its chief licensing executive, Bill Jones, has been negotiating with a leading marketer of anticancer drugs, BMX Pharma, and he has been offered a royalty of 8 percent of net sales, which are estimated to be $100 million two years from now, rising linearly to $200 million 12 years hence, when MabPharma's patent will have expired, and no further royalties would be paid. At a recent meeting, Jones was surprised to receive an offer of a paid-up license for $40 million.

1

MabPharma will soon need to raise cash for its future research investments, and because of its current and past research and development (R&D) expenses, does not expect to pay taxes on its licensing income. MabPharma's treasurer, Sally Molnar, informs Jones that MabPharma's cost of capital is 22 percent. How she derived this number is important, and will be discussed later in this chapter.

Should Jones accept this offer to buy the license or insist on 8 percent for 12 years, assuming all forecasts and data are accurate?

Solution to Case 1

This is a basic problem in discounted cash flow analysis.[1] The central concept is that a sum earned in a future year must be discounted to the present at the rate required to earn that sum in the future year. If $1.00 is a sum that will be earned one year from now, a firm whose cost of capital is 22 percent would have to invest $1.00/(1.22) = $0.82 today at a 22 percent rate of return to have that dollar next year. In other words, a dollar earned next year is worth 82 cents today. If a 22 percent rate of return cannot be achieved, an 82-cent investment to earn that dollar should not be made.

What about two years hence? A dollar earned two years out is worth $0.82/1.22 = 1.00/(1.22)^2 = $0.671. Each subsequent year's earnings will be similarly discounted. Figure 1.1 summarizes the cash flows; let's focus first on Jones' decision.

From the point of view of absolute dollars, Jones' first instinct is to reject the offer. He is being asked to trade $40 million for a revenue stream of $132 million (column 3 of Figure 1.1, "Subtotal" line). It seems blatantly unfair.

But Sally Molnar explains why factoring in a cost of capital of 22 percent puts the choice in a different light. MabPharma will have to raise at least $40 million to support its future research, and receiving cash from BMX avoids the sizable cost of that capital. At a 22 percent discount rate, the revenue stream from a running royalty is worth only $34.8 million (column 4), meaning that $40 million up front is $5.2 million better. In financial parlance, the present value (PV) of the cash flow stream is $34.8 million, but the net present value (NPV) is a positive $5.2 million.

This offer is worth $5.2 million and if it is a final offer, Jones should accept it. But we shall soon see that he has considerable negotiating room.

Discussion

The value of a technology breakthrough, even when risks are fully accounted for, is subject to the cost of capital. Ralph Landau, one of the

FIGURE 1.1 Licensing Revenues

Royalty Rate as Percent of Revenues	8%
MabPharma Cost of Capital	22%
BMX Cost of Capital	12%

Year	Revenues	Cash Flow from Royalties	DCF MabPharma	DCF BMX
0	$ 0	-$ 40,000,000	$40,000,000	-$40,000,000
1	$ 0	$ 0	$ 0	$ 0
2	$100,000,000	$ 8,000,000	-$ 5,374,899	$ 6,377,551
3	$110,000,000	$ 8,800,000	-$ 4,846,221	$ 6,263,666
4	$120,000,000	$ 9,600,000	-$ 4,333,431	$ 6,100,974
5	$130,000,000	$ 10,400,000	-$ 3,847,992	$ 5,901,239
6	$140,000,000	$ 11,200,000	-$ 3,396,714	$ 5,674,269
7	$150,000,000	$ 12,000,000	-$ 2,983,063	$ 5,428,191
8	$160,000,000	$ 12,800,000	-$ 2,608,143	$ 5,169,705
9	$170,000,000	$ 13,600,000	-$ 2,271,436	$ 4,904,296
10	$180,000,000	$ 14,400,000	-$ 1,971,352	$ 4,636,415
11	$190,000,000	$ 15,200,000	-$ 1,705,632	$ 4,369,637
12	$200,000,000	$ 16,000,000	-$ 1,471,641	$ 4,106,801
Subtotal 2–12 Present value	$132,000,000	$ 92,000,000	-$34,810,525	$58,932,744
Net present value		$ 92,000,000	$ 5,189,475	$18,932,744
Internal rate of return (IRR)		19.1%		

greatest technical innovators in the petrochemical industry, eloquently explained his illuminating and expensive experience with his firm Halcon (the technology innovator) and its joint venture partner, Arco, in just these terms. Describing the circumstances when interest rates soared in 1979, Landau relates, "Technology strategy, which had built Halcon's past successes, gave way to concerns for sheer survival; could the next interest payment be met? Arco reopened the original partnership agreement, and I vividly remember Arco's financial head saying, 'I'll teach you the value of money.' . . . Arco had much deeper pockets and a greater ability to make the interest payments. Finance was decisive over even great technology. These circumstances forced Halcon to sell out its 50 percent interest to Arco."[2]

Finally, a word about internal rate of return (IRR). IRR is defined as the rate at which a string of positive and negative cash flows has an NPV of zero. Calculating IRR is often a revealing exercise, for it is another measure of how well a project is achieving a return that meets investor expectations. In the present example, discounting by the IRR of 19.1 percent makes the present value of the running royalties exactly $40 million. Since the initial investment is $40 million, the NPV is zero. (Excel has an algorithm for calculating IRR in its "Functions" menu.)

Because the IRR (19.1 percent) of the initial offer is intermediate between the costs of capital of the two parties (BMX's cost of capital is 12 percent), it makes financial sense to transfer the investment opportunity to the financially stronger party. These rates indirectly reflect an investor preference for commercialization by the more stable and experienced firm.

COST OF CAPITAL

This section discusses the practical aspects of estimating cost of capital, and introduces templates for users to apply to their own situations.

Case 2: Why MabPharma's Money Seems So Expensive

Sally Molnar has a difficult job. MabPharma's top management is dominated by its founders, two distinguished professors from Allstate University, who are not only pursuing their lifetime dream of an important cancer cure, but also hoping to profit from it. The company recently went public with the assistance of its venture capital investors. The chief financial officer (CFO) is an accountant who joined the company when it was young, having impressed one of the founders by his tax acumen. Sally was hired, on the suggestion of one of the directors, to complement the CFO's accounting skills with a deeper knowledge of corporate finance, which she gained based on her MBA and three years' experience with an investment bank. Both the founders and the staff scientists intuitively think the cost of capital should be related to interest rates they pay or receive from banks. Their instinct is to walk away from the BMX deal. Nor are they receptive to suggestions that the company must quickly find sources of cash, or that some favorite long-term projects may be financially unsupportable. "Short-term thinking," they snort. Sally determines to prove her value by assisting Bill Jones with the BMX deal, and later apply financial analysis to the R&D portfolio to be sure the firm's reach does not exceed its grasp.

The BMX offer is a shrewd one. The BMX financial team understands that MabPharma is the weaker party, and proposes to take most of the value created by transferring the technology. Sally determines to get some of it back, reasoning that each party wins over a fairly broad range, and in the end, the pressure of investors on both parties may drive them into the middle ground.

Sally does some research. She finds that the market value of BMX stock is $40 billion, its shareholder's equity is $12 billion, and it holds $8 billion in long-term debt. The volatility of BMX stock is about average for an S&P 500 company and is characterized by a beta of 1.00. The volatility of MabPharma stock is typical for a biotechnology company; its beta is 2.00.

The interest rate on bonds for companies with BMX's credit rating is currently 7 percent. Absent any operating cash flow, MabPharma has no significant borrowing capacity. The current interest on Treasury bills is 5 percent. Stocks on average have earned a premium above Treasury bills of 8.4 percent over the past 70 years. The corporate tax rate is 38 percent.

Based on this data, what amount should Sally advise Bill Jones to counteroffer?

Solution to Case 2

Sally's first task is to calculate the weighted average cost of capital (WACC) for BMX and MabPharma. For this purpose she chooses the widely understood Capital Asset Pricing Model (CAPM),[3] reasoning that her financial counterparts in BMX will probably accept arguments based on it.

Her first step is to determine the weight of equity to debt in each company's financing plan. The calculation is trivial for MabPharma. The only way it can raise money is to sell equity through a secondary stock offering. It has no significant receivables, property, or inventory to support collateralized debt. It will be 100 percent equity financed until it becomes a profitable operating company.

The BMX calculation is more complex (see Figure 1.2). As stated in its annual report, its book value (value of its shareholder's equity) is $12 billion, and it has $8 billion in outstanding debt. So it appears as BMX is financed at 40 percent debt and 60 percent equity, and indeed cites that ratio in its financial reports. But in fact CAPM uses *market value* to determine the weighting. (After all, if BMX seeks to sell shares, it will do so based on the fair market value, not the "book" or accounting value.) The value of BMX's outstanding shares is $40 billion. The market value of its debt will also differ from the accounting value, but usually only slightly, so assume it remains $8 billion. For purposes of calculating WACC, BMX is 83.3 percent equity financed ($40B/$48B) and 16.7 percent debt financed.

FIGURE 1.2   Weighted Average Cost of Capital by the
Capital Asset Pricing Model

WACC = % Debt × After-Tax Cost of Debt + % Equity
             × Cost of Equity
Cost of Equity = Risk-Free Rate + Beta × Risk Premium

Item	BMX	MabPharma
Tax rate	38%	0%
Book value	$12 billion	$0
Market value	$40 billion	$0
Debt	$8 billion	$0
Bonds interest rate	7%	—
Risk-free rate	5%	5%
Beta	1.00	2.00
Risk premium	8.4%	16.8%
WACC	11.89%	21.80%

The after-tax cost of BMX debt will be 62 percent of the pretax interest: 0.62 × 7 percent, or 4.34 percent. It's too bad it's such a small part of
the weighted equation.

The cost of equity will be the 5 percent risk-free rate (Treasury bills)
plus the calculated risk premium. The difference between the risk-free
Treasury bill rate and the return on market has averaged to be 8.4 percent over a period of 69 years.[4] For BMX (beta = 1.00) the risk premium
is 8.4 percent, and for MabPharma (beta = 2.00) it is 16.8 percent, giving costs of equity of 13.4 percent and 21.8 percent, respectively. Using
the weighting factors referred to earlier, the respective WACCs are then
11.89 percent and 21.8 percent (which round to 12 percent and 22 percent, respectively).

Sally next considers the transaction from the BMX viewpoint. BMX is
a multibillion-dollar drug company with a diversified product line. Its cost
of capital is only 12 percent—lenders and underwriters alike will support
either a debt issue or a secondary stock offering, and its retained earnings
will in any case support $40 million investments[5] in promising new tech-
nology. BMX is very excited by the potential of this new drug to add to its
product revenues, its growth rate, and shareholder value. For BMX, a $40
million outlay will avert paying a cash flow stream valued at $58.9 million,
giving a positive NPV of $18.9 million (Figure 1.1, column 5). The up-
front payment is utterly rational, and BMX knows it presents a win-win

situation for both sides. But BMX gets the better of the deal, gaining $18.9 million versus MabPharma's $5.2 million.

Sally advises Jones that there is a total of $24.1 million of value on the table that can be negotiated without either party being hurt. She suggests that Jones counteroffer $47 million, which would split the difference.

On the lower end, an offer of at least $41 million would correspond to the "25 percent rule," which suggests 25 percent of $24 million or $6 million as the minimum fair share of the value due the licensor. But if Jones is persuasive, he may well get the offer raised to $43 million and obtain one-third or $8 million of the $24 million.

Test these solutions in the software version of Figure 1.2.

DISCUSSION OF BETA AND ANOTHER EXAMPLE

Behind CAPM is the plausible notion that investors demand a risk premium for volatility, and that the premium will be higher for more volatile stocks. Beta is basically a measure of the volatility of a stock, or a class of stocks, as compared to the volatility of the average S&P 500 stock. More mathematically, beta is the ratio of the covariance of the return on a specific stock to that of the S&P 500 index, divided by the variance of the S&P 500. Brokerage reports generally include an estimate of beta, though these may differ slightly based on the methods of calculation. But it is quite possible to calculate it directly, as in the following example, which tracks a real case.

As shown in Figure 1.3, the first step was to obtain the value of the S&P 500 index for each applicable year (available on the Internet). The year-to-year S&P 500 return is calculated in the next column. The stock price of the firm (developed by an independent appraiser) was obtained from the company's records, and a column of year-to-year returns for its shares is calculated. Beta is calculated using two functions in Excel, COVAR(S&P 500 Return, Firm Return) divided by VARP(S&P 500 Return). This quotient gives beta as 0.757.

The right-hand side of Figure 1.3 gives the rest of the CAPM calculation. The 10-year bond rate was 4.2 percent. The equity premium was taken as 5 percent, the high end of the range recommended by Copeland and others.[6] CAPM gives a cost of equity of 7.99 percent. The cost of debt was estimated from the firm's financial statements by dividing the interest paid by the debt.

To get the weighting factors, the market value of equity was calculated from the most recent stock price times the number of common shares,

FIGURE 1.3 Cost of Capital for Defense/Aerospace Firm

Year	30-Jun S&P 500	S&P 500 Return	Stock Price	Firm Return	Item	Firm Value	Sector Value
1990	358.02		$ 5.62		Beta	0.757	0.8
1991	371.16	3.67%	$ 4.60	−18.15%	10-year bond	4.20%	
1992	408.14	9.96%	$10.48	127.83%	Risk premium	5.00%	
1993	450.53	10.39%	$ 4.30	−58.97%	Cost of equity	7.99%	7.99%
1994	444.27	−1.39%	$ 4.62	7.44%	Interest	$827	
1995	544.75	22.62%	$ 4.62	0.00%	Debt (M$)	$9,824	
1996	670.63	23.11%	$ 7.82	69.26%	Cost of debt	8.42%	
1997	885.14	31.99%	$ 9.22	17.90%	Shares		
1998	1,133.84	28.10%	$12.58	36.44%	outstanding	1,781,673	
1999	1,372.91	21.08%	$14.28	13.51%	Market value		
2000	1,454.60	5.95%	$16.98	18.91%	of equity	$29,790	
2001	1,224.42	−15.82%	$18.22	7.30%	Percent debt	24.80%	
2002	990.64	−19.09%	$15.92	−12.62%	Percent equity	75.20%	67.82%
2003	974.50	−1.63%	$16.72	5.03%	Tax rate	39.00%	
					Cost of		
					capital	7.28%	7.25%

Defense/Aerospace Sector (August 2003) Number of Firms	Beta	Cost of Equity	E/(D + E)	Cost of Capital
77	0.8	7.99%	67.82%	7.25%

Source: A. Damodaran, www.stern.nyu.edu/~adamodar/New_Home_Page.

while the market value of the debt was assumed to equal the book value of the debt. The calculated cost of capital or WACC is 7.28 percent.

These numbers, generated from financial records alone, correlate very well with a data base[7] of 77 apparently comparable companies, as shown in the bottom of Figure 1.3. The agreement is sufficiently close to be partly fortuitous, although there was no attempt to select data to improve the fit: Beta for the comparator companies was 0.8 (versus 0.757), the cost of equity was 7.99 percent versus 7.99 percent, and the cost of capital 7.25 percent versus 7.28 percent.

As the example shows, the CAPM is straightforward and user-friendly but some caveats should accompany this discussion. First, while CAPM is broadly understood and used in the financial community, it has critics, and there are alternate theories. Second, cost of capital changes with market conditions, and so one must really consider average cost of capital over a business cycle. There will be times when MabPharma will simply not be able to raise equity, and other times when its high stock price will make equity cheap. The corporate treasurer in practice has a broad choice of financing vehicles, and, within constraints, will shop for the least expensive alternative.

It is also quite clear from our examples that debt financing, with its tax shield, is initially very inexpensive. Some debt is very attractive. However, there are limits to how much one can obtain at affordable rates. Too much debt, and rates will approach junk-bond levels. A heavy interest burden may constrain management from making the best decision from a value standpoint. Therefore, corporate cost of capital is largely driven by the equity portion of its capitalization.

CHAPTER 2

Horizon Value by Five Methods

A central issue in technology valuation, and especially with early-stage technology, is how to treat cash flows that will occur well into the future. Such cash flows may account for a significant portion, even a dominant portion, of project value. The purpose of this chapter is to introduce the critical concept of horizon value, suggest five methods for calculating it, and discuss how to select the most appropriate method.

In addition to addressing one of the central problems in project valuation, this chapter is valuable because it relates a number of alternative approaches to valuation: liquidation, transactions involving comparable assets, and cash generation. The same general principles apply whether the transaction is a real one in the current year or a hypothetical one in the horizon year.

The placement of this chapter in the book may be problematic to some readers. The material is essential to the following chapters, but is highly technical, and the detail may not seem important until the reader has confronted this problem. Skimming this chapter and returning to it later may be a good strategy for such readers.

Case 3: Horizon Value For A New Engineering Plastic

The research department of Performance Plastics, Inc. (PPI), has completed development of a new lightweight engineering polymer that has a clear track for replacing metal parts in automobiles. Parts made from this plastic have already passed stringent torture tests with automotive majors, who are anxious to use it to lower their average fleet mileage standards. The product is patented, and after achieving full marketplace acceptance, likely to take 10 years, it is expected to grow indefinitely at 5 percent per annum, in line with other engineering plastics.

PPI's financial evaluation team, following corporate guidelines, has developed a detailed cash flow projection for the first 10 years of this product's life (the details of which are discussed in Case 8 in Chapter 5), and has calculated an NPV of –$7.23 million at PPI's 12 percent cost of capital and an IRR of 7.1 percent. With a negative NPV, the project is under threat of being shut down. R&D's finance chief, Louise Thomas, argues that the guidelines are wrong, that this project is very attractive and will earn more than the cost of capital even in a liquidation scenario. She politely suggests that the approach to horizon value in the guidelines is outdated, and requests the opportunity to make her case.

An agreement is reached where horizon value will be calculated in year 12 by five different methods, so that the decision makers can view the results. Accordingly, the financial projection is extended for another three years, assuming 5 percent revenue growth. The results are shown, in millions of dollars, in Figure 2.1. Louise explains her logic in the following sections, and the solution to Case 3 is given at the end of the chapter.

As a start, no one wants to look at a spreadsheet with 30 or more years of projections, particularly if the outermost years add little to the analysis. So most calculations cut off at a "horizon year," which is equivalent to selling or liquidating the business at that time for an amount of cash equal to its "horizon value."[1] One of the central issues in valuation is how to treat cash flows that will occur in the distant, or somewhat distant, future. Just because the future is distant and murky does not mean it is unimportant. Hindsight tells us that many seminal inventions, from electricity and the railroad in the nineteenth century to jet airliners and genetically engineered crops in the twentieth, struggled for a dozen years or more before they brought significant profits to their owners. Delays can be imposed by the need to make an invention customer-friendly; for the resolution of legal, safety, and regulatory issues; and by the daunting investments required to build a manufacturing and

FIGURE 2.1   Case 3 Financial Outlook at Horizon Year ($ Millions)

Year	Free Cash Flow	EBITDA	After-Tax Income	Working Capital	Total Capital
11	$15.8	$27.6	$16.1	$12.0	$30.6
12	$16.7	$29.1	$16.8	$12.6	$30.7
13	$17.6	$30.5	$17.6	$13.2	$30.7

marketing infrastructure. Even when penalized by the time value of money, for some projects a large portion of the total value will be incorporated in the horizon value.

Moreover, the method of calculation can be a target for skeptics and the basis for it questioned, so the analyst should be prepared to defend his work.

I use five different methods of calculating horizon value, all of which key off the same financial statement. Two of these assume a liquidation scenario, while the remaining three assume an ongoing business. Typically, the former two give a significantly lower figure than the latter three, which in turn should produce results that are fairly close to one another. The choice then boils down to a judgment about which method best fits the business scenario and/or the client's preferred way of thinking.

LIQUIDATION APPROACHES

It has been held that for purposes of being conservative, horizon value should be taken as zero. This is nonsense. In a real-world liquidation one will sell or convert the last of the inventory, and one will certainly collect the receivables. Therefore, at a minimum, the working capital will be converted to cash. This simple scenario defines horizon value Method #1.

It is likely as well that fixed assets, such as property, plant, and equipment, can be sold or salvaged. If the accounting value of these assets, based on initial cost less depreciation, is reasonably accurate, the business can be liquidated for the book value of the assets—that is, its working and fixed capital. This scenario defines horizon value Method #2.

Both of these scenarios implicitly assume that after a certain time a business cannot be run for profit and is better off liquidated. The general reason is that an ongoing business is soon expected to incur operating losses (or at least sufficiently low profits that liquidation is the better economic course). Some of the specific reasons might be: natural resource depletion, patent expiration, contract expiration, a new environmental standard, the expected loss of a key supplier or customer, and the arrival of a formidable competitor. If these conditions apply to the business in question, an investor in a project will prudently assume liquidation at the time of the unwelcome event in his horizon value calculation. As a consequence of such reasoning, the owner of an aging plant may cease making capital investments aimed at productivity improvement, because shutting down will soon offer the best economics.

There are even some assets that may have a negative horizon value. A depleted strip mine or a chemical manufacturing site must be remediated before the land can be sold. A nuclear power plant or an offshore oil production platform must be safely decommissioned. Increasingly, accounting standards are requiring firms to establish reserves for these situations, and this amount, if accurate, would logically be deducted from final cash expected from sale of the assets. There may be other closing costs as well, such as termination packages for employees.

In such complex situations, it is reasonable to estimate horizon value by developing a likely liquidation scenario and calculating its financial impact.

COMPARABLE TRANSACTIONS

The use of comparables for valuation purposes is a widely accepted business practice. For example, in real estate, one way of valuing your unique home would be to look at the prices for transactions of comparable pieces of real estate, and then adjusting for the differences. Stock pickers have long relied on price-earnings (P/E) ratios to value stocks. If Company X is the leader in a stable industry and has a P/E ratio of 15 times earnings, Company Y, which is considered to be not quite as well managed, may be valued at 14 times earnings. The stocks are likely to move in tandem with the overall stock market, but be individually adjusted for favorable or unfavorable developments when they are material.

Anticipated growth rates are important: Other factors being equal, P/E ratios are higher for more rapidly growing businesses. Typically, single-digit P/E ratios are applied to companies that experience low or negative growth; large multiples (30+) can occur in aggressive growth situations, while a large band of companies with moderate to strong growth cluster at multiples in the 12 to 25 range.

The P/E ratio, then, becomes Method #3 for estimating horizon value. Based on an industry category and long-term growth rate, the analyst estimates a reasonable ratio and multiplies it by the net income projected for the horizon year. The major advantage of the P/E method is that it is intuitive; every investor has a sense for what is reasonable. The drawback is that the standard may be implicitly flawed: A publicly traded company is not a perfect analogy for a business unit or project because the net income of the company includes charges for interest on a level of debt that may exist for reasons unrelated to the business or the project. The publicly traded company may also incur other charges to net income due to special circumstances, such as ongoing expenses related to litigation. While a business unit should properly be charged for the cost of capital and for reasonable administrative costs, nonoperating costs are irrelevant, and would not be considered if the unit were to be sold to a very different company.

These problems with P/E are largely averted when one uses earnings before interest, tax, depreciation and amortization (EBITDA) as the basis of comparison. EBITDA is the portion of pretax operating cash flow that excludes changes in working capital. In fact, the EBITDA method is the preferred approach of valuation professionals: When businesses are bought and sold in an industry, the transactions usually fall within a narrow band of EBITDA ratios unless there are special circumstances. In the chemical industry, an EBITDA of 6 to 7 has been established over a long history of transactions. The beauty of the EBITDA approach is that a company can be valued as the sum of its component businesses less the overall corporate liabilities, including the debt, which are not allocated to individual businesses. The EBITDA ratio is Method #4 for estimating horizon value, and may be the safest. The reason is that pretax cash flow can finance the interest payments in a leveraged buyout (there are no taxes when operating income is offset by interest payments). This condition sets a floor price at which the business is attractive to a financial buyer.

DISCOUNTED FREE CASH FLOW

Current financial parlance recognizes two types of cash flow: operating cash flow and free cash flow.

The definition of *operating cash flow* is net income plus depreciation minus changes in working capital. In other words, an increase in annual working capital requirements, which is a typical consequence of business growth, reduces operating cash flow. A smart business will learn methods to reduce its needs for working capital, resulting in positive (and highly valuable) contributions to operating cash flow. Though these improvements are very valuable, they are ultimately not sustainable, since minimum inventory levels are required to maintain operational efficiency, and payment terms for receivables are affected by competitive considerations.

The concept of free cash flow (FCF) recognizes that for a business to continue a pattern of healthy growth, it must also reinvest capital for fixed assets. First, there is the practical matter of replacing obsolete or worn-out assets. Second, new capacity must be added to accommodate growth. Spending zero is equivalent to a strategy of "milking" the business with an eye toward eventual liquidation. In other words, if one intends to remain in business, the funds that are still available to investors are the free cash flow. They can be used for any purpose whatever (hence "free") without affecting the business that creates them: for new investment opportunities (if investors want to create yet more wealth) or for cash dividends (if investors want to spend their wealth).

This concept is crucial, since from an investment viewpoint, the ultimate value of a business is the cash that it throws off. More specifically, *the value of an investment is the discounted value of the free cash flow* it generates.

The definition of *free cash flow* is operating cash flow less capital expenditures. In developing a business plan, the assumed growth rate becomes critical to the estimates of free cash flow, since business growth implies higher capital investment. The higher the growth rate, the lower the FCF; the lower the growth rate, the higher the FCF.

These points come into focus when one considers the nature of a growing perpetuity, our next subject.

THE NATURE OF GROWING PERPETUITIES

A perpetuity is a financial instrument that throws off a constant stream of cash forever. Its value, though, is quite finite, since its owner has the option of selling it at some price and buying another instrument that throws off more cash sooner. Consider this choice: Would an investor prefer to pay $25,000 for a perpetuity of $1,000 per year (4 percent) or for a safe 30-year bond paying $1,250 per year (5 percent)? Any astute investor would choose the latter, reducing the value of the perpetuity to $20,000, more or less. This situation is reflected in the equation for the value of a perpetuity: It is free cash flow divided by the weighted average cost of capital (Value = FCF/WACC). In this example, the cost of capital is defined by an alternative investment paying 5 percent, so the value of the perpetuity is $1,000/0.05 = $20,000. The "more or less" is defined by the perception of a pessimistic investor that few 5 percent reinvestment opportunities will exist when the 30-year bond expires, while an optimist believes she might be able to do even better. The market value will reflect the balance between these viewpoints. The take-home point is that the existence of a comparable investment of similar risk defines the cost of capital.

The concept of a perpetuity, however, is mostly abstract and few perpetuities exist in practice. They are interesting only because many corporations may be viewed as perpetuities, and successful ones can be modeled as *growing perpetuities*. For a corporation or a business has no defined term of existence, and it is not unreasonable to expect it to grow as fast as or faster than the economy as a whole. Of course, in this day of global-scale deal making, many companies are merged out of existence, but it is rare that they are acquired just to be liquidated; most of the employees and facilities will be retained with the intent of improving profit growth and creating wealth. The name may be gone, and owners change increasingly frequently, but the underlying business soldiers on.

Another rationale for assuming a growing perpetuity model is that the assumption of indefinite life need not be critical to the valuation; it is only important that the business persists long enough that the discounted value of any further additional years is minor; 40 years may be as good as a thousand in financial terms.

A formula[2] links the free cash flow in the horizon year of a business to its value in that year. It is:

$$\text{Value} = \text{FCF}/(\text{WACC} - \text{Growth Rate})$$

where the percentages in the denominator are expressed as decimals.

As a very simple example, a free cash flow stream of $1 million growing at 5 percent per year, with a cost of capital of 15 percent, is worth $10 million ($1M/0.10 = $10M) in the horizon year. It must, of course, then be discounted back to the present in calculating NPV. The power of this algorithm is that it makes no difference what year is chosen as the horizon year—as long as the growth rate is constant. This feature is illustrated in Figure 2.2. Remember that year 0 in this context is the horizon year, not year 0 of the project. If it takes 12 years to get to the horizon year, horizon year 0 will be project year 12, and all horizon values will discount[3] to the present by $1/(1 + \text{WACC})\wedge 12$.

Figure 2.2 shows the value in year 0 of a perpetuity with an initial payment of $1.00 growing at 5 percent per annum when the cost of capital is 20 percent. It is designed to be easily followed, and to make the correct answer obvious. Note the first 20 years are shown, and then each succeeding decade. The next three columns show the cash flow, the discounted cash flow, and the cumulative discounted cash flow of this stream. (The accompanying spreadsheet version permits the reader to insert his own combination of growth rate and cost of capital.)

It is immediately apparent that while the cash flow increases steadily, the discounted cash flow decreases even more strongly. The cumulative

FIGURE 2.2   A Growing Perpetuity

Horizon Value = FCF/(WACC − Growth Rate)
Growth Rate   5%
Cost of Capital   20%
Initial Value $1.00

Year	Cash Flow	Discounted Cash Flow	DCF Sum	Horizon Value	Total Value	Horizon Value as % of Total Value
0	$ 1.000	$1.000	$1.000	$7.000	$8.000	12.50
1	$ 1.050	$0.875	$1.875	$6.125	$8.000	23.44
2	$ 1.102	$0.765	$2.640	$5.359	$8.000	33.01
3	$ 1.157	$0.669	$3.310	$4.689	$8.000	41.38
4	$ 1.215	$0.586	$3.896	$4.103	$8.000	48.71
5	$ 1.276	$0.512	$4.409	$3.590	$8.000	55.12
6	$ 1.340	$0.448	$4.858	$3.141	$8.000	60.73
7	$ 1.407	$0.392	$5.251	$2.748	$8.000	65.64
8	$ 1.477	$0.343	$5.594	$2.405	$8.000	69.93
9	$ 1.551	$0.300	$5.895	$2.104	$8.000	73.69
10	$ 1.628	$0.263	$6.158	$1.841	$8.000	76.98
11	$ 1.710	$0.230	$6.388	$1.611	$8.000	79.86
12	$ 1.795	$0.201	$6.590	$1.409	$8.000	82.38
13	$ 1.885	$0.176	$6.766	$1.233	$8.000	84.58
14	$ 1.979	$0.154	$6.920	$1.079	$8.000	86.51
15	$ 2.078	$0.134	$7.055	$0.944	$8.000	88.19
16	$ 2.182	$0.118	$7.173	$0.826	$8.000	89.67
17	$ 2.292	$0.103	$7.276	$0.723	$8.000	90.96
18	$ 2.406	$0.090	$7.367	$0.632	$8.000	92.09
19	$ 2.527	$0.079	$7.446	$0.553	$8.000	93.08
20	$ 2.653	$0.069	$7.515	$0.484	$8.000	93.94
30	$ 4.321	$0.018	$7.872	$0.127	$8.000	98.41
40	$ 7.040	$0.004	$7.966	$0.033	$8.000	99.58
50	$11.467	$0.001	$7.991	$0.008	$8.000	99.89

payout, on a discounted basis, is shown in the column labeled "DCF Sum." By the fourth year half the value has been received, and 80 percent is paid by year 11. Only 0.11 percent is paid after year 50! There is no reason to worry here about perpetuity implying centuries of time.

If year 0 is considered as the horizon year (the last year for which a calculation is needed), then the free cash flow is $1.00 and the horizon value (from all succeeding years) is $7.00, giving a total (net present value) of $8.00. This simple case made a legitimate assumption by using the first year as the horizon year since the growth rate is constant. If year 5 had been used as the horizon year, the contribution from cash flows received in years 0 through 5 would be $4.41 and the horizon value would be $3.59, again totaling $8.00. Indeed, any year gives exactly the same result.

How was the horizon value calculated? The cash flow in the following year (year 1) was divided by cost of capital minus growth rate. For year 0, it was $1.05/0.15 = $7.00. The numerator is the same as the year 0 cash flow ($1.00) multiplied by a year of growth or 1.05. That is all that is needed to make the calculation. But be careful. If you use year 5 as the horizon year, you must use the *discounted* cash flow for year 5, $0.5129; then multiply by 1.05, and divide by 0.15 to yield $3.59.

The algorithm has a major weakness: It works well only for growth rates that are substantially less than the cost of capital. When the growth rate equals or exceeds the cost of capital, the value becomes infinite. When it is very close to the cost of capital, it is astronomical. Under these conditions the algorithm fails to converge, or converges very slowly.

This mathematical phenomenon corresponds to a hypothetical situation where a business grows to the point where it eventually consumes all the money in the world. Such growth rates cannot be sustained in reality, even though some of the more successful growth companies, such as Microsoft or Amgen, have sustained high growth rates for a decade or more. A colleague once described these happy circumstances as a "high-class problem." There are two ways to handle it analytically. One is to take the horizon year to a more distant time when the market need is substantially satisfied and the growth rate drops. The other is to fall back to comparables, such as P/E or EBITDA ratios characteristic of high-growth businesses.

At the top of the Internet bubble, some analysts grasped at weird comparables such as "eyeballs" and "click-throughs" in the absence of earnings or even significant revenues. There was no need for such wild metrics. A much sounder approach would have been to construct a pro forma business plan based on reasonable revenues and margins out to a reasonable horizon year, and correct the result for the risks involved. This is the approach that will be followed in this book.

When does a business become a growing perpetuity? The question is equivalent to asking what is a good choice for a horizon year. One would be tempted to say that it would be when revenues can be assumed to grow at a constant rate, and that is not a bad approximation. But with financial accounting, this condition will not be mathematically precise until all capital invested at earlier growth rates has been depreciated, since depreciation affects tax, and tax affects free cash flow. McKinsey's authors, in a popular text about valuation, advise, "When in doubt, make a longer rather than shorter forecast."[4]

The issue of convergence can be measured, for example, by how many years are required to realize 80 percent of the ultimate horizon value. This was only 11 years in the preceding example. A number of other cases are displayed in Figure 2.3, which shows that as the free-cash flow multiplier increases, so does the number of years required to reach 80 percent realization of the theoretical horizon value. In summary, this handy formula seems to give reasonable results when the growth rate is less than the cost of capital by 5 percent or more, and becomes very dicey when growth is within 2 percent of the cost of capital. I advise switching to one of the "comparable" approaches before the FCF multiplier reaches 25 or the time to 80 percent convergence exceeds 30 years.

TIMING CONVENTIONS

It is easy to get lost in timing issues when one deals with NPV and horizon value. Specifically, does one discount the first year? In Figure 1.1, the first year was not discounted because the investment was made immediately. Instead, NPV was calculated by discounting each successive year and summing the values. Excel's NPV function was not used, since it automatically discounts the first year; had it been used, the result could have been multiplied by (1 + WACC) to reach the correct answer. However, the Excel NPV function is too useful to ignore, so the following convention is adopted in this book.

FIGURE 2.3   Convergence: Years to 80 Percent Realization as a Function of Growth Rate and Cost of Capital

	Cost of Capital 12%		Cost of Capital 20%	
Growth Rate	FCF Multiplier	Years to 80%	FCF Multiplier	Years to 80%
2.5	11.8	17	6.9	9
5.0	16.0	24	8.0	11
7.5	24.9	38	9.6	14
10.0	56.0	88	12.0	18
15.0	NA	NA	24.0	37

Year 0 Convention

Assume for planning purposes that a decision is being made today in year 0 with regard to cash flows beginning in January of year 1. The cash flows in year 1 will be spread from January to December, with the average at midyear. So if they are discounted by a year's cost of capital, one is assuming a vantage point of being in midyear of year 0. That is, the value of this project today is the discounted value of cash flows in year 1 and beyond. This convention may actually be convenient from an R&D planning viewpoint, since budgets for the following year begin to crystallize in June. Any other perspective in time can be reached by applying the discount factor over the appropriate interval.

Horizon Year Conventions

Five different methods have been described for calculating the horizon value. With the growing perpetuity method (Method #5) it is now quite clear that the full free cash flow of the final year shown on the spreadsheet plus the value of the cash flows thereafter are captured. In comparing the result to the other four methods, we must make an apples-to-apples comparison from a timing viewpoint. This requirement implies that for the liquidation or sale of business scenarios to be in a comparable time frame, the transactions must occur on December 31 of the horizon year.

For a liquidation scenario (Methods #1 and #2), the cash received is the average of horizon year and horizon year +1 values (implying one must calculate one more year beyond the horizon). It is also deferred by six months, since other cash payments are assumed to occur at midyear. Hence, they must be further discounted by a half-year's cost of capital.

For a phantom sale of the business based on comparables, the EBITDA or P/E ratios applied would refer to past-year income multiples (Wall Street analysts make the distinction between trailing P/E ratios, and P/E ratios based on next-year earnings), and again be deferred by six months to be discounted by a half-year's cost of capital. These conventions will be followed in subsequent project analysis.

Solution to Case 3 and Discussion

Let's return to our example. Louise has just elaborated on some of the important considerations in calculating horizon value. They are important because horizon value may constitute most of the value of a project, as will prove the case here.

Louise won a victory when she gained agreement to extend the financials from year 10 to year 12. Her argument was that the patent would still be in force and it would be premature to liquidate the business. By doing so she gained two additional years of discounted free cash flow, for year 11 and year 12. Figure 2.1 shows that the free cash flow in those years was $15.8 and $16.7 (in millions) respectively. Discounting them back to the present yields $14.9/1.12 ^ 11 = $4.6 and $15.7/1.12 ^ 12 = $4.3. The sum of discounted free cash flow now turns positive. It is –$7.2 + $4.6 + $4.3 or $1.6 million. This number is the NPV assuming *zero* terminal value, and it will be our starting point for the following calculations.

The choice of horizon year is critical under this assumption, since each additional year is adding about $4 million in value!

Liquidation Scenarios

But no horizon value has yet been added. Method #1 is to add back the end of year 12 working capital, ($12.6 + $13.2)/2 = $12.9 million. That value, discounted 12.5 years, is $3.1 million, the Method #1 horizon value. The total value for the project using Method #1 is $1.6 + $3.1 = $4.7 million.

Method #2 adds back Total Capital Employed, that is, working capital plus undepreciated fixed capital. Again you must use the average of years 12 and 13 or $30.7 million. Its discounted value is $7.4 million, the Method #2 horizon value. The total value of the project is $1.6 + $7.4 = $9.0 million.

Thus the two liquidation scenarios both give substantial net present value in a 12-year scenario. The IRRs (not part of the case) were in fact 14.2 percent and 15.8 percent, bolstering Louise's argument that this plant is a fine investment even in the worst-case scenario of a liquidation. Indeed, even if the calculation were restricted to the 10-year case, there would be enough cash flow from the liquidation of the inventories to overcome the slightly negative NPV that was originally calculated under the corporate guidelines. Note again that the NPV will depend heavily on the choice of horizon year, because each year throws off additional free cash flow. In fact, if a very long horizon were to be chosen, say 50 years, the results of either Method #1 or Method #2 would converge on Method #5.

Liquidation, though, is quite a different story than a healthy business growing at 5 percent per year!

The Growing Perpetuity Model

Let's turn next to Method #5, the growing perpetuity method.

Again, the base calculation starts from the $1.6 million NPV without horizon value. The horizon value in year 12 is the year 12 FCF of $16.7 million plus 5 percent growth, $17.5 million, divided by 0.07 (WACC – growth rate) or $250.6 million. In other words, sitting in year 12, it would be considered fair to sell the growing future cash flows of this business for $250.6 million, the Method #5 horizon value. Discounting back to the present, the total value of the business by the growing perpetuity method is $64.3 + $1.6 = $65.9 million.

This answer is virtually independent of the choice of horizon year. If it were calculated for year 11 it is $65.6 million, and for year 13 it is $66.2 million. The method is invariant to within 0.2 percent, a precision much higher than the many uncertainties built into the financial projection! The small difference arises from the fact that while year-to-year revenue growth is 5 percent, the FCF does not grow at exactly 5 percent owing to the lagging effects of depreciation and taxes. (It will completely smooth out by the time the horizon year is 20 or so.)

Another very important observation is that horizon value in year 12 is 97.5 percent of the total value. In other words, for some long-term projects it takes quite a bit of time to reach cash flow breakeven, but once that point is reached the value creation is enormous. This project is calculated to have an IRR of 26.8 percent; Louise knew it was a big winner. Of course, if year 20 had been picked for the horizon year, the horizon value would be considerably smaller; it is total value that should be essentially independent of horizon year choice. Also note that for this project the total value by Method #5 is about 14 times the liquidation value (Method #1). The message is that a short time horizon and overly conservative assumptions can make a superb project look very ordinary.

Comparables

The remaining two methods for calculating horizon value are as multiples of after-tax income (Method #3) and earnings before interest, tax, depreciation, and amortization (EBITDA) (Method #4). Like the growing perpetuity, they reflect the value of an ongoing business. For each case start with the end of year 12 value, apply the appropriate multiple, discount 12.5 years, and add it to the net present value of the free cash flows for years 1 through 12 ($1.6 million). Figure 2.1 shows that the year-end values of after-tax income and EBITDA are $17.2 and $29.7 million respectively. These numbers reflect the end-of-year *rate* at which income and cash are being generated, and therefore approximate the average of years 12 and 13 full-year results (given in Figure 2.1). What multiples should be applied?

For EBITDA, I have seen many transactions in the chemical industry take place at a multiple close to 7. Price-earnings ratios are more variable, since they depend on perceptions of quality of business, management quality, the stage of the business cycle, and the overall stock market averages, which alone can easily swing 20 to 40 percent. However, few would argue that a 12.5 multiple is too much to pay (absent extraordinary negative factors) for a quality chemical company that has managed to raise dividends regularly over a half-century.

Using these ratios, the calculations suggest a buyer at the end of year 12 would be willing to pay $215.2 million for this business using the price-earnings method or $208.2 million using the EBITDA approach. Discounting them back to the present gives Method #3 (P/E) horizon value of $52.2 million and Method #4 (EBITDA) horizon value of $50.5 million. Adding $1.6 million to each (and rounding), total value becomes $53.7 million and $52.0 million, respectively.

These answers agree with each other quite closely, although that agreement depends heavily on my choice of P/E ratio. Since I have more confidence in the EBITDA method, I prefer to use it and then apply the P/E ratio method as a reality check.

For both Methods #3 and #4, the total value results are almost as insensitive to choice of horizon year as is Method #5, again generating confidence in the methodology. There is an important conclusion to be drawn: *All of the ongoing business methods are insensitive to choice of horizon year, while liquidation methods are very sensitive to this choice!*

Note also that the values obtained by Methods #3 and #4 are almost 20 percent less than that obtained by the growing perpetuity method (see Figure 2.4). First comment: Since the comparable methods are intuitive, while the perpetuity method is mathematical, it is reassuring that the results are at least in the same ballpark.

Second Comment: The difference is probably significant, and either or both of two factors may explain it. Mathematically, what accounts for the difference is the high long-term growth rate of 5 percent assumed in the model. If the rate had been 3 percent, all three ongoing business

FIGURE 2.4 Case 3 Project Values by Five Methods

	1 Working Capital	2 Book Value	3 P/E Ratio	4 EBITDA Ratio	5 Growing Perpetuity
Internal rate of return	14.2	15.8	24.9	25.2	26.8
Net present value	$4.7	$9.0	$52.0	$53.7	$65.9

methods would give results within $1 million of each other (check it using the input/output spreadsheet for Figure 2.4). Or, turning the issue on its head, 12.5 is too low a P/E ratio for a business reliably growing at 5 percent. From a psychological vantage (business risks being what they are), investors, who in the last analysis establish the comparable multiples, are building in a bit of a cushion for uncertainty.

CHAPTER 3

Factoring in the Risk

Every industrial R&D project plan envisions a reward. In financial terms, the payoff can be represented by the project's net present value in the year it is commercialized. But that payoff is further and invariably diminished by what might be called "The Three Horsemen of the R&D Apocalypse," (1) the time value of money; (2) the risk of technical failure; and (3) the cost of the R&D program itself. Given the value-destroying potential of these three factors, senior management will wish to determine whether its continuing investment in R&D is creating value, and, if so, how much. A linear approach to this judgment is inevitably flawed, since it does not include the value of management's flexibility to respond to changes in the marketplace or in the technology outlook.

The prior two chapters discussed in some depth the valuation of a riskless project, or at least one where market risk is wrapped up in the cost of capital, and the cash flows are predicted with confidence. While this first step toward a financial model is necessary (and not all that simple) it is still far from the norm in the world of technology, where unique risks are extraordinarily high.

This chapter presumes the payoff, but introduces two critical analytical tools that are central to a *risk-adjusted* valuation: decision trees (DT) and real options (RO).[1] The value calculation is basic, once the input parameters have been established. Why might this be important? The discounted cash flow (DCF) approach discussed in Chapters 1 and 2 is well established and beloved of finance executives, but is known to systematically underestimate the value of R&D projects (and other intangible assets). The decision tree approach, sometimes expanded as "decision and risk analysis," captures the substantial value of the option to abandon. It quantifies *unique risk* and creates value by structuring R&D programs into a series of go/no-go decision points that define the abandonment options.[2] The power of this approach has been one reason for the widespread adoption of stage-gate methodology, although the rationale has been largely qualitative.[3]

The real options approach has hitherto been treated independently from decision trees. It captures value from the management of *market risk,* risk that cannot be diversified.

In reality, the two approaches are additive and compatible, and form a powerful combination. Technically, the real options method is more appropriate for valuation of R&D project plans, because plans are options, not assets.[4] The best arguments for pure discounted cash flow analysis or DCF plus decision tree analysis are their broad acceptance and familiarity.

This chapter separately introduces decision trees and real options, and later describes how they can be combined into a single calculation (DTRO), reducing valuation to two steps: (1) the calculation of NPV using DCF, followed by (2) DTRO analysis. The integration of these methods will be completed in Chapter 4, by capturing full value from both unique and market risk using a compound option on the business plan NPV.

While this approach was developed with industrial R&D in mind, it is quite general and well fits other situations with high risk, exposure to volatile markets, long time horizons, and progressively increasing development costs. Other such applications include venture capital, petroleum exploration, and even screenplay development. The methods are particularly useful when a historical database is available regarding the odds of project success, as in the pharmaceutical industry or the drilling industry. Serious thought is being given to the possibility that R&D project termination factors are predictable.[5] So, if the calculations are performed correctly, those using them may invest in selected opportunities that competitors pass up, a potential source of competitive advantage.

DECISION TREES

The decision tree is a classic tool[6] for estimating the payout of a project where unique risk is involved. The term *tree* refers to a series of branches and branch points. Each branch represents an activity and has an associated cost and duration. Each branch point has associated probabilities. The sum of all terminal branch probabilities is 100 percent.

At the end of each final branch is a payoff, which can be positive, negative, or zero. The probability of that payoff is calculated from the combined probabilities of reaching it through each branch point on the path. The expected value of the overall project is obtained by summing each possible payoff with its associated probability.

Let's review the logic with a simple example containing a single 60/40 branch point. John sees an advertisement offering a $200 discount on a new television set, on a "while supplies last" basis, at a store that is two hours away. He estimates there is only a 40 percent chance one of the new TVs will be available when he gets to the store. He also values his time and the cost of the trip at $90 (the cost associated with the first branch of the project). Should he go? On one of the two final branches there is a 60 percent chance of a zero payoff, giving a net loss of $90. On the other, there is a 40 percent chance he will get a net payoff of $110 ($200 less the $90 cost). The expected value of the situation is calculated by multiplying each payoff and its probability and adding: (60% × –$90) + (40% × $110) = –$54 + $44 = –$10. John chooses to mow the lawn.

While this problem can be worked in one's head, with more branches the answer will be less obvious. Let's look at a more complex case, where time is an important element.

Case 4, Part One: Bioremediation with Decision Tree Alone

John Hamilton, who heads an R&D team at the fictional bioremediation business unit of Acme Chemical, proposes to develop a new microorganism that its microbiologists have identified as having excellent potential to bioremediate refractory chlorinated waste, an environmental hazard.

The business plan calls for two R&D stages over three years: a laboratory feasibility study followed by a two-year field test. In year 4, when technical risks have been eliminated, the technology will be commercialized at three Superfund sites. The feasibility study will take one year and cost $500,000, and is given a 50 percent chance of technical success. The field test will take two years and cost $1 million, and have a 75 percent chance of success. Deployment of the technology at three commercial sites will require an investment of $5 million.

The R&D team believes the technology, if successful, would offer customers a large cost saving versus the best alternative technology, while earning Acme an adequate return on investment. Specifically, Acme's economic evaluators estimated the enterprise would have a value of $8 million, giving a net present value in year 4 of $3 million.

Should Hamilton's project be approved given the costs and risks involved? Assume Acme has a 12 percent cost of capital. See Figure 3.1 for a graphical depiction of the situation.

Solution to Case 4, Part One

Note that in developing this case, the timing convention of being in year 0 is used. Since the payoff of $3 million NPV is in year 4, its present value is

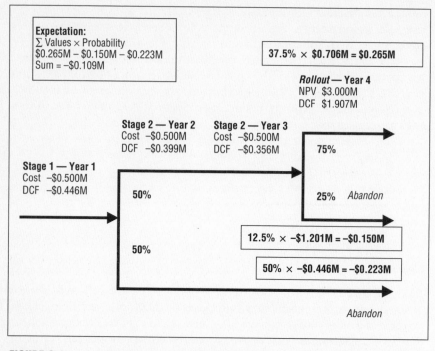

Expectation:
Σ Values × Probability
$0.265M − $0.150M − $0.223M
Sum = −$0.109M

37.5% × $0.706M = $0.265M

Rollout — Year 4
NPV $3.000M
DCF $1.907M

Stage 2 — Year 2
Cost −$0.500M
DCF −$0.399M

Stage 2 — Year 3
Cost −$0.500M
DCF −$0.356M

75%

Stage 1 — Year 1
Cost −$0.500M
DCF −$0.446M

50%

25% *Abandon*

12.5% × −$1.201M = −$0.150M

50%

50% × −$0.446M = −$0.223M

Abandon

FIGURE 3.1 Project Outcomes by DCF/Decision Tree Analysis. The project has abandonment scenarios after Stages 1 and 2, and one successful outcome with a 37.5 percent chance of success. The expectation value (upper left) is the weighted sum of the three possible outcomes.

only $1.907 million. Similarly, the discounted cost of Stage 1 is −$0.446 million, and that of Stages 1 and 2 is −$1.201 million. Also, the payoff of the "success" branch must be reduced by the costs of the R&D program that leads there, and is only $0.706 million. The project has three possible outcomes: a 50 percent chance of failure after the feasibility stage, a 12.5 percent probability of failure after the field test (the worst outcome), and a 37.5 percent chance of success. They add to 100 percent. Thus decision tree analysis tells management the project is a marginal loser, with a weighted value, or expectation, of −$0.109 million.

In short, because of the development costs, the high unique risks, and the element of time, the project has negative economic value when evaluated by a decision tree (Figure 3.1). Time in fact proves critical, for, had the cost of capital (which heavily penalizes the commercial NPV) been ignored, the project value would be marginally positive at $0.125 million.

Even so, Hamilton's team has created value by adroitly managing the option to abandon after the uncertain stages. If the stages were combined with a commitment to roll out this technology in year 4 regardless—for example, by signing a fixed-price contract with a contract research organization—the expected reward would be 37.5 percent × $1.907 million, or $0.715 million, versus a certain cost of $1.201 million, giving a far worse expectation of a $0.486 million loss. Mitigating the unique risk with the option to abandon adds a great deal of value but is of itself not enough to justify the project.

We shall come back to this case later in the chapter.

OPTIONS

Real options is the name being given to the application of options theory to everyday business situations. It is a field that is not much more than 15 years old, and one that has seen explosive growth in interest only in the past five years. The term is used in contrast to *financial options*, a much older and better-developed craft that involves speculative and hedging transactions on currencies, securities, and commodities. But to understand a real option it is very helpful to first understand a financial option. Fortunately, while few of the readers of this book will be active traders of financial options, many more will have been granted stock options by their employers, which are an excellent primer for understanding the nature of options, real or financial. The following case and discussion are meant to illustrate some of the differences between options and assets (the underlying security on which the option is written).

Case 5: Are Julia's Options Golden Handcuffs?

Julia is a research director at Acme Chemical, and exactly one year ago she received her first stock option award, covering 10,000 shares. At the time of the award Acme was trading at $45 per share. (Acme's generous policy is to grant 10-year stock options with a face value of three times salary to employees of Julia's rank, and Julia's salary is $150,000.) Also, under Acme's policy, employees who leave the company are given only one year in which to exercise their options. Since her grant, Acme's stock has dropped to $40.

Julia, however, is worried about her financial future, and is evaluating a job offer from another firm. Analysts speculate that Acme faces a takeover threat and that the stock would trade at $60 if it materialized. But Julia could well lose her job as a result. As part of her thought process, she wants to know what her options are worth today. She additionally wants to know what she would lose if she left the company today, reducing the remaining term of her award from nine years to one. Doing a little financial sleuthing, Julia learns that Treasury bills with a 10-year term are paying about 4 percent, and that the volatility of Acme stock is fairly low, 20 percent.

Black-Scholes Option Pricing Model

The Black-Scholes formula, a Nobel Prize–winning (1997) algorithm, is our tool of choice to address Julia's questions. Brealey and Myers[7] describe this mathematical formula as "unpleasant-looking" but one that on "closer acquaintance [the user] will find exceptionally elegant and useful." There is nothing really magical about Black-Scholes: Option values may also be calculated using the older "risk-neutral" binomial method[8]—and as a practical matter the binomial results usually track the Black-Scholes values closely and are based on similar assumptions. Some real options specialists argue for the risk-neutral method. But in engineering parlance, the beauty of Black-Scholes is "plug and chug"—a closed-ended calculation.

To apply the Black-Scholes formula, five numbers are needed: (1) the value of the underlying security, (2) the strike or exercise price, (3) the time period of the option, (4) the volatility, and (5) the risk-free rate. All of the numbers are already in hand. The underlying security is valued at $40. The exercise price is $45. The duration is nine years—by which time Julia must invest the strike price or walk away. The risk-free rate, as published in the *Wall Street Journal*, is 4 percent. A critical parameter in options analysis is the volatility (σ). Technically, it represents the annual standard deviation of the price of the security under option. The historical monthly volatilities, on an annualized basis, of listed stocks are available under "Market Data" at the Chicago Board Options Exchange web site (www.cboe.com); Julia averages some recent months to estimate Acme's volatility.

Solution to Case 5

The answers to Julia's questions are calculated in Figure 3.2, which also walks through the mathematics[9] of the Black-Scholes formula step by step, for readers who may wish to follow the calculation more closely. The software version of Figure 3.2 is a very useful template for analyzing a variety of financial and real options. In addition, another Excel-based Black-Scholes calculator is included in the accompanying software as BLACKSCHOLES.xls.

Julia's options are out-of-the-money, or in common parlance "under water," owing to the decline in Acme's stock since the grant. But they are very valuable ($132,543) because there is an excellent chance that Acme will move higher in the ensuing nine years. For example, should the

FIGURE 3.2 Incentive Stock Options

Item	Symbol	Current Price	High Price	Shorter Term	Deep-Out-of-the-Money
Inputs					
Price	P	$40.00	$60.00	$40.00	$10.00
Strike price	X	$45.00	$45.00	$45.00	$45.00
Risk-free rate	r	0.04	0.04	0.04	0.04
Years	t	9.00	9.00	1.00	9.00
Standard deviation of security	σ	0.200	0.200	0.200	0.200
Intermediate Calculations					
Discount factor	$(1 + r)\wedge t$	1.4233	1.4233	1.0400	1.4233
Square root of time	$t\wedge 0.5$	3.00	3.00	1.00	3.00
Present value (PV) of strike price	PV(X)	$31.62	$31.62	$43.27	$31.62
Ratio of price to PV of strike price	Y	1.2652	1.8977	0.9244	0.3163
Log of Y	Ln(Y)	0.2352	0.6407	−0.0786	−1.1511
Risk factor	$Z = \sigma * t\wedge 0.5$	0.600	0.600	0.200	0.600
Black-Scholes D1 factor	$D1 = \ln(Y)/Z + 0.5Z$	0.6920	1.3678	−0.2928	−1.6185
Black-Scholes D2 factor	$D2 = D1 − Z$	0.0920	0.7678	−0.4928	−2.2185
NORMSDIST for D1	N(D1)	0.7555	0.9143	0.3848	0.0528
NORMSDIST for D2	N(D2)	0.5367	0.7787	0.3111	0.0133
Relative value of option	$W = N(D1) − N(D2)/Y$	33.14%	50.40%	4.83%	1.09%
Output					
Value of option	W * P	$13.25	$30.24	$1.93	$0.11
Intrinsic value of option	P − X, when P > X	$0.00	$15.00	$0.00	$0.00
Number of shares under option		10,000	10,000	10,000	10,001
Value of option grant		$132,543	$302,392	$19,334	$1,085
Intrinsic value of option grant		$0	$150,000	$0	$0
Option delta		$0.76	$0.92	$0.41	$0.06

takeover bid at $60 soon materialize, they could be cashed in for their intrinsic value, now $150,000. And, if the stock just moved to $60, the option, too, would appreciate, to $302,392, on the basis that further gains would be possible. Thus, because options theory is based on a random walk or "markets have no memory" approach, the options would then be valued $152,392 above the intrinsic value.

Julia's more burning question, however, is what she would lose if she left the company, reducing the term of her options to one year. Now they would be worth only $19,334; she would be giving up over 85 percent of the theoretical value of the grant, amounting to more than $100,000. The golden handcuffs are quite material in her case.

Business conditions can change rapidly. Assume that Acme suffers a serious adverse development and the stock drops to $10. Julia's options would be deeply out-of-the-money and would be worth only $1,085, less than 1 percent of their current value. The handcuffs would be removed. The lesson is that deep-out-of-the-money options have little value.

The last row in Figure 3.2 is labeled "Option delta." It represents the change in the value of the option with each dollar change in the stock price. For example, if Acme rose from $40 to $41, Julia's options would increase in value by $0.76 per share, and her grant would be worth $7,600 more. If the stock price were $60, however, the option delta would increase to $0.92, almost a dollar-for-dollar change in the underlying security. In other words, the Black-Scholes value is starting to track the stock price very closely—if the stock goes up a dollar so does the value of the option. So, the deep-in-the-money option begins to behave increasingly like a stock.

At the other extreme, at a stock price of $10, well out-of-the-money, the option delta is just 0.06—the option will barely move with a small increase in stock price; the algorithm is essentially telling us that the stock price still has too far to go to have much chance of getting into the money. These characteristics of financial options will apply in important ways to real options situations.

REAL OPTIONS

Let's now see how options analysis can throw new light on a business strategy.

Case 6: The Mark I Microcomputer

The first real options case is adopted from the fictional Blitzen Mark I microcomputer case from the corporate finance textbook of Brealey and Myers.[10] The proposition is as follows: there is a proposal to produce a new computer model, the Mark I, which will require a first-year investment in capital and net start-up costs of $450 million. The business runs for six years, and is harvested in the fifth and sixth year, according to the schedule of cash flows in Figure 3.3.

CEO John Clark turns down the project because he has set a hurdle rate of 20 percent, and using that rate as a discount rate the net present value of the cash flows is negative, –$46 million. (This figure implies that the cash flow stream in years 2 through 6 has a present value of $450 million – $46 million or $404 million.) Is this the right call in view of the uncertainty of the cash flow forecast?

Solution to Case 6

Judy Novak, the CFO, is a real options advocate. She argues that the Mark I project carries with it an option to build the Mark II three years hence. The Mark II is forecast to be no more profitable than the Mark I (!!), but because of the high growth rate of the industry, it will be double the scale of the Mark I; that is, it will require a $900 million investment in year 4, and throw off double the cash flows in years 5 through 9. Therefore, its cash flow stream will be worth $808 million in year 4 or $468 million when discounted back to year 1.

Judy characterizes the Mark II as a three-year call option on an asset valued at $468 million with a strike price of $900 million. Using the Black-Scholes formula she finds [11] that this option is worth $55 million, assuming a volatility of 0.35, which is reasonable for a computer stock. (See Excel workbook BLACKSCHOLES.xls, worksheet "Mark I.") This volatility is a proxy for the fact that it will be even more difficult to forecast Mark II revenues and margins in years 5 through 9, but they are likely to correlate with results for the Mark I, which are themselves uncertain. Only if the Mark I performs better than forecast will the option to build the Mark II be exercised.

Her argument is that, with the embedded option to build the Mark II,

FIGURE 3.3   Schedule of Cash Flows from Mark I Case ($ Millions)

	Year 1	Year 2	Year 3	Year 4	Year 5	Year 6
After-tax operating cash flow	–$200	$110	$159	$295	$185	$ 0
Capital investment	$250	$ 0	$ 0	$ 0	$ 0	$ 0
Increase in working capital	$ 0	$ 50	$100	$100	–$125	–$125
Net cash flow	–$450	$ 60	$ 59	$195	$310	$125

the real value of the Mark I is the sum of the pro forma enterprise value of –$46 million and the $55 million option value, or a positive $9 million. The textbook story even contains a rather coy (but correct) remark by Ms. Novak, that the Mark II carries with it a call, which she ignores, to build a Mark III, Mark IV, and so on. Hence, the total value could in effect consider a cascade of compound options, which could justify even higher valuations.

Hence, the decision should be to move ahead. This result is typical of situations where a consideration of market risk will turn a marginally negative NPV into a winner.

Note that Judy's analysis depends critically on both the growth rate of the computer industry and the volatility.

Consider the growth rate first. If the growth rate were zero, then the Mark II would be the same size as the Mark I, and the option value would be halved: $55 million ÷ 2 = $27.5 million. Without growth, the option value would not have been enough to offset the negative $46 million enterprise value, so the decision would remain no.

Discussion: Options under Internet Speed

As an exercise, it is very illuminating to consider what this decision would look like if the growth rate were at "Internet speed," say 10× in three years (a growth rate of 115 percent, more than doubling revenues annually) instead of 2× (a growth rate of 26 percent). Then the option value would be 5× as large as the 2× case, or 5 × $55 million = $275 million. This large value swamps the –$46 million, and gives a total value of $229 million. Mark I now looks like a great project based on options thinking and growth alone.

But there is more to come, for volatility has yet to be considered. The value of an option increases with volatility, the annual standard deviation of the stock price. In 1999, it was not unusual for Internet companies to reach volatilities of 1.0 or higher (100 percent). Let us consider the implications of a volatility of 1.0. (See again Excel workbook BLACKSCHOLES.xls, worksheet "Mark I.") The Black-Scholes value of this option is now $1,263 million, and the value of the proposal is $1,263 million – $46 million = $1,217 million. In this scenario, the negative value of the cash flow stream is completely swamped by the option value.[12]

The larger lesson is that optionality can create enormous wealth under circumstances of high growth and high volatility, and it does not even require a change in the basic economic assumptions to do so.

All of this reasoning is of course entirely orthodox, as long as the circumstances of high growth and volatility are maintained. The ancillary caveat is that options expire. If the projected trajectory of growth does not materialize, the options value will sink like a stone. When the "broadband revolution" hit a speed bump, the options value contained in the share prices of Internet companies evaporated even more quickly than it had formed. Not only was the extraordinary growth rate of Internet stocks unsustainable, but in the aftermath of the crash, their volatilities also dropped sharply.

In a sense, the bubble could be explained as well by rational behavior of investors being offered large but very risky opportunities as by "irrational exuberance." The latter explanation of the bubble would hold only if a rational person could determine the point at which the economic fundamentals of Internet commerce were unsustainable. But there was plenty of conflicting opinion about that estimate, and such rational and knowledgeable players were few. Instead, money managers were under pressure not to underperform their peers. The larger lesson is that similar circumstances are likely to result in similar patterns, despite investor resolutions to be more prudent and cautious next time.

COMBINING DECISION TREES WITH REAL OPTIONS (DTRO)

A unique feature of this book is the demonstration that market risk can be combined with unique risk by reframing the decision tree as a compound series of real (call) options. Best of all it can be handled automatically, rather than as a series of consecutive calculations. Since R&D plans are in reality options (there is no obligation to exercise them), market risk can only create positive value.

Case 4, Part Two: Bioremediation Solution Revisited
with DTRO

When this case was introduced earlier in this chapter, the conclusion was that, even though the project had an attractive NPV, its overall value was negative after the costs of R&D, the risks of failure, and the time value of money were factored in. Does options thinking change anything? In the context of our problem, market risk means the planners don't really know the prices and costs that will affect the business four years hence, but assume they will be subject to factors that have affected the industry in the past. Examples of such factors could include supply and demand for remediation services, changes in regulatory climate, and the aggressiveness of competitor activity.

Solution to Case 4, Part Two

Two additional parameters are needed for options analysis, the volatility and the risk-free rate; both concepts have been previously introduced. There are a number of possible proxies for volatility, but let's choose the volatility of a proxy bioremediation industry, which is determined as the average annual volatility of three comparable publicly traded bioremediation companies. Our (fictional) survey indicates that a volatility of 50 percent appears reasonable. Assume the risk-free rate is 5 percent.

To restructure the analysis in options terms (Figure 3.4), consider Stage 2 as a two-year call option to invest $5 million, the strike price to begin commercial operations. The underlying security for this option is valued at $6.442 million—that is, the present value of the strike price at the risk-free

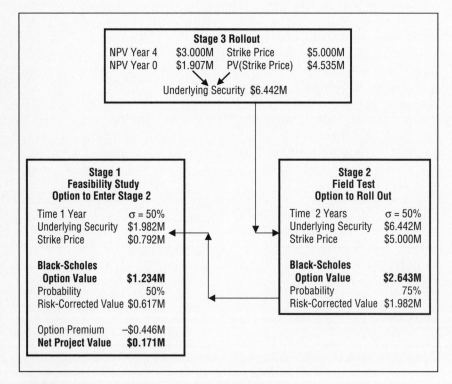

FIGURE 3.4 Project Outcome by Real Options Analysis. The real options calculation begins with the value of a successful rollout (top). This value is the underlying security for the field test option (lower right), which is in turn the underlying security for the feasibility study (lower left).

rate, $4.535 million, plus the discounted net present value, $1.907 million, of a successful project. This option is worth $2.643 million by the Black-Scholes formula at a market volatility of 50 percent. When corrected for the unique risk implied in a 75 percent probability of success, the project value is $1.982 million.

Next consider Stage 1 as a second option to enter Stage 2, for which the underlying security is the value of the Stage 2 option, or $1.982 million. This option has as its strike price[13] the discounted cost of the field test, $792,000.

Plugging into Black-Scholes gives a value of $1.234 million. But there's unique risk of 50 percent at this stage, so this option is worth $617,000. Its discounted cost is –$446,000, so the project has a positive value of $171,000.

Let's do the reality check (Figure 3.5) and assume zero volatility. A reasonable expectation should be that there will then be zero benefit from market risk, and the result should not differ from the decision tree. Could this prove true even though the methodology looks very different? The underlying security and the strike price are the same as in Figure 3.4, and unsurprisingly Black-Scholes gives an option value for Stage 2 of $1.907, exactly the year 0 net present value! Correcting by 75 percent for unique risk gives $1.430 million. Feeding this value into the Stage 1 calculation computes a second option valued at $675,000. Correcting by 50 percent probability of success gives $338,000. Subtract the discounted project cost of Stage 1 ($446,000) and the net value is –$109,000. This result is identical to that obtained from the decision tree analysis described earlier. Despite the fact that the numbers passed twice through the Black-Scholes equation in the second case, the result is accurate within the reasonable precision of the computer.

The difference between the decision tree and the decision tree/real options results is significant, $279,000, and suffices to make Dr. Hamilton's project a winner. That vital difference was created by market volatility. Looking at the project overall, it took a combination of serial options to abandon (DT) and the value of market risk (RO) to ensure a positive economic outcome.

Discussion: Perspectives on Real Options

Does adding real options to the economic analysis make a difference? Although the answer is "sometimes," it makes the most difference with respect to the toughest decisions. Since options algorithms are readily integrated into an analytical package and their use is conceptually sound (since plans are options), there is little reason not to do so. Certainly, achieving turbocharged valuations via real options will not be a universal result, since that outcome depends on exceptional conditions.

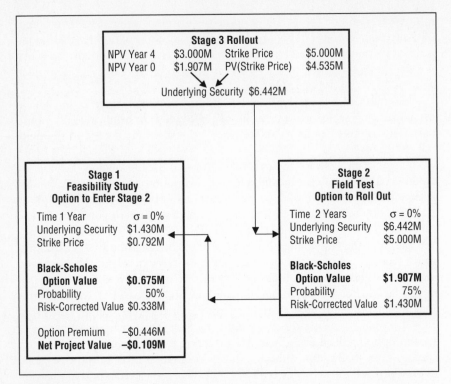

FIGURE 3.5   Project Outcome by Real Options Analysis—Zero Volatility. The dynamics are identical to Figure 3.4, with volatility set equal to zero. The result equals that of Figure 3.1.

In particular, an option that is deep-in-the-money—that is, where the present value far exceeds the strike price—will receive little additional benefit from real options. This circumstance should not disappoint, since a deep-in-the-money option is a happy circumstance and should always be exercised. Deep-out-of-the-money options likewise will get only a small boost from real options treatment; but these are generally foolhardy projects that rightfully should be rejected or rethought. Projects that are at-the-money or slightly out-of-the-money (zero or slightly negative net present values) are the ones that have higher real options values, and benefit most from being viewed through the real options lens. Indeed, for any project there is a range of NPVs for which decision tree analysis gives a negative result but decision tree/real options gives a positive result. These are opportunities that should not be lightly discarded. Again, decision tree/real options will help with the close calls.

CHAPTER 4

Medical Device Case Study: A New Product for a New Application

The toolbag is now full. All of the critical analytical concepts needed to perform risk-adjusted valuations on project proposals have been introduced. The book will now turn to several different types of technology projects, and tailor the methods to the nature of the problem. This chapter presents a five-part problem set derived from a real case, and has been used as a teaching tool in four-hour workshops. Many of the assumptions have been simplified to facilitate analysis in the time given.

Case 7: Implantable Artificial Pancreas

The central research laboratory of BMX Pharma has identified a business opportunity in the treatment of diabetes.

Diabetes, after cardiovascular disease and cancer, is probably the third most serious disease affecting human health in Western countries. The most dangerous form, type 1 or insulin-dependent diabetes, was until the discovery of insulin invariably fatal within a few weeks of onset. Now, administration of insulin controls its most serious symptom, hyperglycemia (excess blood sugar), and significantly prolongs life, but many diabetics experience deteriorating health because the degree of control is far from satisfactory. They are likely to experience cardiovascular disease, loss of sight, and kidney disease (many patients on dialysis are diabetic).

In a healthy individual, the pancreatic islet of Langerhans cells have a well-tuned feedback mechanism for increasing insulin in response to elevated glucose levels, say after a meal, then turning it off when glucose levels drop, thus preventing the opposite condition, hypoglycemia. Patients administering insulin attempt to minimize these fluctuations, but often fail to achieve full control. The excursions into hyperglycemic conditions gradually take their toll. A number of mechanical or biological approaches to improved control have been proposed, one of which is an implantable artificial pancreas (IAP).

Technical Description

The concept is to implant a polymeric device, smaller than a hockey puck, which forms a reservoir of disease-free porcine islet cells. A tubular ultrafiltration membrane that is permeable to glucose and other nutrients, permeable to insulin, and impermeable to components of the immune system passes through the device, in contact with the islet cells. Blood flows through the tubular membrane, which is connected surgically to the circulatory system via an arteriovenous shunt. This device will provide natural feedback by producing insulin in response to circulating glucose levels, and deliver it to the blood stream. It is important that the foreign (porcine) islet cells not be subjected to, or create, an adverse immunological reaction. However, because insulin is a small protein, it can pass through the pores in the membrane, while the large proteins and cells that comprise the human immune system will not. The cells are intended to remain alive for five years, after which the device will be replaced or recharged.

Marketing Plan

Market research indicates that there will be overwhelming demand for a device with these characteristics within a group of Type 1 diabetics, estimated to number 1.2 million U.S. patients 12 years from now (when the rollout is completed). Owing to the emergence of competitive technologies and structural market limitations, only 50 percent of this population is targeted. The business expects to charge $10,000 per device, and there is a high probability of reimbursement from medical insurance given the device's ability to defer future medical costs of diabetes such as dialysis.

The cost of implantation surgery and other medical costs will be billed separately by the participating hospitals and physicians, and are not part of the IAP business plan. In association with these hospitals, the IAP business will build and maintain 24 regional implantation centers each capable of servicing 5,000 implants each year (20 per day for 250 days). These centers will be built and staffed at a rate of four per year, so that in six years, there will be capacity to perform 120,000 implants annually. At this point the business can service a patient population of 600,000. No new centers will be built thereafter and further growth will be accommodated by expanding the existing centers. A long-term growth rate of 5 percent will be assumed after year 6; any further expansion of the business will occur by expanding the initial 24 centers.

Summary of Timing Assumptions

As always, in a valuation problem based on cash flow analysis, it is critical to keep track of what year you are in. It is project year 0. This means analysis of a proposed expenditure of R&D funds for next year's budget, year 1. Assume the R&D program, completed on obtaining FDA approval, lasts six years (Years 1 to 6). If successful, in year 6 the business should have strong indications that it has a solid plan, and it will make its capital investments then, expecting the first commercial revenues in year 7. Therefore, project year 6 is commercial year 0, and project year 7 is commercial year 1. The last four implantation centers will come on line in project year 12, after which the business will enjoy 5 percent revenue growth.

Case 7, Problem 1: Revenue Model

Forecast the revenues from the IAP for the first 10 years of commercial operations.

Solution to Case 7, Problem 1 and Discussion

Because this is a new-to-the-world product, there are major uncertainties in the business model. Nevertheless, a starting point is needed and is shown in Figure 4.1.

The business will open four centers in the first year, each near a teaching hospital in a different region of the country. Because a portion of the potential target population, "brittle diabetics," would be very anxious to receive the device, meeting the patient goal will not be difficult. The real concern is more likely to have a fair system for rationing the device! In the first year, four centers will be opened, relying on surgeons trained during the clinical trials. They will perform 20,000 implants. Revenues will be $200 million. In the second year, with four new centers, an additional 40,000 implants can be performed. By year 6, capacity will be at 120,000 implants per year, and importantly, cumulative implants will have reached 420,000.

Because of the nature of the product and associated services, a change in business dynamics occurs in year 7. In that year, the business would expect 20,000 implant replacements, in addition to 106,000 first-time im-

FIGURE 4.1   Revenue Model for Implantable
Artificial Pancreas (IAP) Business

Implants per Center (Years 1–6)	5,000
Revenues per Patient	$10,000
Long-Term Growth	5%

Year	Centers	Implants	Revenues (M$)
1	4	20,000	$ 200
2	8	40,000	$ 400
3	12	60,000	$ 600
4	16	80,000	$ 800
5	20	100,000	$1,000
6	24	120,000	$1,200
7	24	126,000	$1,260
8	24	132,300	$1,323
9	24	138,915	$1,389
10	24	145,861	$1,459

plants. In year 8 it would expect 40,000 replacements, and a declining number of first-time patients, as the initial target market begins to saturate. There will be a number of other complicating effects that are not in this model, but would in time be included as the nature of the market is clarified by time. Some patients will not seek a second implant, while others may need them sooner. Population growth and an aging population will contribute to long-term growth. Some penetration may be expected into a much larger population of Type 2 diabetics. All of these factors are bundled into a 5 percent long-term growth rate. Clearly, there is considerable uncertainty about the longer horizon.

However, the business plan considers the chief limitation to growth to be providers, not patients. The key task will be in having enough physicians and technicians trained in implantation procedures. Also, the IAP business team believes it must control the IAP facilities and procedures to ensure safety, quality, and efficiency, much as is done in chains of dialysis clinics. Therefore, it must invest not only in production facilities for devices and islets, but in transplant clinics. It does not wish to be in the business of employing surgeons, though, other than those required for supervisory roles. Hence, the surgeons will bill patients directly and separately, while the patients are charged for the device and the use of the clinical facility.

With this business model, revenues can be expected to grow to $1,459 million in year 10 of commercial operation.

Case 7, Problem 2: Cash Flow Model

Forecast the cash flows for this business for years 1 to 10. This task will require us to build a pro forma financial statement to estimate potential income and cash flows from manufacture and sale of the IAP device. (This is the most valuable and most time-consuming part of the exercise.)

Assume the initial investment will include a $75 million porcine islet good manufacturing practices (GMP) facility,[1] a $15 million medical device GMP facility, and $40 million for four regional surgical centers, paid for in the year prior to commercial operation. There will also be $20 million in one-time start-up costs (staffing and training). Investments in subsequent regional centers will be made one year prior to their coming on line.

Also assume the following:

Gross margin (selling price less variable costs): 80 percent of revenues.

Fixed cost (factory overhead): 25 percent of gross fixed capital.

Depreciation: 10-year straight line.

Net working capital: 15 percent of revenues.

Selling, administrative, and R&D expenses (SARD): 25 percent of revenues.

Tax Rate: 38 percent.

Estimate the potential free cash flows from manufacture and sale of the IAP device for the first 10 years of commercial operation.

Solution to Case 7, Problem 2 and Discussion

This problem requires the construction of a pro forma financial statement, which is shown as Figure 4.2. It will be reviewed line by line, to cover both the mathematics and the business logic.

Revenues. This topic was covered under Case 7, Problem 1.

Variable cost of goods sold. This heading represents the incremental cost of producing goods and services. For the IAP, it is $2,000 per device. It would include raw materials, such as plastics, chemicals, and porcine pancreases; the direct labor involved in producing membranes and plastic housings and extracting the islet cells; and utilities used directly in manufacturing, including waste disposal costs. It might also include technicians in the clinic who directly assist the medical team. The principle that determines whether wages and salaries are treated as fixed costs or variable costs is whether the staffing would be maintained or

FIGURE 4.2 Calculation of Cash Flows for IAP Business

Implants per Center	5,000		Gross Margin Percent	80%			Investments	M$
Revenues per Patient (M$)	$10,000		Factory Fixed Cost	25%			Islet Facility	$75
Long-Term Growth	5%		SARD	25%			Device Facility	$15
Cost of Capital	12%		Depreciation (Years)	10			Surgical Center (Each)	$10
Tax Rate	38%		Net Working Capital	15%			Start-up Expense	$20

Year	0	1	2	3	4	5	6	7	8	9	10
Centers	0	4	8	12	16	20	24	24	24	24	24
Implants	0	20,000	40,000	60,000	80,000	100,000	120,000	126,000	132,300	138,915	145,861
Revenues (M$)	$ 0.0	$200.0	$400.0	$600.0	$800.0	$1,000.0	$1,200.0	$1,260.0	$1,323.0	$1,389.2	$1,458.6
Variable cost of goods sold	$ 0.0	$ 40.0	$ 80.0	$120.0	$160.0	$ 200.0	$ 240.0	$ 252.0	$ 264.6	$ 277.8	$ 291.7
Variable margin	$ 0.0	$160.0	$320.0	$480.0	$640.0	$ 800.0	$ 960.0	$1,008.0	$1,058.4	$1,111.3	$1,166.9
Fixed costs	$ 0.0	$ 42.5	$ 52.5	$ 62.5	$ 72.5	$ 82.5	$ 82.5	$ 82.5	$ 82.5	$ 82.5	$ 82.5
Depreciation	$ 0.0	$ 13.0	$ 17.0	$ 21.0	$ 25.0	$ 29.0	$ 33.0	$ 33.0	$ 33.0	$ 33.0	$ 33.0
Operating profit	$ 0.0	$104.5	$250.5	$396.5	$542.5	$ 688.5	$ 844.5	$ 892.5	$ 942.9	$ 995.8	$1,051.4
Selling, administration, and R&D	$ 0.0	$ 50.0	$100.0	$150.0	$200.0	$ 250.0	$ 300.0	$ 315.0	$ 330.8	$ 347.3	$ 364.7
Start-up expense	$ 20.0	$ 0.0	$ 0.0	$ 0.0	$ 0.0	$ 0.0	$ 0.0	$ 0.0	$ 0.0	$ 0.0	$ 0.0
Pretax income	–$ 20.0	$ 54.5	$150.5	$246.5	$342.5	$ 438.5	$ 544.5	$ 577.5	$ 612.2	$ 648.5	$ 686.7
EBITDA	–$ 20.0	$ 67.5	$167.5	$267.5	$367.5	$ 467.5	$ 577.5	$ 610.5	$ 645.2	$ 681.5	$ 719.7
Taxes	–$ 7.6	$ 20.7	$ 57.2	$ 93.7	$130.2	$ 166.6	$ 206.9	$ 219.5	$ 232.6	$ 246.4	$ 261.0
Net income	–$ 12.4	$ 33.8	$ 93.3	$152.8	$212.4	$ 271.9	$ 337.6	$ 358.1	$ 379.5	$ 402.1	$ 425.8
Gross fixed capital	$130.0	$170.0	$210.0	$250.0	$290.0	$ 330.0	$ 330.0	$ 330.0	$ 330.0	$ 330.0	$ 330.0
Working capital	$ 0.0	$ 30.0	$ 60.0	$ 90.0	$120.0	$ 150.0	$ 180.0	$ 189.0	$ 198.5	$ 208.4	$ 218.8
Accumulated depreciation	$ 0.0	$ 13.0	$ 30.0	$ 51.0	$ 76.0	$ 105.0	$ 138.0	$ 171.0	$ 204.0	$ 237.0	$ 270.0
Net fixed capital	$130.0	$157.0	$180.0	$199.0	$214.0	$ 225.0	$ 192.0	$ 159.0	$ 126.0	$ 93.0	$ 60.0
Total capital	$130.0	$187.0	$240.0	$289.0	$334.0	$ 375.0	$ 372.0	$ 348.0	$ 324.5	$ 301.4	$ 278.8
Increase in working capital	$ 0.0	$ 30.0	$ 30.0	$ 30.0	$ 30.0	$ 30.0	$ 30.0	$ 9.0	$ 9.4	$ 9.9	$ 10.4
Capital expenditures	$130.0	$ 40.0	$ 40.0	$ 40.0	$ 40.0	$ 40.0	$ 0.0	$ 0.0	$ 0.0	$ 0.0	$ 0.0
Operating cash flow	–$ 12.4	$ 28.3	$ 83.1	$137.9	$192.8	$ 247.6	$ 302.5	$ 339.5	$ 355.8	$ 373.0	$ 391.0
Free cash flow	–$142.4	–$ 23.2	$ 40.3	$103.8	$167.4	$ 230.9	$ 340.6	$ 382.1	$ 403.1	$ 425.2	$ 448.4

adjusted with changes in factory output. There is often an element of judgment involved.

Variable margin. Variable margin, sometimes called contribution margin, is defined as revenues less variable costs of goods sold. I no longer use the term *gross margin*, as I find some inconsistency in its use; sometimes it refers to revenues minus variable costs, and sometimes to revenues minus all manufacturing costs. This product, like many medical products, requires a high variable margin, estimated at 80 percent, to recoup R&D expenses and to cover high fixed costs associated with safety and quality.

Fixed costs. Fixed costs are in principle costs that will continue even if the operation is temporarily idle. Some costs, such as property taxes, insurance, and security may be truly fixed. But most fixed costs involve people: supervisors, professionals, and office staff, who in principle will be retained if the operation shuts down for a time. In a medical operation, the quality assurance function can be a large fixed cost. In this calculation assume fixed costs are 25 percent of gross fixed capital.

Depreciation. Depreciation is an accounting charge for aging capital assets. It is not itself a cash item. Since net income includes a charge for depreciation, cash flow is equivalent to the sum of net income and depreciation. Most industrial equipment is depreciated on five- or seven-year schedules, while buildings are depreciated in decades. In a more detailed financial statement, separate schedules would be used for each class of assets.[2] Here, average depreciation is simulated using a 10-year schedule to account for the fact that some of the IAP assets are buildings. Another detail that is ignored is that tax laws allow accelerated depreciation, creating a liability called deferred taxes. The principal effect of this detail is to reduce the effective tax rate for a growing business, since new deferred tax liabilities are created each year. Note also that no depreciation charge was taken in year 0, since the assets were not yet in use.

Operating profit. This item is revenues less variable costs, fixed costs, and depreciation. No corporate charges have yet been assessed.

Selling, administrative, and R&D expense (SARD). In a more detailed financial statement, these items may be broken out as separate lines. Selling expense is the cost of the sales force, marketing team, and the technical service staff, plus advertising and promotional costs. (These items are not part of cost of goods sold, a term that refers to manufacturing cost.) Administrative expenses takes in the cost of headquarters operations, including executive salaries, legal expenses, and miscellaneous corporate functions. R&D expense should include all costs required to support the business plan. An R&D "tax" to support other corporate initiatives is not necessary, since the precommercial phases of each project are accounted for explicitly and separately in this model.

It is expected that considerable selling expense will be incurred in winning and maintaining the confidence of the medical profession. It is also likely, based on past experience in preclinical trials, that incremental improvements in the device will occur frequently, adding up to major gains in performance over a decade. R&D budgets will need to be substantial, so 25 percent of revenues are budgeted for SARD.

Start-up expense. These are extraordinary expenses, such as training the clinical staff and validating equipment, which are connected with the start-up of this business and are not capitalized.

Pretax income. The pretax profit is operating profit less corporate and nonoperating expenses or income. Since this is a pro forma financial statement for a business unit, it is necessary to subtract only SARD and start-up expense. No interest charges are assessed, since they are included implicitly in the cost of capital. Hence, in our case pretax profit is equivalent to earnings before interest and tax (EBIT). Had the case dealt with a company rather than a business unit, interest would be charged and nonoperating income and expense would be recorded before arriving at pretax profit. (One form of nonoperating income for a technology company might be licensing income.)

EBITDA. It was noted earlier that earnings before interest, tax, depreciation, and amortization (EBITDA) is a measure of pretax cash flow, and is obtained by adding back depreciation to pretax income.

Taxes. An average corporate tax rate is used, and it is also assumed that tax credits generated when net income is a loss are usable. This assumption may not be appropriate for a firm that will generate losses over a long period of time. For global projects, remember that foreign tax rates may be quite different from U.S. rates.

Net income is pretax income net of taxes. It is synonymous with net earnings or aftertax income.

Gross fixed capital is the sum of the business's property, plant, and equipment at original cost.

Working capital is the sum of accounts receivable and inventories less accounts payable. In a more detailed financial statement, each of these elements will be given its own line. In this example an amount of working capital equal to 15 percent of revenues is used.

Accumulated depreciation is the sum of each successive year's depreciation.

Net fixed capital is gross fixed capital less accumulated depreciation.

Total capital is net fixed capital plus working capital. It is the accounting or "book" value of the business, and is fundamentally based on historical cost.

Increase in working capital is the year-to-year increase in working capital. When this number is positive, as it usually is for a growing business, it signifies that the owners are investing additional capital to finance business operations. Hence, it must be subtracted from cash flow.

Capital expenditures or capex represents additional expenditures for plant, property, and equipment. Capital expenditures are required for growth beyond initial capacity levels, and will also be required to retire outworn equipment. It is a negative cash flow item.

Operating cash flow is defined as net income plus depreciation less increase in working capital. This is the amount of cash a business throws off in a given year.

Free cash flow is operating cash flow less the capital expenditures needed to execute the business plan. This is the amount of cash available to the owners to spend as they please. If the owners choose to expand the business more slowly, the initial effect will be to increase free cash flow. In the IAP business plan, in the first two years free cash flow is negative. In years 2 through 5, increases in cash flow of about $60 million each year are driven by rapidly growing net income. However, in year 6 it gets a big boost from a reduction in capex. In year 7, it gets another boost, because a lower growth rate generates a reduction in the rate at which working capital increases. Thereafter, free cash flow grows with the business at about 5 percent per annum.

Case 7, Problem 3: Net Present Value and Internal Rate of Return

Calculate NPV and IRR for this project. This question seeks to measure the value of a successful project, once the time, cost, and risk of the R&D phase is behind us. Figure 1.2 established that the cost of capital for BMX Pharma is 12 percent.

Solution to Case 7, Problem 3 and Discussion

The key item missing is the horizon value, which will now be calculated by the growing perpetuity method. It should be familiar. In year 10, free cash flow is $448.4 million per Figure 4.2. With long-term growth at 5 percent, the horizon value in year 10 is then $448.4 \times 1.05/(0.12 - 0.05) = $6,725.3 million. Including horizon value, year 10 FCF is $448.4 + $6,725.3 = $7,173.7 million. Discounting each year's cash flow back to year 0, NPV is calculated to be $3,151.5 million. Similarly, the internal rate of return is a stupendous 66.9 percent. These calculations are shown in the worksheet "Problems 2&3" within the Excel workbook Medical.xls.

For this case, 68.7 percent of the NPV is in the horizon value. This result suggests that even if the rollout goes more slowly than planned in the first few years, the economics will still be fine.

Is our valuation with the growing perpetuity method excessive? I think not. This valuation works out as 9.3 times EBITDA and 15.8 times net income (price-earnings ratio).

Undoubtedly, given success of this magnitude, the IAP would be a very attractive business; the question now revolves around whether it is worthwhile in view of the long, expensive, and risky R&D program required to bring it to fruition. We turn to this question next.

Case 7, Problem 4: Expected Value via the Decision Tree Method

Assume BMX's internal experts expect this project will require six more years of effort before commercialization, with three logical stage gates. **What is the current value of this project?** The R&D plan is based on the following stages:

> *Stage 1:* Years 1 and 2—preclinical development in animals: duration two years; $10 million per year, probability of success 40 percent.
>
> *Stage 2:* Year 3—Phase I clinical trial: duration one year; $20 million per year; probability of success 60 percent.
>
> *Stage 3:* Years 4 through 6—Phase II and III clinical trials and FDA approval; duration three years; $30 million per year; probability of success 80 percent.

Solution to Case 7, Problem 4 and Discussion

The development of a decision tree analysis proceeds in three steps, each shown as a tier of Figure 4.3. The first tier looks at the R&D costs *by year* and groups them by stages. From a present value viewpoint, they may be less than they seem. First, R&D costs are tax deductible to BMX, so the real cost is on an after-tax basis. Second, future expenses, just like future income, must be discounted by the cost of capital. When the NPV calculated earlier is discounted for a six-year delay, its value is halved, to $1,596.7 million.

The second tier of the chart looks at costs *by stage*, adding together the appropriate discounted costs in tier 1. It also indicates the probability of success at each stage gate—that is, the probability of advancing from one stage to the next.

FIGURE 4.3   Decision Tree for IAP Business Plan ($ Millions)

Year	Pretax Cost	Annual After-Tax Value	Discounted After-Tax Value	Stage
0	$ 0.0	$ 0.0	$ 0.0	—
1	–$ 10.0	–$ 6.2	–$ 5.5	1
2	–$ 10.0	–$ 6.2	–$ 4.9	1
3	–$ 20.0	–$ 12.4	–$ 8.8	2
4	–$ 30.0	–$ 18.6	–$ 11.8	3
5	–$ 30.0	–$ 18.6	–$ 10.6	3
6	–$ 30.0	–$ 18.6	–$ 9.4	3
NPV		$3,151.5	$1,596.7	

Stage	Cost	Cumulative Cost	Probability of Success	Probability of Failure
1	–$ 10.5	–$ 10.5	40%	60%
2	–$ 8.8	–$ 19.3	60%	40%
3	–$ 31.8	–$ 51.1	80%	20%

Outcome	Probability	Cumulative Value	Weighted Value
Failure after Stage 1	60.0%	–$ 10.5	–$ 6.3
Failure after Stage 2	16.0%	–$ 19.3	–$ 3.1
Failure after Stage 3	4.8%	–$ 51.1	–$ 2.5
Success after Stage 3	19.2%	$1,545.5	$296.7
Total	100.0%		$284.9

Value		$284.9
Value as rifle shot		$255.5
Difference		$ 29.5

The final tier addresses costs *by outcome*, of which four are possible in this scenario. The first is a 60 percent probability that the project fails in two years, after the animal trials have been analyzed. The second is that the project is dropped after the Phase I (human safety) clinical trial. With its 40 percent probability of failure, this stage is seen as riskier than the next, since not only will safety be assessed but it will be quickly clear whether the device is functioning satisfactorily. The overall probability of this outcome is 16 percent.

The third, and worst, possible outcome is that the project fails after Phase II and III clinical trials, which involve a huge ($90 million) expense. But the probability of this happening is only 20 percent if the trials begin, and only 4.8 percent overall. Structuring the project in stage gates is the technique that mitigates this risk. (Note in the fourth column that the weighted exposure to risk is actually highest in Stage 1.)

The final outcome is successful commercialization after Stage 3. The associated value is the NPV less all R&D costs incurred.

It is straightforward to calculate the probabilities of each outcome using the individual probabilities given. (Just to be sure, they are added to confirm the sum is 100 percent.) The expected value of the project[3] is then the probability-weighted sum of each possible outcome (column 4), and adds up to $284.9 million.

For reference, I routinely calculate a "rifle shot" alternative—meaning that there is a commitment to see the project through to the end (no exits after Stages 1 and 2), assuming the same final probability of success. This approach is more expensive by $29.5 million, which is to say that risk management adds that amount of value.

Note that this analysis depended on only 10 parameters—the cost, duration, and estimated probability of success for each of three stages, plus the project NPV. How are these parameters to be estimated in the real world? The short answer is to ask the research managers. The longer answer is a process of determining the objectives of each stage, which include not only a demonstration of the technology at the appropriate scale, but also all of the technical information required for the next stage to begin. This last point is particularly important when a technology transfer step is involved, say from laboratory to pilot scale. These needs can be reduced to time lines and resource commitments. Nearly all laboratories account for professional time at a man-year rate that includes overheads to cover laboratory fixed costs. Extraordinary costs, such as animal experiments, clinical trials, outside testing services, raw materials, and so on, will need to be added separately.

The "probability of success" input, however, raises other issues. It reduces a complex situation defined by multiple specifications to a single number. Will those responsible for deciding to advance a project be satisfied with substantially meeting the specifications, or will they insist on meeting them fully? Unfavorable variances from specification may translate into lower revenues, additional cost, or higher capital investment than contemplated in the original business plan. (An acceptable degree of variation may be predetermined by calculating the sensitivity of plan economics to scale, cost, and capital.)

Once a basic definition of success is agreed, there are two ways to estimate it: (1) ask the experts, or (2) review the statistics. The expert approach should manifestly include individuals who are not project champions or who do not otherwise have a stake in continuing the project. The statistical approach can work when the statistical base is adequate, and the comparisons are essentially apples-to-apples. I strongly recommend that every company create a database on its past projects and determine what percentage of candidates has advanced to each next stage. Drug companies have excellent statistics of this type, and have generally published them quite freely. There are a few generic studies that can give a clue to the overall situation.[4] In other situations, the database may be scanty, or projects may be so varied in character that apples are being compared to oranges. But even if agreement on probabilities or other R&D inputs cannot be reached, the method described in the next chapter still enables sensitivity tests on profit based on all three R&D variables (duration, cost, and probability) at each stage.

Case 7, Problem 5: Using Real Options to Address Patent Issues

Advise top management on whether to protect its intellectual property in Europe.

BMX faces an immediate decision whether to maintain its patents on the medical device and porcine islet isolation technologies in the European Union (EU). The question arises because management questions whether the European market is economically attractive.

Here are the known facts: The patent lawyers estimate that filing fees, legal fees, and patent maintenance costs will require an investment of $300,000 over the next six years. Commercialization will require a total investment of $150 million to gain approvals, build manufacturing facilities, and set up the first regional centers (simultaneously with the U.S. centers). Unhappily, because of current reimbursement policies in key countries and other business issues, a conservative estimate of the NPV for this project is a negative $20 million. Nonetheless, this estimate is highly uncertain, and depends on public attitudes and national politics. A consultant has been monitoring the European opportunity for several years, and his periodic updates have shown annual fluctuations of 30 percent or more. Many of the issues will be resolved over the next six years, and indeed may be shaped by developments in the U.S. market. Optimists in the company suggest the game shouldn't be abandoned yet, while others argue that any project that doesn't earn the cost of capital should be dropped and the money invested in projects that do. (Assume the risk-free interest rate is 5 percent.)

Solution to Case 7, Problem 5 and Discussion

A classic problem in R&D management is the cost of foreign equivalents to U.S. patents. In addition to the cost of drafting and filing the foreign applications, many countries charge escalating maintenance fees, which can become quite onerous after a few years. Because the commercial value of a patent is usually poorly understood at the time of filing, many companies try to file overseas on their most promising inventions. Unmanaged, the costs can become very heavy, so it becomes critical to review the overseas patent estate and to prune those patents now believed to have no strategic or commercial value.

The problem as written is probably a no-brainer. Given the uncertainties, protect your position. At worst, you may be able to license European partners or imitators. But the situation is an option and it is interesting to value it.

This is a six-year call option to invest in a European business. The present value of the underlying security is the initial investment plus the NPV. But the NPV is negative, so the option is currently out-of-the-money: strike price $150 million, underlying security $130 million. Assume the risk-free rate is 5 percent.

The remaining input is the volatility. Typically, with real options, this choice is critical and deserves thought. In the IAP case, many factors come into play: volume, pricing, currencies, and so on. The uncertainties could be modeled by a sensitivity analysis using a pro forma financial statement similar to the one created earlier in the chapter, or with a Monte Carlo calculation based on it. However, to keep this problem simple, assume that based on our consultant's inputs, our financial analysts have reestimated the opportunity for each of the past several years, and are beginning to get a measure of the volatility of the forecast. Use 30 percent. Then it is a straightforward shot through the Black-Scholes formula (see workbook "MedicalPatentCaseBS.xls worksheet "Problem 5").

The answer is $44.4 million. This is a longish (six-year) option, not seriously out-of-the-money, and therefore very valuable. Because of the uncertainty in the volatility, a sensitivity analysis is run showing that the option is still worth $33.5 million at a more conservative 20 percent. At 50 percent volatility, the value is $65.0 million. Of course, options deal with market risk—there remains the unique risk that the project will fail. Multiplying by the overall probability of success of 19.2 percent calculated in Figure 4.3, Stage 3, the value is $8.5 million.

There is an additional way to manage risk available here, also involving options thinking. While protecting the patent will cost $300,000 over the next six years, only the initial cost of filing must be paid now. There will be exit points corresponding to the project's stage gates along the way, and a formal analysis of cost using decision tree methods would be straightforward.

Finally, this analysis would help guide our strategy should some expensive patent litigation ensue—patent suits typically cost a few million dollars. Because the value of this option would appear to greatly exceed the cost of defending it, the business should defend it aggressively.

CHAPTER 5

A New Product for an Existing Application

In the previous chapter, as in my book *The Valuation of Technology*, I worked through the logic of project valuation in four steps: (1) revenue model, (2) financial plan, (3) decision tree/stage gate analysis, and (4) real options. While this approach is good for understanding the process, it has the drawback that a lot of recalculation is necessary if one wishes to change a parameter. Project planners like to test sensitivities, such as the effects of lower first-year sales, a lower sales price, or a one-year delay. Accordingly, an Excel template has been created (FSDTRO.xls) where all project inputs and outputs appear on a single worksheet that links to the detailed financial statements and DTRO calculations. It is also possible and convenient to designate input and output variables for a Monte Carlo calculation, if the user has the necessary software.[1] This chapter introduces and discusses this template.

The discussion will focus on some of the critical questions that arise in planning an R&D project where the application is known, and on the excitement and pressure of bringing an innovation to fruition.

Case 8: Inventing an Engineering Polymer

Now run the time machine backward: In Case 3 the research department of Performance Plastics, Inc. (PPI) had completed development of a new lightweight engineering polymer, aimed at replacing metal parts in automobiles. Go back eight years earlier, when a young polymer scientist, Dr. Charlie Lamb, has an idea that he thinks could lead to a new product line for his company. He has discovered a catalyst that combines two monomers that could never be copolymerized before, and speculates that this combination will provide great stiffness, unprecedented toughness, and the processability required to manufacture rigid auto parts. Management is skeptical; auto companies are known to be ruthless negotiators, and since most raw material costs will be known to them, large profit margins are not to be expected. Still, the need is real, as federally mandated pressures to increase gas mileage and decrease emissions are relentless.

Another problem is that the R&D program will be long and expensive. First, the physical properties of the product will need to be optimized, and a patent estate created for it. Then enough sample must be made for initial molding trials to confirm that the promised properties and processability can be realized on commercial equipment; a few tons will be needed. Customers will receive samples, but they will soon request prototype parts for various torture tests and ultimately for test-track vehicles. Their tests are likely to take years, because parts failures (and recalls) create massive liabilities. A conceptual manufacturing process must be developed, and its key steps tested at a scale that gives confidence that the manufacturing plant will run as designed. The customers will not commit firmly for large orders until supply is assured.

Charlie's invention, dubbed polyarothene, is a real headache for management. An internal debate rages between those who believe the auto companies are just too tough to deal with and the risks far too high, and those who point out that the growth rates of PPI's existing products are inexorably slowing, that the stock price is going nowhere, and that it was research followed by years of struggle that created PPI in the first place. The CEO concludes that the arguments and the counterarguments are in part emotional and are disrupting the company, and calls for analysis.

The question before the analytical team is whether Charlie's idea is valuable, even after all the risks are taken into account. The goal is to calculate the *risk-adjusted value* of a decision to proceed.

Revenue Model

At this early stage of the project, it would be virtually impossible to build a revenue model on a customer-by-customer and part-by-part basis. That task would be undertaken perhaps four or five years out as the auto manufacturers define their new model introductions. What is known is the weight of parts in existing automobiles that might be replaced by performance plastics. This number must exclude parts that may be replaced by cheaper commodity plastics with which the firm cannot compete on price. A conservative approach would also assume that the customer will not pay more for a better or lighter part; that is, the customer's value proposition will initially be driven by better performance at equal cost. Price and volume estimates should reflect this logic.

PPI's initial thinking about price is that it should be at about $1 per pound. This offers a 43 percent "gross margin," (variable cost of goods sold), more than auto companies are accustomed to pay for a commodity plastic, but not in the "greedy" zone. Also, Charlie's patent and polyarothene's performance advantages serve to justify this price. PPI's calculations indicate that, on an equivalent volume basis, structural steel and aluminum would each cost about 90 percent more than polyarothene,[2] and weigh 7.8 and 2.7 times as much respectively. So even if the plastic part needs to be somewhat heftier than its metal equivalent, the opportunity is real—at least up to the constraint that the application cannot use 90 percent more polymer (on a volume basis) than the metal being replaced. Fortunately, the proposed price is also well below any competing engineering polymer.

The business engages a consulting automotive engineer, and his analysis indicates polyarothene has an excellent opportunity to reach a level of 100 million pounds of annual sales in the United States within 10 years of commercial entry, or about 6 pounds per vehicle in a market of 16 million vehicles.

The next question is, how fast can the business reasonably get there? Because of the conservatism of the customers, a rapid penetration of this market cannot be expected at the outset. But if the business dawdles, with its plant running at a fraction of capacity, the economics will turn sour. PPI finally settles on a goal of selling six million pounds in the first year, enough for one million vehicles.

This decision is a big one and is supported by the type of sensitivity analysis I described in the introduction to this chapter. Six million pounds is an ambitious goal and implies the plastic is specified on several different makes and models. It is clear that the early commercialization stage of the project must prepare the way for that transition, and that a critical step will be to achieve a sales level representing about 100,000 vehicles in the final year of that stage. If this level of success is not in sight, management proposes the project would be terminated at the stage gate leading to early commercialization. The pressure is building.

The pro forma model now has two volume numbers (for years 1 and 10), and needs two more to pin down the revenue model. One is the intermediate year 5 volume, which is critical to determining the size of the initial manufacturing investment. The second is the long-term growth rate, which affects the horizon value, which in turn is very critical to the net present value.

After much discussion the year 5 sales are estimated at 48 million pounds, or about half the potential market, based on the notion that the product would by then be in use by about half the eventual adopters. It takes four or five years to design a new model in Detroit, so the year 5 sales would be of a product that is already on the drawing boards. But that industry would still have laggards, owing not only to conservatism, but to contractual arrangements with other suppliers and competitor actions to forestall switching. But a better new material always wins: That is why in the United States there are no more steel beer cans and very few glass soft drink bottles. By year 5 it also would be expected that the rest of the market would already contemplate switching to polyarothene.

Generally business planners are comfortable with 5- and 10-year revenue projections. If there is any plan at all, these numbers are usually available. The methodology in my template is to interpolate the growth between years 1 and 5, and years 5 and 10, on a geometric basis. Growth from 6 to 48 million pounds is at 68 percent per annum (it is not unusual to double annual sales in the early stages of a successful new product), and it is about 16 percent for years 5 through 10.

The longer-term growth rate chosen is 5 percent. It is considered that the automotive market, in volume terms, can grow at best at only 2 to 3 percent per year. But the experience in engineering plastics, and even commodity plastics, has been almost 5 percent annual growth owing to the opening of new applications and to product improvements no longer attainable by more mature technologies such as steel and aluminum.

There are obviously many other ways to structure a revenue projection (I used a different algorithm in *The Valuation of Technology*), and the template is readily modifiable to accommodate situational preferences.

Fixed Capital Model

The importance of the year 5 sales projection was mentioned earlier. It derives from the concerns of the planners about building a plant of the correct scale. The decision involves a trade-off: A large plant operating at a small percent of capacity incurs enormous unrecovered fixed costs. But a large plant enjoys great economies of scale in fixed capital and fixed operating costs. For example, the control system and the office are likely to be the same size, but spread over more pounds. The surface area of steel in a reactor vessel or tank increases with the 2/3 power of the volume; thus the surface-to-volume ratio is reduced. In the chemical industry, it is believed that the cost of a new plant varies with 0.6 power of its volume. PPI's engineers considered a 12-million-pound plant that would be filled in two years, a 48-million-pound plant that would be filled in five years, or a 100-million-pound unit that would not be fully utilized until year 10. The costs for the middle case were estimated by PPI's engineering staff to be $33.6 million or 70 percent of annual revenues at capacity.

Figure 5.1 depicts the economics of larger and smaller plants. The algorithm used is that Plant Cost = K × Capacity ^ Exponent. K is an arbi-

FIGURE 5.1 Polyarothene Fixed Capital Investment versus Volume

Based on Algorithm That Plant Cost = $K \times$ Capacity ^ Exponent

Exponent			0.6			
Standard Cost (M$)			$33.6			
Standard Capacity (M Units)			48			

	Capacity	Capacity ^ Exponent	K	Cost	Cost per Unit	Percent of Standard
Standard plant	48.00	10.20	3.29	$33.6	$0.70	100.0%
Small plant	12.00	4.44	3.29	$14.6	$1.22	174.1%
Large plant	100.00	15.85	3.29	$52.2	$0.52	74.6%

trary constant calculated for the standard case. The exponent is 0.6, but may be varied by the user. The 100-million-pound plant would cost only $52.2 million and reduce fixed capital per pound to $0.52, an impressive 25 percent. Another option might be to build a series of small 12-million-pound plants. These cost only $14.6 million each, but are inefficient from a capital viewpoint: They cost $1.22 per pound of capacity.

The template (Figure 5.1 Polyarothene Fixed Capital Investment versus Volume.xls) then makes it very convenient to calculate the trade-offs. For the large plant, because of the huge capacity unused for a decade, the NPV is $11 million less, but the project has a positive outcome. The small plant case is unacceptable: The NPV for the commercial project is $11.3 million, and is insufficient to recoup the cost of the R&D program. In addition, the company would be burdened by the intangible costs of planning and implementing an endless series of expansion projects.

Another consideration is expansion beyond initial capacity. One process is incremental, and is called "debottlenecking." Plant supervisors often learn that production is limited by a single element, say a pump or a heat exchanger. With a small investment in capital the bottleneck is removed and another unit in the process becomes the bottleneck. This circumstance leads to a condition where incremental capacity costs less than initial capacity. Most producers take advantage of these cheap opportunities to increase real capacity above planned or "nameplate" capacity. Another popular option is to add new production lines to an existing plant; often the new lines are larger than the old, and they will be more efficient as production technology improves. Since many assets from the plant will be shared, this option also will come at a lower cost per unit of capacity.

The template is based on this concept. (See Figure 5.2.) It contemplates an initial investment with a given capacity (48 million pounds), at a given

FIGURE 5.2   Master Template

Inputs (Millions)		Outputs ($ in Millions)		
Units Sold Year 1	6	Growth Rate Years 1–5	68.18%	
Units Sold Year 5	48	Growth Rate Years 5–10	15.81%	
Units Sold Year 10	100	Long-Term Growth Rate	5.00%	
Long-Term Growth Rate	5.00%	FCF Multiplier (MF)	14.29	
Sales Price/Unit	$1.00	Var. Cost as % Revenues	57.00%	
Variable Cost/Unit	$0.57	Mfg. OH as % Fixed Capital	11.43%	
Manufacturing Overhead/Unit	$0.08	Turnover Ratio	142.86%	
Initial Fixed Capital/Unit	$0.70	Initial Investment	$34.28	
Initial Annual Capacity (Units)	48			
Incremental FC/Unit	$0.50	**Business Value in First Commercial Year**		
Asset Life (Years)	10	*Horizon Value Method*	*IRR*	*NPV*
Selling, Admin., and R&D	10.00%	1. HV = Working Capital	14.19%	$ 4.73
Days Inventory	30	2. HV = Book Value	15.82%	$ 9.04
Days Receivables	36	3. HV = EBITDA * ME	24.93%	$52.02
Days Payables	25	4. HV = Net Income * P/E Ratio	25.17%	$53.73
Tax Rate	35.00%	5. HV = FCF * MF	26.76%	$65.94
Cost of Capital	12.00%	ROIC (Average)	18.55%	
EBITDA Multiplier (ME)	7	10-Year IRR	7.07%	
P/E Ratio	12.5	10-Year NPV (no HV)	($7.23)	
Risk-Free Rate	5.00%			
Volatility	30.00%	**Current Value**		
Choice of HV Method (1–5)	5	Current Value as Rifle Shot		($ 1.01)
		Current Value by DT		$ 1.76
R&D Parameters		Value Added by DT		$ 2.77
Duration Stage 1	2	Current Value by DTRO		$ 1.82
Duration Stage 2	2	Value Added by RO		$ 0.06
Duration Stage 3	2	Cumulative Probability		10.42%
Duration Stage 4	2	Cumulative R&D Cost (AT)		$ 7.31
Pretax Cost Stage 1	$0.75			
Pretax Cost Stage 2	$1.50	**Value Progression**		
Pretax Cost Stage 3	$3.00	Current Value		$ 1.82
Pretax Cost Stage 4	$6.00	Value after Stage 1		$ 6.63
Probability Stage 1	33.33%	Value after Stage 2		$14.60
Probability Stage 2	50.00%	Value after Stage 3		$20.83
Probability Stage 3	75.00%	Value after Stage 4		$65.94
Probability Stage 4	83.33%			

initial cost ($0.70 per pound of annual capacity). When initial capacity is exceeded, new fixed capital is added at an incremental cost ($0.50 per pound) to keep sales and production in balance. Obviously, the user of the template has the choice of making the incremental cost equal to, or even greater than, the initial cost or adding large new plants when required, by modifying the template. The model is flexible, and the planner is encouraged to experiment with it.

There are some timing considerations. In this template the initial investment in the plant is shown in year 1, and since the plant is operating in that year, depreciation is charged. In reality, capitalizable expenses associated with this plant, starting with design engineering and proceeding through site preparation, construction, and commissioning, will be incurred over a period of two, three, or more years. The spending schedule is likely to be back-loaded, with the greatest expense in the final year. Because of the time value of money, the initial investment should include "interest" (at the cost of capital) on these earlier expenses.

Working Capital Model

Working capital is defined as accounts receivable less accounts payable plus inventories. This template measures working capital in "days" of revenues, a very intuitive measure. For example, assume that receivables are collected in a little more than 30 days (industrial companies will seldom pay earlier than the contract stipulates and some will pay later owing to billing disagreements). Payables, which include raw materials and accrued payroll expense, will be somewhat less than 30 days. Inventories of all kinds—raw materials, work in process, and finished product—are taken as 30 days. All in all, this combination amounts to 11.4 percent of revenues, or a "cash flow cycle time" of about 42 days, fairly typical for the chemical industry. Aggressive cash managers, however, have been able to reduce cash flow cycle time below 30 days.

Net Present Value

This subject has been reviewed as Case 3, in the context of analyzing the contribution of horizon value to NPV. The detailed financials are on worksheet "Proforma" of the Figure 5.2 template. Note that some of the input parameters, such as selling, administrative, and R&D expenses (at 10 percent of revenues) and manufacturing overhead (11.4 percent of gross fixed capital), reflect the much leaner operating philosophy of a business where sales are concentrated at a few customers and gross margins are quite thin.

R&D Model

The model requires three R&D inputs per R&D stage (12 numbers for a four-stage process). These are simply the estimated duration of that stage, the estimated after-tax cost of the stage, and the probability of success defined as the probability of advancing through the current stage gate to the next stage. The probabilities of success and cost estimates used in the following pages approximate those from a database that I developed on about 100 projects over a five-year period.

An example of a four-stage process begins with a "conceptual" stage involving range-finding experiments, small-scale tests, and intellectual property development. At this point, Dr. Lamb, the inventor, is the protagonist. His team must test variations in catalyst structure, ratios of monomers, polymerization conditions, and additives. These experiments ensure obvious improvements are not missed and will help create a "patent fence." The resulting polymers must then be tested for physical properties and rheology (processability). The best combinations will be selected for further work. The conceptual stage is important, because the hurdles to overcome are high and because it sets up the conditions for increasing levels of investment. In addition, the costs of laboratory work are very low compared to the investments that will follow, so this is the time to eliminate as many unknowns as possible.

It should also be recognized that every experiment Lamb's team runs affects the value of his project. If the result is worse than expected, value decreases and the project is jeopardized. If it is better than reasonably expected, value has been created. Even if it is exactly as expected, value is created, because uncertainty has been reduced!

The conceptual stage is estimated to take two years, cost $750,000 (three man-years), and have a one-in-three (33 percent) chance of advancing through the stage gate. However, when the probabilities of success at each stage gate are cumulated, the overall chance of achieving commercial success from this point is only 10.4 percent.

When they are ready, Charlie and his troops will request a stage gate meeting to decide whether the project should move to the "feasibility" stage. Present at the meeting will be R&D executives, corporate engineering staff, business unit marketing staff, and a financial analyst assigned to the project. The feasibility stage will involve more people and an increase in scale. One task will be the conceptual design of an efficient manufacturing process, which will be tested in a pilot plant in the following stage. This will require data about mixing conditions, heat transfer, and purification procedures needed to select equipment for pilot-scale operations. Larger-scale laboratory equipment will be operated to produce the pounds of material needed for small-scale extrusion and molding trials. Contact may be made with potential customers to understand their expectations regarding physical properties; any shortcomings will be addressed, and specifications will eventually be established for a dozen key physical properties, ranging from stiffness to color. The feasibility stage is estimated to take two years, cost $1.5 million, and have a 50 percent probability of advancing into development.

The next stage gate meeting authorizes the "development" stage, which will cost $3 million over two years and is rated at a 75 percent probability of success. Laboratory science will now play a smaller role, and the engineers will take charge. They have three key tasks. The first is to test the proposed process at a scale large enough to design a production line. The second will be to produce increasingly larger amounts of polymer, for testing in commercial-scale molding equipment. Sample prototype parts will soon be made available to customers, and molds will need to be designed and fabricated for that purpose. Third, they must ready PPI's semiworks to produce a ton a day or so of material for the early commercialization stage. Note that the need to produce test material is quite different from the task of designing a process. Sample production can be improvised using separate pieces of equipment on a batch-to-batch basis. However, process design will involve testing on scaled-down versions of the equipment to be used in the final process, demonstrating continuous operation, and focusing on minimum operating and capital costs. Common problems such as plugging, corrosion, or poor mixing must be identified and fixed now. Meanwhile, assuming the initial samples were well received, contact between the technical service staff and the customer's research unit has become intense. Some specific target parts, selected based on a strong customer need, have been identified and are being translated into mold design. Custom molders, selected by the original equipment manufacturers (OEMs),[3] are in the loop, as well as the purchasing staffs of the OEMs. There will inevitably be questions, problems, delays, and misunderstandings.

The stage gate authorizing the "early commercialization" or "launch" stage is truly a critical one, since a failure in this stage will be financially expensive as well as a blow to PPI's reputation. Not only are the ongoing R&D costs high, but at some point there may be a risk of writing off some capital. The cost is estimated to be $6 million, its duration is two years, and it has a five-in-six (83.3 percent) chance of succeeding. The chances of success are good, because the stage gate team, which now includes the president of the operating division, has verified that the pilot data are sound, the cost estimate is reasonable, and enough customer commitments are in hand to assure adoption of the technology. Product is being made in the semiworks and is being sold to customers in increasingly large quantities. But despite a small revenue stream that offsets raw material costs, the semiworks is inefficient and PPI loses money on every pound. Within PPI the semiworks, or market development plant, is part of R&D, and R&D is in effect subsidizing the project. However, the relationship with customers is controlled by the business unit, so a spirit of teamwork is essential. Considerable technical support is also required since any molding problems encountered in the field must be solved quickly. Finally, a marketing and sales team is lining up new opportunities to ensure the year 1 production target is met or exceeded.

Exposure to R&D risk in this process is managed carefully even though costs double at each stage. In the context of a portfolio of similar projects, unique risks are diversified, and it is justifiable to think in terms of probability of loss rather than maximum loss. For example, at the end of the conceptual stage the project will have a two-in-three chance of losing $750,000, or a probability-weighted loss of $500,000. At the feasibility stage, the cumulative R&D expense will be $2.25 million, and the probability-weighted loss is half that, $1.125 million. Similarly, at the end of development the weighted loss is $1.31 million, and at the end of early commercialization it is $1.88 million. These numbers are further mitigated by tax deductibility and by the time value of money, which is quite substantial for the later stages.[4] So, in economic terms, the real risk stays under about $1 million! It is the combination of successively increasing costs and sharply reduced relative risks that powers value creation.

Results of Case 8 and Discussion

The outputs from this exercise include the value of the project today and the value to be expected at the completion of each stage. The calculated value of the project is $1.82 million, of which $0.06 million comes from real options. A great deal of value, $2.77 million, is derived from the decision tree structure with its abandonment options. This converts the project from a loser as a rifle shot to a winner.

The real option contribution is small because I used the growing perpetuity method for calculating NPV, which put the option well into the money (by $65.9 million). Had I used the most conservative approach, liquidation of working capital (which has an NPV of only $4.7 million, barely in-the-money), real options would add considerably more value, $0.49 million.

Is it fair to conclude that real options are unimportant? Not really. There is a substantial range of NPV (from $17 million to $24 million) where the real options contribution puts the project in the black. Below an NPV of $17 million the project is no longer able to bear its R&D costs.

It is also interesting to look at the progression of value at the completion of each project stage.

Current value	$ 1.82 million
Value after Stage 1	6.63 million
Value after Stage 2	14.60 million
Value after Stage 3	20.83 million
Value after Stage 4	65.94 million

It can be seen that after Stage 1 is completed the project will be worth $6.63 million. This largely explains why it is worth $1.82 million today: The one-in-three chance is worth about $2.2 million, but it will cost $0.4 million (discounted, after-tax) to get there. So this lottery ticket should be worth about $1.8 million. The value after Stage 4 is, as expected, the commercial NPV.

Return on R&D Investment

An additional calculation can lead to one of the most sought after, and elusive, parameters in R&D analysis: the return on R&D investment. The main reason for this parameter being elusive is that the value created by R&D effort often cannot be separated from the efforts of marketing, sales, and manufacturing, nor from the capital investment that follows from R&D success. In this model the separation is, in an analytical sense, quite possible! In no way does this negate the fact that a commercially successful R&D program is totally dependent on a team effort, and that crediting R&D alone for success is wrongheaded.

The calculation is relatively simple. The annualized gain in Stage n is:

$$\mathrm{Exp}[\ln(V_{n+1}/(V_n + I))/t_n] - 1$$

where V_n is the premoney value at the beginning of the stage, I is the R&D investment, V_{n+1} is the value achieved at the successful completion of the stage, and t_n is the duration of the stage. The R&D returns in each stage of the example are listed in the last column of Figure 5.3, and an average weighted by the amount of R&D spending is calculated.

The R&D return for the duration of this project is 37.16 percent.

Note that while the return in Stage 3 is quite low, it enables Stage 4, which is very attractive. However, to this point each calculation assumed project success. In Figure 5.4, the calculation is repeated to correct for probability of success. The R&D return is 30.6 percent on a weighted basis.

Is this case economically reasonable? It is in line with other studies. Aboody and Lev have calculated an internal rate of return of 26.6 percent for chemical industry R&D.[5] Their estimate was derived from a regression analysis of corporate earnings versus R&D spending. Carter and Edwards[6] have discussed evidence that returns on R&D investment may be expected to be in the 20 to 30 percent range. This estimate is based on Carter's personal studies plus an extrapolation from the Securities Market Line. They

FIGURE 5.3   Return on R&D Investment

Investment Round	Value Premoney (Millions)	R&D Investment (Millions)	Value Postmoney (Millions)	Duration (Years)	Annualized Return
1	$ 1.82	$0.75	$ 2.57	2	60.58%
2	$ 6.63	$1.50	$ 8.13	2	34.00%
3	$14.60	$3.00	$17.60	2	8.80%
4	$20.83	$6.00	$26.83	2	56.77%
	$65.94				
Weighted Average Return					37.16%

FIGURE 5.4   Probability-Weighted Return

Annualized Return	Probability of Success	Probability-Corrected Annualized Return
60.58%	33.33%	20.19%
34.00%	50.00%	17.00%
8.80%	75.00%	6.60%
56.77%	83.33%	47.31%
Weighted Average Return		30.60%

also quote John Gibbons,[7] former science adviser to President Clinton, as estimating R&D returns at 30 to 50 percent.

Clearly, the expected return on R&D investment will be project-specific, company-specific, and industry-specific. Its calculation by the methods given here does, however, offer an indication of whether a project proposal is consistent with industry norms.

SUMMARY

The methodology built into this master template gives an instant picture of the risk-weighted value of a project. It allows the analyst to quickly determine which project characteristics are critical. The program generates a financial statement based on estimates of revenues and growth rates, and simple parameters to estimate capital intensity and overhead costs. Five alternatives are available for calculating horizon value. The program then accepts inputs describing the estimated cost, duration, and probability of success for each project stage, to calculate a risk-weighted value using decision tree methodology. With the addition of a volatility parameter and the risk-free interest rate, the options value of the project is automatically added to the valuation.

CHAPTER 6

Start-Ups

The prior chapter demonstrated that, while R&D is a very risky investment, the returns can be high! This observation has not escaped entrepreneurs, venture capitalists (VCs), and even institutional investors, such as university endowment funds, whose investments in emerging technologies have increased dramatically in the past decade. Increasingly, R&D investment opportunities are being packaged as "pure plays" in the form of discovery-based start-up companies. (They may later be syndicated by venture capitalists into diversified R&D funds.)

Correspondingly, many large company R&D projects can be valued as if they were spun off into a start-up—a realistic option, and an attractive one under certain circumstances. As a result, one must now look at an internal project from the perspective of an independent, pure-play start-up, and have the ability to switch perspectives at a glance, since a project can move from one arena to the other in a heartbeat. The comparison provides considerable intellectual insight into how value is created in R&D. Welcome to the technology marketplace, where value is created as the big players maneuver for advantage with the small and nimble.

The same forces—R&D cost, the risk of failure, and the time value of money—impact a start-up and a behemoth, but not necessarily in equal measure. In addition, the life of a start-up is much more directly concerned with the perceptions of investors. Unlike mature companies, start-ups lack the cushion that reasonably predictable cash flow provides to the stock price. Finally, to a much larger degree, younger companies are subject to issues relating to ownership and control. Excessive control by founders may be anathema to investors, yet founders have legitimate reasons to fear being forced out by investors on unfair terms. Fortunately, the very tools we have just developed apply directly to the evolving financial structure of a successful start-up, although they are in practice not yet as often applied.

Indeed, it is not uncommon for technology entrepreneurs to get their start in large company laboratories. Some leave for financial opportunity, others out of frustration that their ideas are not adequately supported. Sometimes the departure is contentious, but in other cases, such as the one described in this chapter, the originating company views an independent start-up as the best vehicle for maximizing a new technology's value, and actively seeks to facilitate its success.

A start-up typically evolves in one of three modes. The classic mode, although not the most common, is the one described in the company's prospectus. It is to proceed through several rounds of venture capital and private equity financing, during which period the company's technology and business model will be proven. It will then raise enough money in an initial public offering (IPO) to survive and prosper as an independent company. As part of the IPO process, early-stage investors and founders find their "exits," although IPO investors will be concerned that key management is retained for the first crucial years as a new publicly traded company. There are many role models: Amgen, Biogen, Apple Computer, and so on. Venture finance equity tables for a number of successful technology companies are available in the Appendix of John Nesheim's excellent book *High Tech Start-Up*.[1]

An even more attractive exit mode can be acquisition by a strategic buyer. This outcome may be the real intent of the founders and early-stage investors, and offers two special bonuses. First, the technology developed can be leveraged by the commercial resources of the buyer (inaccessible or very expensive for the start-up). These resources might included testing expertise, development skills, a sales force, brand names, and manufacturing facilities. Second, a lower element of market risk will be reflected in a more favorable cost of capital when the project is within the walls of a strategic buyer, if that buyer is viewed by the market as a stable operation. A lower cost of capital automatically increases the net present value of any business plan; in principle this gain should be shared by buyer and seller.

The benefits can be dramatic if the cost of capital is reduced from the 20 to 40 percent range (start-up) to 10 to 15 percent (strategic buyer). This effect is closely analogous to the "free lunch" that accrues to investors who diversify their portfolios.[2] In this case, however, the value is driven by eliminating the enormous premium paid for venture-stage capital as a class, and reducing the cost of capital to that of a competent operating company, performing business as usual. Note it is not simply a financial manipulation, such as the hypothetical acquisition of a biotech wild card by a regulated utility. Such an irrational transaction should properly result in an increased cost of capital for the utility that offsets the lower cost of capital for the project—with zero or even negative net value creation. But the same biotech property in the hands of Big Pharma can be a value story.

An example of the strategic buyer exit mode is described by Bob

Kunze[3] in the Agrion case, in which I participated as the representative of a major early-stage investor, W. R. Grace & Company. In this example, Agrion, a start-up with rights to a novel approach to immunization, acquired an operating veterinary vaccine company, Diamond Laboratories, which was subsequently purchased by a strategic buyer, the German chemical giant Bayer.

The third mode is the path of failure. For big companies, failure is a simple problem. The project is shut down and the scientists and engineers are reassigned. There are few financial consequences since R&D is expensed; hence there are no write-offs to declare. There is a question as to whether to salvage the intellectual property values through license or sale, or to leave the intellectual property on the shelf to be revived under more promising circumstances. The chief technical officer (CTO) can handle the whole affair, and routinely winds down dozens of programs annually.

It is far more complicated for a start-up that is in trouble delivering its hoped-for promise, since there are disappointed investors, albeit sophisticated ones. Liquidation is a possibility if there is considerable cash on hand and the technology is virtually worthless. Cut your losses and return the cash to the investors.

A delaying tactic is the "cram-down," issuing new equity at a much lower price than the previous round. The massive dilution involved is uncomfortable for existing investors, but it allows a troubled firm a second chance.

Far more likely is a merger with a still-viable competitor. Antitrust is not a problem because start-ups are below the radar screen. But a competitor may be very interested in acquiring patents that could affect its position, and ensuring that key scientists do not create the nucleus for yet another competitor in the field. At the same time investors in the failing company get a bite of a new apple—the equity they receive as a result of the merger, and the hope that the combined companies now have the resources to succeed. This exit strategy also applies to companies well past the start-up stage: Many companies get through the IPO stage, only to find that they are not truly viable, and end up being acquired by stronger firms.

EVOLUTION OF THE TECHNOLOGY MARKETPLACE

A vigorous and healthy, if highly volatile, marketplace for technology has emerged in the past 40 years wherein the sellers are typically scientists, engineers, and entrepreneurs, and the buyers are venture capitalists, established companies desperate to acquire technologies they have been unable to create, and general investors with a taste for technology speculation. Investment bankers specializing in technology mediate many of these deals.

The marketplace for technology in the United States was first actively developed in 1946, when Harvard professor General Georges Doriot and a small circle of Boston-area bankers and industrialists founded American Research and Development (ARD), the first U.S. venture capital firm. Using start-up funds of less than $5 million, ARD began mining the fertile fields of postwar technological development then taking place in and around Harvard and MIT. ARD's great moment of fame occurred in 1957, when it invested heavily in a venture spearheaded by a young MIT researcher named Kenneth Olson. Olson called his company Digital Equipment Corporation. By 1971, ARD's investment of $70,000 had grown almost 5,000-fold, and hundreds of other venture capitalists were eagerly attempting to clone its success.[4]

Since the founding of ARD, venture capital has been associated with virtually all of the major technology-driven new industries in the United States: semiconductors; super-, mini-, and microcomputers; medical devices; software; biotechnology; and wireless telecommunications. Venture capital industries have emerged in Great Britain, continental Europe, Asia, and Australia, but all on a much smaller scale.[5]

A major event in the valuation of technology-based companies was the initial public offering of the stock of Genentech, a company without a single salable product and only the prospect of running at a loss for several years. Nevertheless, its market capitalization on going public exceeded that of American Can Company, a Fortune 100 company with more than 100 years of operating history.

Of course, venture capitalists do not share their funds with a start-up company out of the goodness of their hearts. Because the risks are high, they demand in return a significant ownership stake in the venture, evidenced by shares of founders' stock. In some cases, they will advance new money to the firm in exchange for convertible preferred stock, a bondlike hybrid security that can be converted into common stock at the option of its holder. Both common stock and convertible preferred stock give their holders an interest in the future fortunes of the enterprise. The goal of the venture capitalist is to help the struggling start-up develop its technology and business to the point at which it becomes either (1) an attractive item for purchase by a larger company or (2) capable of selling its shares through an initial public offering of stock (IPO). In either case, the venture capitalist hopes to harvest his or her investment for much more than its initial cost. The VC will almost always focus on his exit strategy, and cannot be regarded as a long-term investor.

Venture capitalists know from experience that many start-up investments fail to pay off. By investing in a number of start-ups, however, they expect to achieve superior average returns. A few outstanding successes will make up for a number of failures. ARD provides a perfect example. Over the years of its activities and many investments in small companies, ARD[6] earned a compound annual return of 14.7 percent; almost half of this was due to its major hit with Digital Equipment.

Since almost no banks or other institutions will provide capital to a start-up company, the VC is often in a good position to get what he wants (hence the term *vulture capitalist*). The high cost of VC financing induces some company founders to hold out for other sources of capital. In their view, giving large blocks of dirt-cheap founders' stock to the venture capitalist is like giving away much of the upside potential of their company and their ideas.

However, it is worthwhile to remember that venture capital is itself a competitive business, subject to enormous volatility. In the market bubble of 2000, venture capital firms raised over $107.5 billion, more than 10 times the level of a decade earlier. The reason was that the best performers in the industry had been achieving annual returns on capital of 50 percent or more as the bubble picked up steam. Investors could not resist such seemingly easy money. But demand quickly overtook supply, and venture capitalists found themselves bidding more and more for weaker ideas and less experienced management teams. Many of the Internet niches were so oversubscribed by me-too start-ups that it was clear the majority could not survive. The bubble in portfolio values burst shortly thereafter, and the monies raised by the venture capital industry dropped by almost 90 percent. However, venture investment can only rise again; the long-term trend is almost certainly up. Under these volatile circumstances, a demand for average annual returns, over a business cycle, of 20 to 30 percent looks more reasonable.

Case 9: MiracleCure's Financing Process

For technologists, venture capitalists and others like them represent just the first stage of a potential series of markets for invention. To understand how values are determined in this marketplace, it is worthwhile to review the typical stages of financing for successful technology start-ups. Later in the chapter, they will be linked closely to the corresponding stages of technical progress.

Solution to Case 9

Case 9 is a fictional and much simplified case, but the buildup in value and the way value is shared between innovators and investors follows a pattern traced by many innovative companies in the biotech industry.

Stage 1—Seed Capital: Sweat, Angels, and VCs

In the first step, an entrepreneurial group develops an informal strategic intent and identifies the technology assets, ideas, resources, and markets it intends to exploit. Much of the initial investment is represented by so-called sweat equity contributed by the founders on speculation that the core concept will succeed. The founders may also contribute some cash to fund start-up activities such as incorporation costs, design expenses, the building of prototypes, equipment, and the like.

Other cash is often contributed by friends or associates: so-called angels. A venture capitalist (VC) may be affiliated with the founding group as well. While other founders contribute technical knowledge and inventive ideas, the venture capitalist contributes money and, in some cases, contacts in the financial, business, and supplier communities. In other cases, a major corporation may provide seed money to the start-up in return for technology rights. In such cases, a VC may not be needed.

We can take a simple approximation of value at this stage by looking at the R&D funds the company (let's call it MiracleCure) has spent and the amount contributed by early-stage investors, including the founders.

Assume that MiracleCure has already spent $1 million on R&D in its quest for the ultimate cancer cure. Early investors have invested an additional $3 million, for which they have received three-sevenths of the stock. The founders retain control, holding four-sevenths. Using a "step-up ratio" of 4, which is the ratio of premoney valuation to cumulative R&D, we can make a rough estimate of MiracleCure's value using the following formulas (see Figure 6.1):

$$\text{Cumulative R\&D Expense} \times \text{Step-up Ratio} = \text{Premoney Valuation}$$

and

$$\text{Premoney Valuation} + \text{Financing} = \text{Postmoney Valuation}$$

or

$$(\$1 \text{ million} \times 4) + \$3 \text{ million} = \$7 \text{ million}$$

Where did the $4 million premoney valuation come from? In the last analysis it was determined by negotiation between the seed round investors and the founders—but if the parties were sophisticated they might have looked at the step-up ratios in comparable deals for guidance. Just such a proprietary deal database has been created by Recombinant Capital[7] as a

FIGURE 6.1 MiracleCure Capitalization Model ($ Millions)

Stage	Name	R&D	Cumulative R&D	Financing	Step-up Ratio*	Premoney Valuation	Postmoney Valuation
1	Seed capital	$ 1.0	$ 1.0	$ 3.0	4.0	$ 4.0	$ 7.0
2	Private placement 1	$ 3.0	$ 4.0	$ 7.0	2.5	$10.0	$ 17.0
3	Private placement 2	$ 7.0	$11.0	$17.0	2.8	$30.8	$ 47.8
4	Initial public offering	$17.0	$28.0	$40.0	2.5	$70.0	$110.0

*Premoney valuation/cumulative R&D.

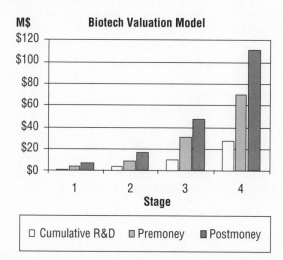

guide for biotech investors, and a step-up ratio of 4 is in the middle of the range for initial financing rounds.

From the point of view of technology valuation, a nominal $1 million of cumulative R&D in sweat equity and founder's cash has been monetized fourfold. While this may seem high, it is worth bearing in mind that the risk of project failure in the first stages of research was also high, and these risks have now been overcome. The markup is appropriate if there was initially a 25 percent chance that $1 million of research would meet the conditions to advance to the feasibility stage of R&D. The goal was met and the probability of the advance to Stage 2 is now 100 percent. A value of $4 million was created through reduction of technical risk.

Stage 2—Private Placement, Round 1

Now assume that the MiracleCure management group has spent some time developing its ideas into a demonstration of technical feasibility, and that these ideas continue to look promising. However, the initial funding is starting to run out, and it is clear that more investment will be needed. A total of $4 million has now been expended in R&D activities, and the founders have enough data and confidence to write a credible business plan, which will include financial projections and a description of markets, customers, manufacturing plans, patents, competitors, and risks. This business plan will be presented to venture capitalists and other sophisticated investors.

Venture capitalists typically not only invest their own money, but manage funds placed with them by sophisticated private and institutional investors. Among the latter may be large corporations that are cash rich but idea poor, and looking for a "window on technology." Venture capitalists also often syndicate their investment favorites with other venture capital funds in order to diversify their risks. They say, "I'll buy a piece of your company if you'll buy a piece of mine." Many of these investors do not intend to stay for the long term; rather they expect to sell their shares at high markups at the initial public offering or sooner.

The amount raised in the first round of financing is usually only enough to see the company through a few years of its business plan and negative cash flow. In fact, investors characterize start-ups in terms of a "burn rate"—a company with $9 million in cash on its balance sheet and a burn rate (projected annual cash loss) of $3 million will be out of cash and back for a new round of financing in three or fewer years. The short window between financing rounds is actually rational for all concerned. Founders do not want too much venture investment because it is relatively expensive compared to capital they may be able to raise later. And by making smaller investments, venture capitalists both gain greater diversification and increase the benefits of the option to abandon.

Assume that MiracleCure has burned through the $3 million invested by its angels and is eager to begin developmental stage R&D. The strength of its business plan, the prominence of its scientific staff, and general optimism about the anticancer drug market induces one of the behemoths of the pharmaceutical industry to make an investment of $7 million—a modest investment for a big drug company, but significant money for MiracleCure.

The value of MiracleCure can once again be estimated using the same formula used earlier. Now, however, cumulative R&D has grown to $4 million. And while the continued R&D progress in the feasibility stage is very encouraging, it is not as startling as the brilliant discovery that quadrupled the investors' original stake. A premoney valuation of the company of $10 million is negotiated, representing a step-up ratio of 2.5.

Postmoney Valuation = ($4 million × 2.5) + $7 million = $17 million

Figure 6.1 categorizes MiracleCure's financing through this and subsequent rounds, indicating the postmoney valuation in table and graphic form.

Stage 3—Private Placement, Second or Mezzanine Round

Many start-ups go through several rounds of private placement and engage in other financing activities, such as spinning out technology to joint ventures and limited partnerships or performing contract research for industrial partners.

For simplicity assume that none of these other financing techniques is needed, and that after a time MiracleCure has spent the $7 million it raised from the first-round investors on more R&D (cumulative R&D is now $11 million), and that its prospects look sufficiently attractive to warrant another round of investment. Specifically, in this example, investors are assumed to view the company as being worth $30.8 million, the new premoney valuation, representing a step-up ratio of 2.8. Another $17 million is raised and postmoney valuation rises to $47.8 million, as shown in Figure 6.1.

While these are increasingly larger sums, the company is also growing and has a higher burn rate. Specifically, the burn rate has increased from the initial $1 million to $2 million per year to $5 million or more as early products move into clinical trials, and new, promising second-generation products are added to the R&D pipeline.

At this point, a new piece of nomenclature enters the vocabulary: "mezzanine financing"; this is the financing round immediately preceding the IPO.

Stage 4—Initial Public Offering (IPO)

With its credibility established by successful test results in human subjects, MiracleCure is ready to go public—that is, to make its first public offering of stock through an IPO. Indeed, it must attract more investment if it hopes to complete the clinical trials and build the manufacturing capacity it needs to produce, sell, and deliver finished products. At this stage $28 million has been spent on cumulative R&D, and the firm is valued by the investment bankers promoting the offering at $70 million. New funds of $40 million are being raised to support growth, but in all likelihood some of the initial investors—including the founders and early employees—will be using the IPO as an opportunity to harvest some of the profits on their early investments. This is when people who were recruited for modest salaries plus stock options at 20 to 30 cents per share see a chance to cash out at $20 or $30 per share and become instant millionaires.

Secondary Offerings

If MiracleCure continues to grow, it will need still more capital. If cash flow remains negative it may be necessary to offer more shares of stock to the public through what are called *secondary* offerings. Also, as tangible assets grow and operating cash flow turns positive, MiracleCure may be able to raise new capital through borrowing.

In the real world, not every successful start-up makes the transition through these many financing steps. As noted earlier, promising start-ups are, instead, often acquired and absorbed into larger companies eager to capture their technology and human talent. MiracleCure, for example, may be the target of a strategic acquisition by a larger firm attracted to its technology and to the markets it is addressing. That larger firm might be the major drug firm that provided much of its early funding. Acquisition may be the best possible exit strategy for the venture capitalists, founders, and early employees. While some may mourn the loss of MiracleCure's independence, these individuals may celebrate its acquisition as the biggest payday in their lives.

In summary, investments in technology start-ups, often companies with no real operating components, have been highly rewarding for sophisticated investors. Step-ups in value of more than 100 percent are common between first and second financing rounds, another 80 percent step-up can occur in the third round, and another 35 percent at the IPO level. IPO returns on some companies have been sensational—Apple Computer rewarded early public investors 235 times over.

One of the most important determinants of returns, according to a study by William Bygrave and Jeffry Timmons, is the health of the IPO market at the time a company goes public. That market is notoriously volatile (some say fickle), enjoying, in turn, periods of euphoria and of retrenchment. As they state, "When the IPO market is buoyant, it's comparatively easy to float new issues of venture capital–based companies at high valuations. This causes venture capital returns to rise, because . . . IPOs, on average, provide the most bountiful harvest of venture capital."[8]

However, they also found that during the long periods in which the IPO market has been unenthusiastic, returns were far lower.

Case 10: A Start-up Markets a New Analytical Instrument

Case 10 is part fact, part fiction. Part One is fact, based on my own personal experience. Part Two is fiction, where numbers and history not available to me are reconstructed as they might have occurred. Case 10 differs from Case 9 because it goes beyond the details of financing to the excitement of launching a very successful new enterprise.

Industry Background

Analytical instruments form a highly specialized market, not only serving the scientific community, but providing routine analyses for medical, environmental, and quality applications. When a chemist mixes two compounds in a beaker, it is to an analytical instrument he or she turns to find out precisely what happened. When regulators want to know the quantity of polychlorinated biphenyls (PCBs) in a contaminated disposal site, they need an analytical instrument. Patients suffering from diabetes need analytical instrumentation to monitor their blood sugar. The applications are virtually endless.

For many instruments, such as polymerase chain reaction (PCR) analysis of DNA, the technology can be extremely sophisticated. Research instruments used by scientists are often exquisitely sensitive, highly specific, and very flexible. Some require enormous magnets or high vacuum. Instruments for routine analysis may be highly automated to provide rapid throughput, relying on automatic sample changers and computerized reports. What do they cost? Anywhere from a few thousand dollars to several hundreds of thousands of dollars, depending on the degree of technical sophistication, the size of the market, and the bells and whistles (such as the computer system and the sample changer). The number of analytical instruments in a modern laboratory may outnumber the scientists and technicians, and as such represent a considerable investment in fixed capital.

Case 10, Part One: A Surprise Phone Call

My Dionex saga began with a call from one of Dow Central Research's laboratory directors, Bill Burgert, in 1972. Burgert told me one of his research scientists, Hamish Small, had invented a new form of chromatography dubbed ion chromatography, and thought (correctly) that it would have applications in environmental analysis. Since that was my department, he asked my help. I met with Hamish, liked the idea, and asked a young analytical chemist, Tim Stevens, to help define some initial applications. Tim took to the assignment with great enthusiasm, and soon we built several prototype units and moved them into division laboratories. The initial technical feedback was very positive.

Demand was rising, and we outsourced manufacturing to a small machine shop on the outskirts of Midland, Michigan, and soon had almost 20 units in the field. The instruments were functional, constructed using rack-mounted components, and the tubing, valves and plastic bottles were in plain sight. They were not very pretty, but perfectly appropriate for a laboratory environment. Money was very tight then, so we learned how to make ion chromatographs for less than $3,000 apiece. Soon they would be sold for 10 or more times that price!

Small's invention occurred only because Dow Central Research offered seed money to creative scientists like himself. But the invention posed a classic dilemma for his boss (Burgert): Small's discovery was a classical example of "a solution looking for a problem." Many business gurus advise against such investments. This case, however, shows the opposite side of the coin—that fundamental science can lead to excellent returns on relatively modest investments, especially when intellectual property protection is solid. But when the project moved to my analytical group, it became essentially self-financing: Dow's internal customers paid for each instrument and for Stevens' time. We did find many problems for which ion chromatography was an effective solution. This real-world condition at the outset ensured that we learned the value equation at the customer level, and was, in hindsight, a key to the success of the project.

I also worked closely with George Rock, a Dow licensing executive, on how to commercialize this discovery—because Dow, as a matter of policy, didn't want to be in the instrument business. We visited Waters Associates (now part of Millipore). Waters had previously licensed Dow's earlier invention of gel permeation chromatography, but they unexpectedly turned ion chromatography down because they were riding another tiger—liquid chromatography. Dow reviewed some other alternatives.

A Technical Breakthrough

What is ion chromatography? Ions are charged participles ubiquitous in aqueous environments, whether these be environmental waters, body fluids, or foods and beverages. Ions come in matched pairs; each positive ion (such as sodium, ammonium, calcium, and a host of other metals) is balanced by a negative ion (such as sulfate, chloride, or acetate). Prior to Small's invention, each ion had to be measured by its own specific analytical technique. His breakthrough was that a single analytical measurement could measure all the positive ions, and a parallel instrument, if so desired, could detect all the negative ones. From a technical viewpoint, the breakthrough invention was to enable the use of a conductivity detector, an inexpensive but accurate device, to measure the output of a chromatographic separation. From an economic viewpoint, many independent analyses could be replaced by one (or two), and these were very susceptible to routine analysis on a simple instrument equipped with an automatic sample changer. Why hadn't this been achieved before? Because a large quantity of "eluent" made up of strong acids and bases, themselves ionic, was required to move the ions of the sample down an analytical ion exchange column. This created an enormous background that made the targets virtually invisible to the conductivity meter, and the method impractical. Small's elegant invention was to simply strip the eluent on a second ion exchange column placed directly before the detector.

Strategic Considerations

Chemical companies have a love-hate relationship with the instrument business. Their analytical chemists regularly invent new and ingenious ways to make measurements more accurately or with greater sensitivity than ever before. They create competitive advantage. Should these advantages be shared with the world? That is both an economic and a strategic issue. The first is basically a question of comparative NPV, the subject of this book. But in addition, the culture of an instrument company that sells a single instrument to a single analytical chemist is very different from a business that sells hopper cars of nylon or tank cars of styrene to a factory. DuPont created a sizable and well-respected instrument business based on its R&D discoveries, but eventually concluded that greater value would be created by divesting it to a party more in tune with the philosophy of one-time sales to very specialized and demanding customers.

Dow had made a strategic decision not to enter the instrument business, but to license its key inventions. In view of the DuPont history, Dow was likely right. Prior to ion chromatography there were at least three prior inventions, and each had been licensed to a different instrument company. Two were in the field of analyzing wastewater—the total oxygen demand (TOD) analyzer and the total organic carbon (TOC) instrument. Each was a standard in water laboratories. The third was gel permeation chromatography (GPC), a method for analyzing the molecular weight of polymers based on liquid chromatography, which had been successfully licensed to Waters Associates and was once Waters' core business. The fit of ion chromatography and the history of the Dow-Waters relationship seemed so logical it appeared to be a sure thing. But it was not.

As noted earlier, I participated in the initial presentation to Waters, and they turned down the Dow proposal on the basis that their resources were fully consumed by the fast-growing field of high-pressure liquid chromatography (HPLC). Waters may well have been right, for HPLC became a multibillion-dollar industry, arguably the most important analytical technique ever invented. Nonetheless, ion chromatography was itself a gem, and offered far higher exclusivity.

Solution to Case 10, Part One

Dow decided to spin the technology out to a new company, Dionex, which was founded in 1975 and has prospered. It currently has revenues of nearly $200 million. My direct participation with ion chromatography ended before this time, but it is interesting to map how the value creation process might have occurred given the situation going in. The imaginary scenario that follows fully justifies the valuation of Dionex stock (about $130 million) at its IPO in 1982. It assumes the project went through four stages, culminating in the IPO.

Case 10, Part Two: IC Corporation—A Fictional Case

The case history in Part One involves two real companies, Dow and Dionex. But since I have had to fill in much data, I will rename Dionex as IC Corporation and Dow as Acme Chemical to avoid any impression that the following financial case is a real one. This device also allows me to simplify what can only have been a very complex business process, giving greater clarity to how value is created through research and development.

In the real case, as well, we never performed any financial analysis. At the time, I didn't have the skills, and the first electronic spreadsheet (remember Visicalc?) wasn't to appear for five more years. But now that the tools are available (hence this book), I advocate using them. I agree that at the early stages of a project, it is probably fruitless to worry about the fine detail of its evolution—the business never evolves like the plan. But it is extremely important to understand the magnitude of the potential, and to confront the key issues in quantitative terms. The beauty of a fast electronic spreadsheet is that project valuation can be upgraded rapidly after every technical or market development. Even though the valuation is bound to change, there is little reason to be concerned when the light is clearly green. When it turns red the course is obvious. When it is in the yellow zone, a careful reappraisal is warranted, and each assumption needs careful scrutiny, lest one be trading cash for hope.

Solution to Case 10, Part Two

As before, the analytic process works backward, starting with a commercial business plan, then outlining the R&D/investment stages, and finally calculating the payoff for founders and investors alike.

IC Corporation's Business Plan

Figure 6.2 summarizes the premises of this plan.

FIGURE 6.2 Ion Chromatography Project

Inputs		Outputs		
Units Sold Year 1	1,000	Growth Rate Years 1–5	25.74%	
Units Sold Year 5	2,500	Growth Rate Years 5–10	9.86%	
Units Sold Year 10	4,000	Long-Term Growth Rate	5.00%	
Long-Term Growth Rate	5.00%	FCF Multiplier (MF)	10.00	
Sales Price/Unit	$25,000	Var. Cost as % Revenues	18.00%	
Variable Cost/Unit	$4,500	Turnover Ratio	250.00%	
Mfg. OH as % Fixed Capital	60.00%	Initial Investment	$30,208,333	
Initial Fixed Capital/Unit	$10,000			
Initial Annual Capacity (Units)	2,000	**Business Value in First Commercial Year**		
Incremental FC/Unit	$5,000	*Horizon Value Method*	*IRR*	*NPV*
Initial Cash	$5,000,000	1. HV = Working Capital	49.01%	$ 60,280,562
Asset Life (Years)	10	2. HV = Book Value	49.11%	$ 61,328,822
Selling, Admin., and R&D	15.00%	3. HV = EBITDA * ME	53.91%	$124,529,867
Days Inventory	50	4. HV = Net Income *	54.46%	$133,733,367
Days Receivables	50	P/E Ratio		
Days Payables	25	5. HV = FCF * MF	53.79%	$122,505,597
Tax Rate	35.00%	ROIC (Average)	65.70%	
Cost of Capital	15.00%			
EBITDA Multiplier (ME)	7	**Current Value**		
P/E Ratio	12.5	Current Value as Rifle Shot	($ 4,617,188)	
Risk-Free Rate	5.00%	Current Value by DT	$ 1,939,330	
Volatility	40.00%	Value Added by DT	$ 6,556,519	
Choice of HV Method (1–5)	3	Current Value by DTRO	$ 2,084,121	
		Value Added by RO	$ 144,791	
R&D Parameters		Cumulative Probability	10.42%	
Duration Stage 1	1	Cumulative R&D Cost (AT)	$ 19,825,000	
Duration Stage 2	2			
Duration Stage 3	3	**Value Progression**		
Duration Stage 4	3	Current Value	$ 2,084,121	
Pretax Cost Stage 1	$ 500,000	Value after Stage 1	$ 7,008,512	
Pretax Cost Stage 2	$ 4,000,000	Value after Stage 2	$ 17,668,150	
Pretax Cost Stage 3	$ 6,000,000	Value after Stage 3	$ 25,733,190	
Pretax Cost Stage 4	$20,000,000	Value after Stage 4	$124,529,867	
Probability Stage 1	33.33%			
Probability Stage 2	50.00%			
Probability Stage 3	75.00%			
Probability Stage 4	83.33%			

The input portion of the worksheet begins with the elements required to construct the revenue forecast. The number of units sold in the first commercial year (the year of the IPO), the number sold in year 5 (1,000), the number sold in year 10 (2,500), and a long-term growth rate are projected. Also estimated is an average selling price of $25,000. The volume price relationship might have been developed in the following sequence. Early sales are likely to be to research laboratories and large analytical laboratories that would buy the instrument initially to understand its capabilities. Scientists like something new. The price must be in line with prices for similar instruments, such as those used in HPLC. As the method gains enough credibility to be used routinely, the next tier of sales could be to government and industrial laboratories that perform environmental, boiler, or drinking water analyses. The number of such sites would need to be determined (consultants have this data based on sales of other an ytical instruments), and strategies established for promoting faster penetration. Finally, there would be potentially large new markets where the ultimate utility of the instrument is not yet apparent, such as medical laboratories testing bodily fluids, or industrial quality control laboratories. It would be best to be conservative in estimating sales in these areas, but the upside is huge. Repeat sales are likely; workhorse analytical instruments can be regarded as worn out or obsolete within five years, particularly because improvements in automatic sampling and data analysis capabilities make upgrades imperative.

Next come the costs. Acme has learned that basic models could be made for $3,000 for parts and labor, plus a profit for the subcontractor. There are not yet economies of scale. However, the commercial units are likely to be more expensive, not only because of better cabinetry, but more importantly because instrument companies (like car companies) prosper by selling appealing features, and customers often demand them. Hence a variable cost of $4,500 is assumed, giving a very promising contribution margin of $20,500.

The next decision is whether IC Corporation will do its own manufacturing; assume that (given its handsome margins) it wishes to protect its franchise by building some critical parts, such as control systems, and by controlling final assembly. It must therefore invest in a factory building, process equipment, and a warehouse. However, as assembly is not a capital-intensive operation, $10,000 per annual unit of production might be more than adequate. A 2,000-unit-per-year plant would cost $20 million, giving a manufacturing turnover ratio of 250 percent. In time, this estimate will be refined as equipment lists and architectural drawings are developed.

The choice of a 2,000-unit plant is a decision in itself; it implies that the plant operates at only 50 percent of capacity in the first year, and will not reach full capacity until year 4. This decision can be tested using economic calculations as in Case 8. New capacity can be added more cheaply to an existing facility. Estimate the additional cost as $5,000 per incremental annual unit of capacity. Units of capacity are now assumed to be added as needed, the process referred to as debottlenecking.

The final elements of cost are the fixed expenses or overheads. In this case, I have tied the manufacturing overhead percentage to the size of the plant (60 percent of gross fixed assets). One reason for the large figure is that the gross fixed assets are small relative to the size of the business. Another is that considerable supervision and coordination will be needed, since many of the instruments will be individualized to customer specifications, and quality control must be rigorous.

Selling, administrative, and R&D expenses are taken as 15 percent of revenues. The R&D laboratory will constantly test the technology against new market opportunities, support the sales force in developing and publishing new analytical methods, and suggest improvements in the instrumentation itself. A technical service force must be prepared to cure sick units in the field, and make suggestions to customers as to how to operate their instruments more effectively. The service representatives are also a vital source of strategic intelligence to the company. Finally, there is advertising and promotional expense. Regular ads are needed in chemical trade journals. The instrument must also be shown at trade shows, especially the massive Pittsburgh Analytical Conference (which is no longer held in Pittsburgh); an impressive booth is surprisingly expensive.

The remaining input assumptions (Figure 6.2) deal with working capital, including some spare cash for the start-up year; asset life (10 years); the tax rate; and the cost of capital. For the latter, I use 15 percent, as a blend of the cost of capital for an Acme Chemical and for an instrument company with a proprietary and useful main product.

The result, the project NPV in the year of commercialization (1982) is $124.5 million when using an EBITDA multiplier of 7 to determine horizon value.

Modeling the R&D and Financial Stages

For this exercise, we assume there are five R&D stages, and we wish to track the value of the project as we progress through them. The duration, cost, and estimated probability of success for Stages 1 through 4 are shown on the bottom left of Figure 6.2.

Stage 0   Stage 0 represents the evolution of a raw idea before serious consideration is given to commercialization. For ion chromatography, Stage 0 ended in 1972, and met two key requirements. First, the idea had to be reduced to practice to a degree that other experts considered credible. The inventor had built a "breadboard" instrument that made this clear.

Secondly, a patent position needed to be established—if the idea was not truly novel, operating margins characteristic of open competition (for it would be easy to reverse engineer an ion chromatograph) might not be sufficient to overcome development costs. The patent search looked good, and a patent filing was made. However, the patent had not yet been allowed—still a possible showstopper. More importantly, it was unclear whether there was much of a market for this technology. Here, then, was the first decision point, and the point at which we begin the analysis needed to support Acme's continued funding of ion chromatography.

Acme's Physics Research Laboratory had invested $250,000 in this idea. Although this was now a sunk cost and does not affect future equity calculations, it does establish the reasonableness of the first step-up ratio. The project value derived from DTRO analysis is $2.084 million, of which $0.144 million or 7 percent comes from the real options piece. The project is a loser by rifle-shot analysis (–$4.617 million), but, as is so frequently the case, this is more than overcome by management of risk through the stage gate approach. Hence the first step-up ratio is 8.34.

If one looks at the capitalization table (Figure 6.3) one sees that the founders would receive 17.36 percent of the equity after the successive recapitalizations of the company. These shares would be worth $26.858 million if the project is successful. Presumably, these shares would belong to Acme or the inventor if the election were made to go to start-up mode at this stage. But the Acme decision maker decides to continue playing the hand.

Stage 1   One reason to continue to play is the internal synergies of the big company environment, which creates fast and easy access to potential applications. Acme's analytical laboratory constitutes some 200 scientists and technicians, and provides support to more than 50 manufacturing plants. All environmental analyses, including many performed by plant technicians on-site, are in its purview. The arena of opportunity is vast, though highly diffuse. The question is whether any of these operations can benefit from a radical new instrument. Many laboratories routinely measure a related parameter, total dissolved solids, which reports salt discharged to the environment, a parameter critical to the company's environmental performance. Would it be useful to understand the nature of this salt by identifying its constituent ions?

An expert chromatographer who knows most of the potential customers for the project is chosen and suggests a handful of potential applications. He quickly builds a laboratory instrument, with the inventor's technical inputs, and starts to test it against real-world samples drawn from the manufacturing environment. This constitutes Stage 1, the conceptual stage.

In financial terms, Acme has invested $0.500 million of new money (as the round 1 investor), spent it on R&D, succeeded, and created a new premoney valuation of $7.009 million. This number appears as "Value after Stage 1" in Figure 6.2, and as premoney, round 2, in Figure 6.3. The step-up ratio (reflecting the new premoney valuation divided by the most recent postmoney valuation) is 2.71. This change largely reflects the fact that the

FIGURE 6.3 Capitalization History of IC Corporation

Prior Investment: $250,000   Founders' Shares: 1,000,000

Tier 1

Round	R&D/G&A	Cumulative Expense	Premoney Value	Step-Up	Cash Raised	Postmoney Value
1	$ 250,000	$ 250,000	$ 2,084,121	8.34	$ 500,000	$ 2,584,121
2	$ 500,000	$ 750,000	$ 7,008,512	2.71	$ 4,000,000	$ 11,008,512
3	$ 4,000,000	$ 4,750,000	$ 17,668,150	1.60	$ 6,000,000	$ 23,668,150
4	$ 6,000,000	$10,750,000	$ 25,733,190	1.09	$20,000,000	$ 45,733,190
IPO	$20,000,000	$30,750,000	$124,529,867	2.72	$30,208,333	$154,738,201

Tier 2

Ownership after Round	Founders	Round 1 Investors	Round 2 Investors	Round 3 Investors	Round 4 Investors	Public (New)
1	80.65%	19.35%				
2	51.35%	12.32%	36.34%			
3	38.33%	9.20%	27.12%	25.35%		
4	21.57%	5.17%	15.26%	14.26%	43.73%	
IPO	17.36%	4.16%	12.28%	11.48%	35.19%	19.52%

Tier 3

Value at IPO	$26,857,755	$6,443,425	$19,006,135	$17,763,257	$54,459,296
Investment	$250,000	$500,000	$4,000,000	$6,000,000	$20,000,000
Gain	$26,607,755	$5,943,425	$15,006,135	$11,763,257	$34,459,296
Gain as percent	10,643.1%	1,188.7%	375.2%	196.1%	172.3%
Years to payoff	12.0	9.0	8.0	6.0	3.0
Annual return	47.7%	32.8%	21.5%	19.8%	39.6%

Tier 4

Stock Round	Market Cap Premoney	Market Cap Postmoney	No. of Shares Premoney	No. of Shares Postmoney	Share Price	Reconcile with Cash Raised
1	$ 2,084,121	$ 2,584,121	1,000,000	1,239,909	$ 2.08	$ 500,000
2	$ 7,008,512	$ 11,008,512	1,239,909	1,947,568	$ 5.65	$ 4,000,000
3	$ 17,668,150	$ 23,668,150	1,947,568	2,608,951	$ 9.07	$ 6,000,000
4	$ 25,733,190	$ 45,733,190	2,608,951	4,636,645	$ 9.86	$20,000,000
IPO	$124,529,867	$154,738,201	4,636,645	5,761,397	$26.86	$30,208,333

probability of success has moved from an initial 33 percent to 100 percent (for this stage only!), at a cost of $0.500 million. More good work.

Acme now picks up additional equity in the project as a round 1 investor of 4.16 percent, worth $6.443 million, if the project succeeds.

Stage 2 The conclusion after Stage 1 is that the data are promising and that some prototype instruments should be tested in the field directly by plant chemists. The decision is made to undertake the feasibility stage, at a cost of $4 million and an estimated duration of two years. This is a more expensive proposition—because teams of people are involved, there is an investment in instrumentation, and considerable R&D support and method development are required. Not considered, however, are the offsetting benefits that the instruments in the field are bringing to plant operations. Confidence is gained when a basic patent is issued. Acme elects to stay for one more stage.

The successful completion of this round brings an increase in pre-money value to $17.668 million, an amount noticeable even to an industrial giant such as Acme. Following the same logic, Acme in round 2 has added 12.28 percent to its final share in the equity of a successful company, bringing its total to 33.80 percent. It will be worth $52.308 million upon successful completion of the business plan.

Acme also estimates it will need another $26 million in Stages 3 and 4 to design commercial instruments, to develop new methods for external customers, to promote the concept, and to develop a robust manufacturing process. Start-up of a manufacturing plant could take a capital investment of $30 million more. While all this money and more might well be paid back handsomely, senior executives remind the R&D enthusiasts that they are in the chemical business, not the instrument business, and that the cash could be used more strategically. Furthermore, because the amount of equity Acme is building may soon be a deterrent to other investors, the time to exit is now. They recommend spinning the technology out, and remind the key employees that the licensee (possibly a start-up) would probably want to acquire some of the core players of the chromatography team. For simplicity this analysis ignores the reality that key management and technical employees are likely to be rewarded by stock options and/or restricted stock, which will dilute the stakes of the other equity holders.

Stage 3 It is now 1975. Stage 3 initiates the life of the California-based start-up, IC Corporation. The technical task is to develop and test a product. It will require industrial design, manufacturability, a supply chain for disposables, manuals, and brand recognition. Target customers, such as laboratories performing analysis for the Environmental Protection Agency, must be identified, prioritized, and educated. Wholly different skill sets are required than those needed to place rack-mounted units in Acme's plant sites. A CEO experienced in the instrument business is recruited, and is tasked to put together the nucleus of the new company. Figure 6.2 shows this development stage lasting three years and costing $6 million; the new company at this point has a burn rate of $2 million. While I have classified this money as R&D, it in fact includes many other categories of expenditure. During this period, it will be necessary to place "beta" (prototype) models in the field that are sufficiently robust, and which attract enough customer interest, that commercial viability seems assured. The next milestone will be the early commercialization stage, when customers will be expected to pay for Mark I units. There is much to be done.

Of course development costs money, and Acme offers a deal to round 3 investors for a private placement: Put up the $6 million for this round, accepting our premoney valuation of $17.668 million, and take 25.5 percent of the company. In return Acme will give you a preferred position for financing round 4 ($20 million), and the right to sell your shares as part of the IPO. If our business plan succeeds you should nearly triple your investment. There is nothing surprising in this structure; venture capitalists typically reserve large portions of their funds for second-round investments. In essence they are seeking to sweeten their financial investment with a call option; if things look good they can exercise, if bad they will keep the cash.

The capitalization table in Figure 6.3 shows the investors' situation. It is logical from the viewpoint of managing risk to not put all $26 million at risk, and set a milestone after only $6 million has been spent. But relatively little value is added in the development stage; the big payoff comes after Stage 4. The round 3 investors can expect an annualized return of 19.8 percent—not bad, but their payoff is six years down the line and is at some risk. The round 4 investors get a much better deal: a 39.6 percent annualized return, a lower level of risk, and a payoff in half the time. In fact, they have almost too good a deal, so it is attractive for insiders to reinvest in the company at this point. Giving previous investors an inside position on round 4 makes sense and sweetens the deal for the round 3 investors. Remember that these returns are driven entirely by the NPV and the structure of the four stages of the program: finance follows project economics.

The round 3 investors will undoubtedly ask Acme to take a haircut on its valuation or will look for other concessions (likely relating to control). But if the business plan is correct Acme has no need to budge very far. The technology is largely proven, it is patented, and the chance of commercial success is now well above 50 percent and rising.

Stage 4   Stage 4 is the early commercialization stage, where management has sufficient confidence in its product that it is willing to charge customers for it, but has yet to invest in efficient manufacturing facilities or distribution channels. Extensive technical service and debugging is required, plus there is a constant need to keep improving the technology and respond to information that can only be gained by working closely with customers. In brief, this is the last opportunity to cut one's losses before committing to the facilities and staff envisioned in the business plan. So, even though revenues are being booked, operating losses and start-up expenses far outweigh them. Cumulative losses of $20 million over a three-year period are foreseen. It is an exciting and a rewarding time.

It is 1982. At the end of Stage 4, investment bankers are engaged, a prospectus is written, and management goes on the road to raise the $30.208 million required to build the factory, sign supply contracts, and start the business—the initial public offering (IPO).

Capitalization History

While we have wended our way slowly from "Eureka!" to the birth of what will be a $200 million public company, our viewpoint has moved from one step in the process to the next. It is very worthwhile to look again at the total flow represented in Figure 6.3. Why? Because it is only a spreadsheet, it is prospective, and it evolves according to the inputs we give it—the NPV and the duration, cost, and probability of success at each stage. For a new business idea, the equivalent spreadsheet will be invaluable in structuring a business plan that anticipates problems down the road. Issues such as control (as defined by share ownership and agreements with investors), risk, fair returns for both founders and investors, and the right time to approach VCs or other private equity investors are clarified. Soon some things will be set in stone, but now there is a chance to anticipate and avoid the pitfalls.

We have already described how tier 1 is derived from the successive valuations placed on the company at the time each stage gate is successfully crossed and money is raised to finance the next stage.

Tier 2 describes how the ownership changes in this process. Note that this ownership is itself a decision. Acme could in principle have gone to the outside at the end of Stage 0 or at the end of Stage 1, but chose to do so at the end of Stage 2. This choice was driven by both business judgment and the fact that Acme has ample financial resources. Consider what might have happened had the spin-off occurred after Stage 0. The founder is successively diluted to (approximately) 80 percent, 50 percent, 38 percent, 22 percent, and 17 percent. Clearly, he can retain control through Stage 2, but not much longer. Tier 3 shows that his investment will have grown 100-fold from $0.250 million to $26.857 million in 12 years. This is an annualized return of 47.7 percent (lower than might be imagined), and it is the highest return for any round of investors. And it should be, because it was at the greatest degree of risk. Round 1 investors make only a small investment, and consequently own only 4 percent of the company, but their return is very attractive, 32.8 percent. They are at less risk than round 0 investors, and their return is lower. Similarly, round 2 investors, who make the first sizable cash investment in the company, end up with 12 percent of the company.

Of course, as the scenario is written, Acme makes up the class of round 0, 1, and 2 investors, comprising 33.8 percent of the shares, worth $52.307 million. The round 3 and 4 private investors' 46.7 percent stake is worth $72.223 million based on an investment of $26 million. Both Acme and the investors intend in time to sell their stakes. They may piggyback on the IPO if the marketplace indicates a strong demand for the shares. Their right to do so has probably already been defined in the contractual agreements between the company and each round of investors.

Phantom Shares

If the founder is considered to hold phantom shares as a result of the Stage 0 success, the value of these shares is in principle the value of the project divided by the number of shares issued. It has been determined that the initial value of the project is $2.084 million. The number of phantom shares is arbitrary. Assume there are 1 million, valued at $2.08 per share. (Of course Acme never thought in these terms, but it is not unknown for "intrapreneurs" to be awarded "real" phantom shares.) In rounds 1 and 2, the number of phantom shares rises to 1,947,568, determined by dividing the new money invested by the share price when the investment is made. That share price is calculated from the value of the project at the appropriate stage gate. The phantom share price has risen to $9.07 by the time Stage 3 is complete.

It is time now to issue real shares. Acme issues 1,947,568 shares to itself and awards the round 3 investors 661,383 shares in return for their $6 million in cash. The round 3 investors own about 25 percent of the company at this stage.

At the end of round 3 the shares appreciate to $9.86. Round 4 investors (the mezzanine investors) receive 2,027,693 shares at this price in return for their $20 million. The investors combined now control 58 percent of the company, and, if united, are in a position to call the shots. Finally, there is a happy ending for all when shares are valued at $26.86 at the IPO.

Note that this illustrative example did not consider either management shares or underwriting fees, which are beyond the scope of this book, but which are both material. Nesheim's book offers capitalization tables at this level of detail.[9]

In summary, phantom shares are a useful way to look at the process of value creation as an R&D project proceeds to commercialization, with the recognition that value can be maintained, or even enhanced, by having the right owners at the right stage.

REVERSING THE PLAYERS

The preceding example illustrates how technology is spun out of a large industrial company to create a nimble start-up. But the reverse can be equally true and is now more frequent: A company with a breakthrough cure for cancer can start up in a university environment, then bring on venture capitalists and professional management to reach the stage of Phase I clinical trials. At that point, facing huge costs and risks, they can exit their position and leave the rest of the drug approval and marketing process to Big Pharma, which has the resources, skills, and hunger for the final product. Genentech developed recombinant human insulin, but before attempting to commercialize its own drug was wise enough to sell the commercial rights to Eli Lilly,[10] the leading U.S. player in the insulin market.

CHAPTER 7

Process Breakthrough!

The great process industries of the twentieth century—steel, aluminum, paper, refining, and petrochemicals—enter the twenty-first in a disturbing state of maturity. Competitive advantages (except for location) and scale are rare, and margins are at the mercy of global supply and demand. Overcapacity is a common occurrence, as growth rates have slowed, and basic manufacturing packages can be purchased in the technology marketplace.

Competitors spring up in once-unlikely places: the Persian Gulf, Korea, Brazil. It would seem unthinkable that Qatar, depending on imported bauxite and with no consuming industries within a thousand miles, would invest in an aluminum plant. But electricity, not bauxite, is the key raw material for aluminum, and Qatar can produce plenty from its huge, but largely unmarketable, gas reserves.

The last hope for the scientists and engineers employed in these Western industries is the process breakthrough—that advance which makes every existing manufacturing facility in the world obsolete. It has happened before, and it will happen again.

Undoubtedly, the greatest breakthrough of the twentieth century was in moving the chemical industry from a coal-based feedstock (acetylene and benzene) position to a petroleum (ethylene, propylene, and benzene) base. But this example is almost as ancient in a technological time scale as alternating current (AC) replacing direct current (DC). More recently, refining was revolutionized by the catalytic cracker (Exxon, 1939), and again by zeolites (Mobil and W. R. Grace/Davison) a decade or two later. Pulp mills moved from sulfite technology to Kraft (sulfate) and thermomechanical pulping. Steel evolved from the open hearth to the basic oxygen furnace, while casting economics were transformed by minimills. Aluminum still addresses the challenge of continuous casting. Polyethylene was revolutionized by Dowlex (Dow Chemical) and Unipol (Union Carbide) in the 1970s, and then again by metallocene site-specific catalysts in the 1990s. Acrylonitrile process technology was transformed by Sohio, acetic acid by Monsanto's direct carbonylation process, and adiponitrile (a nylon precursor) by DuPont. Propylene oxide (a polyurethane building block) and styrene were transformed by Halcon and Arco. Exxon has been struggling to commercialize its ambitious AGC-21 project[1] to convert natural gas to liquid gasoline. This technically challenging objective will surely be achieved by a major petroleum company within the next two decades. The list is long but it is not infinite.

To these can be added new processes that enable distinctly new products. Large-scale integrated circuits enabled the personal computer. Drawing and ironing technology created the two-piece aluminum beverage can, and injection blow molding the ubiquitous polyethylene terephalate (PET) beverage bottle. Gaseous diffusion enabled nuclear weapons and nuclear power.

Many industrial companies, as well as technology providers, are still evaluating the possibilities for the next big breakthrough from a technology viewpoint. Advanced catalysts, fuel cells, solar cells, partial oxidation, supercritical fluids, advanced ceramics, biotechnology, and nanotechnology could play enabling roles. Most of the individual efforts seem small, fragmented, exploratory, risky, and above all expensive. But looks can be deceiving. The total effort, and the number of projects, is enormous. And when the economic corner has been turned in a specific application, the trickle of investment tends to become a torrent. For example, during my tenure as R&D vice president for American Can, the company researched seven significant new processes. The outcomes are listed in Figure 7.1. Two never got off the ground, one died after a major development effort, two

FIGURE 7.1 American Can's Process Research Portfolio (1978–1982)

Project	Commercial	Result
Dry papermaking (Bolt towel)	Yes	Product failure in consumer tests
Novel headbox for paper machine	No	Technical feasibility not established
Extrusion blow-molded barrier bottles	Yes	Commercial success
Injection blow-molded plastic cans	No	Technical near miss
Continuous cast aluminum sheet	No	Joint venture with Alcan explored, dropped
Municipal waste recycling	Yes	Uneconomic
Draw/redraw process for food cans	Yes	Commercial success

died in the marketplace (costly failures), and two were commercial successes, but not home runs.

In hindsight, was all this process research a good investment? The answer has to be yes: The program created some viable options for corporate growth and investment with better than commodity returns. Some of the failures were small efforts with considerable scouting value. It should also be noted that American Can would never have had the financial resources to aggressively commercialize seven new technologies. Indeed the costs of converting food can production to draw/redraw technology strained the capital budget. For a time, I thought the injection blow-molded plastic food can would be a home run, but the process was never perfected.

I have been personally involved with many other such projects in the chemical industry, and in particular with the very successful introductions of linear low-density polyethylene and metallocene catalysts. The anecdotal evidence seems to indicate that effort in this area will continue to be significant, and the odds, while long and getting longer, do not rule out big paydays for those both smart and lucky.

The purpose of this chapter is to explore the financial dynamics of changing the dominant process in a world-scale commodity, and the size of the potential economic prize. When is this game worth the candle?

Case 11: Is the World Ready for a New Phenol Process?

Dr. Gina Sanchez is director of process research for Acme Chemical, an important producer of phenol. Her charter includes scouring the world for promising new technologies, and she reads the following item placed on the Web by Argonne National Laboratory.[2]

Phenol is the second-largest commodity produced from the inexpensive raw material, benzene. Currently, the [U.S.] chemical industry uses the three-step "cumene process" to produce 95 percent of the 4.5 billion pounds of phenol it requires annually for manufacturing phenol-formaldehyde resins. A proposed new process would convert benzene to phenol in only one step and would eliminate the need to neutralize acids, to separate organic products, or to be concerned with a potentially unstable intermediate product in the cumene process. Theoretically, the new process also produces no by-products, whereas the cumene process leaves acetone to be sold (in an oversupplied market) to make the process economical, and several other hazardous compounds that must be handled appropriately. Selective oxidation and direct conversion of benzene to phenol were both ranked as high-priority topics for further research by chemical experts in the public and private sectors. The new process could generate considerable energy savings and reduce by-products and hazardous wastes. The bottom line result for industry will be production cost savings, a reduction in environmental impacts, and more effective carbon management.

The announcement catches Gina's attention, but she suspects the new process is mostly conceptual at this point—promising laboratory-stage research. She knows Argonne will need to attract a commercial partner to scale up the process and ready it for commercialization. Its development will be long and expensive. Might Acme be that partner? She also has several projects vying for her limited resources. Her career will hang on her judgment call.

Solution to Case 11

Gina badly needs a working tool for estimating and comparing opportunities to innovate in new processes for commodity chemicals, based on typically sketchy early-stage information. Later, she can again use that tool in negotiating terms with the U.S. Department of Energy, since she is concerned negotiators lacking real-world industrial experience may overestimate the value. The model can then be updated as more accurate information is developed.

Methodology

There is a basic difference between the economic model required to evaluate a new-to-the-world product, such as the artificial pancreas or an ion chromatograph, and a new process that makes an existing commodity. In particular, there is heavily entrenched competition. In general, competitors will not shut down their plants until the prices they receive are below their cash costs, and perhaps not even then. Existing capacity will not go away, absent the technology leader initiating the strategy of a ruinous price war. As an experienced player in commodity chemicals, Acme will probably prefer a more conservative strategy of convincing competitors not to invest further in their obsolete technologies, of waiting for older plants to wear out, and of capturing as much as it can of future volume growth. Acme will also consider a licensing strategy, since geopolitical considerations may prevent it from placing plants in the regions of greatest market growth.

Therefore, the key question is less what a new Acme plant might earn (which in any case involves highly uncertain forecasts of commodity prices) as how much more it can earn than a current state-of-the-art plant earns. It is this difference that drives value creation and determines strategy. A simple way to measure the difference is to build two financial statements ("old technology" and "new technology") into the FSDTRO model, and subtract the NPVs. This difference becomes the total value of a license to the new technology, which will then be shared between licensor and licensee. Acme's own new plants can be considered to be internal licensees.

The costs and unique risks of the R&D program leading to the construction of a commercial plant are estimated by the now familiar decision tree methodology, giving an expected value for the project at each project stage.

Business Assumptions:

The input parameters for this project are summarized in Figure 7.2, and can be tracked as we develop the business assumptions.

■ Acme will market and license this technology nonexclusively worldwide to manufacturers of commodity chemicals through a strategic alliance with a major engineering contractor. The global market is estimated to be three times the domestic market, or six billion kilos.

■ Acme's reward will be a percentage (base case 25 percent) of the value added at the manufacturing level by the new process versus current technology. The engineering contractor will profit through design engineering and construction management but is assumed for now not to have ownership in the technology itself.

This assumption covers the case where the first commercial plant is built and operated by Acme; in effect there is an internal license that captures 100 percent of the value of the technology improvement. All subsequent plants are external licensees. An Acme plant, operating as projected and built within its capital budget, is a virtual necessity for a successful licensing program, and puts competitive pressure on the other suppliers as well.

■ Acme will capture a percentage (base case 50 percent) of the growth (base case 4 percent per year) in that commodity owing to clear economic superiority. This is a plausible but uncertain assumption. Some of the market growth will be met by inexpensive debottlenecking of existing plants—what is called "capacity creep." In addition, some producers are in a captive position—Dow values its phenol primarily as a raw material for a much more profitable product, bisphenol A, the building block for its epoxy resin business. They, and others, could well elect to subsidize phenol manufacture from downstream profits.

FIGURE 7.2   Phenol Scenario

Commercial Assumptions		Derived from Assumptions	
Market Size (B kg)	6.00	Annual Capacity Growth (Mkg)	240
Market Growth	4.00%	New Tech Share (Mkg)	120
New Tech. Share	50.00%	Initial Investment (New) ($M)	$ 85.33
Sales Price/kg	$0.80	Initial Investment (Old)	$133.33
		Pilot Plant Capital ($M)	$ 7.20
Old Technology		Initial Annual Capacity (Mkg)	120
Variable Cost/kg	$0.500	Turnover Ratio	80.00%
Manufacturing Overhead/kg	$0.100		
Fixed Capital/kg Annual Capacity	$1.000	**New Technology**	
		Variable Cost/kg	$0.475
New Technology		Manufacturing Overhead/kg	$0.060
Variable Cost Improvement	5.00%	Fixed Capital/kg Annual Capacity	$0.600
Manufacturing Overhead Improvement	40.00%	**R&D Parameters**	
Initial Fixed Capital Improvement	40.00%	Duration Stage 1	1
Pilot Plant as % of Comm. Plant	10.00%	Duration Stage 2	1
		Duration Stage 3	2
Asset Life (Years)	15	Duration Stage 4	2
License Cents/kg	$0.02		
Acme Value Capture	25.00%	Pretax Cost Stage 1 ($M)	$ 1.21
		Pretax Cost Stage 2	$ 2.42
Business Parameters		Pretax Cost Stage 3	$ 4.84
Selling, Admin., and R&D	10.00%	Pretax Cost Stage 4	$16.88
Days Inventory	30		
Days Receivables	36	Probability Stage 1	50.00%
Days Payables	16	Probability Stage 2	50.00%
Tax Rate	38.00%	Probability Stage 3	75.00%
Cost of Capital	12.00%	Probability Stage 4	83.33%
EBITDA Multiplier (ME)	6		
P/E Ratio	12.5		
FCF Multiplier (MF)	8.33		
Risk-Free Rate	5.00%		
Volatility	30.00%		

Balancing these negative factors is the virtual certainty that plants that are too old or too small to compete will inevitably be shut down.

■ One new plant will be built each year, with capacity equal to the market growth times the fraction of that growth expected to be captured. (This scenario will never play out smoothly owing to considerations of timing and scale; but the total capacity increase should be right, and the fluctuations should average out over time.)

■ Value will be captured through reduced variable costs (base case 5 percent), reduced fixed capital (base case 40 percent), and reduced factory-level overhead costs (base case 40 percent, proportional to fixed capital). The key test will be Argonne's claim, "Reduces industry's capital costs." Basically, Gina is testing the assumption that a breakthrough in capital intensity (reasonable when a three-step process is reduced to one) is the principal value driver, and she is *not* yet assuming a breakthrough in variable cost via yield, raw materials, and so on. She knows that often the lowest variable cost process involves more capital intensity, and that she may be able to engineer her way toward that goal. Each successive engineering improvement must earn a return on capital that meets Acme's hurdle rate. (These are hidden options.)

■ Gina will test the sensitivity of the economic value to penetration rates of 50 percent of market growth (conservative) and 150 percent of market growth (aggressive, implies forced shutdown of now-obsolescent plants).

R&D Stages

The R&D program is currently configured to cost a cumulative $25.35 million, last six years, and have a 15.6 percent overall probability of success. These parameters can be varied for a real case. The four stages are:

1. *Concept development.* This stage will essentially verify and extend Argonne's work: literature review, lab scale reactions, screening of analogous catalysts, and strengthening the patent fence. The probability of success used is 50 percent, higher than usual, since Gina's main goal here is to confirm Argonne's promising results.
2. *Feasibility stage.* This stage involves lab-scale research on reactor design, catalysts, and separations sufficient to demonstrate an economic advantage.
3. *Development stage.* This will involve a bench-scale effort aimed at proof of concept and design of a pilot plant.
4. *Pilot stage.* A pilot plant operating at one-fiftieth of the scale of a commercial unit (assuming[3] a capital cost of 10 percent of the commercial plant) will be operated for one year. Design engineering for the commercial unit will be initiated. The cost of this stage is double the prior stage *plus* the cost of the pilot plant.

Inputs to the Calculation

No attempt will be made to forecast phenol price over the life of the project; we base the price on the current market at $0.36 per pound or about

$0.80 per kilogram. The options value of the project should partly account for phenol price volatility. Variable cost per kilogram is taken as $0.50, and capital intensity at $1.00 per annual/kg. Gina presumably has access to considerable industry data from the *Chemical Economics Handbook* published by SRI and consultancies such as Chem Systems.

Using 0.10 per kilogram for manufacturing overhead (10 percent of gross fixed capital) and 10 percent for selling, administrative, and R&D expenses (lean numbers appropriate for a commodity), one calculates a net present value for a plant built with the "old technology" of –$32.27 million. See Figure 7.3. Here, we used the working capital liquidation scenario for horizon value, assuming that with new technology coming on, the plant's life is limited. This value corresponds to an IRR of 4.95 percent, telling us what we suspected already: that at current prices phenol is marginally profitable but does not achieve reinvestment economics. This conclusion remains true even if we use more generous methods of calculating horizon value.

Next we set up the calculation for the new technology. To simplify it, the spreadsheet calculates variable cost, manufacturing overhead, and fixed capital in relation to the old technology, making it easy to run the necessary sensitivities.

An entry in the new technology pro forma calculations must be made for a royalty payment to Argonne. It is assumed this will be paid directly by the licensee, in recognition of the discovery of the catalyst, and will be separate from the Acme license to the process technology package. This royalty is input at $0.02 per kilogram or about a penny a pound. While

FIGURE 7.3   Phenol: Financial Results for Old and New Plants ($ Millions)

Project Value in First Commercial Year

| Horizon Value Method | Old Technology | | New Technology | | |
	IRR	NPV	IRR	NPV	Delta NPV
1. Working Capital	4.95	–$32.27	18.59	$20.10	$52.38
2. Book Value	6.82	–$26.11	19.36	$23.80	$49.91
3. EBITDA × ME	10.38	–$ 9.82	23.40	$49.39	$59.21
4. ATOI × P/E Ratio	8.73	–$18.19	23.40	$49.38	$67.57
5. FCF × MF	10.29	–$10.37	22.81	$44.90	$55.27
ROIC (average)	6.11		17.30		

ME = EBITDA multiplier; ATOI = After-Tax Operating Income; MF = Free cash flow multiplier; ROIC = Return on invested capital this may be generous in terms of risk-reward ratio, it can be negotiated later; for now the project must be robust under conservative assumptions.

Results for the Base Case

The calculation shows that an investment made with new technology gives an NPV of $20.1 million and an IRR of 18.6 percent, meeting the hurdle rate for anyone's investment in commodity chemicals. It rises to an NPV of $49.4 million assuming a viable, ongoing plant, a reasonable assumption with modern technology.

Of course, any licensor except Acme itself must pay an additional royalty to use the technology. This has been assumed to be equivalent to 25 percent of the difference between old and new ($52.3 million), or $13.1 million. (The most conservative assumption is again used for horizon value.) The licensors can afford this; indeed they cannot afford to reinvest in old technology. The business plan is beginning to look solid at the producer level.

The issue now turns to whether it makes sense to pursue the R&D program to get there. The key driver is the current value of the total royalties paid to Acme over the life of the project. We take the life of the project to be 15 years, with no additional terminal value. By that time Argonne's basic catalyst patent will have expired, and any process improvement patents gained by Acme will be aging quickly.

The net present value of this royalty stream (Figure 7.4), when the R&D phase is complete, is $144.90 million. What is its current value when discounted for the time value of money, the R&D investment, and the risk of failure? Our DTRO analysis (Figure 7.5) indicates the current value is $7.64 million—easily good enough to justify an investment in Stage 1. It rises with each stage gate to $16.57 million, $35.55 million, and $49.65 million.

The final reality check is what the realized NPV of $144.90 million means in cents per kilogram. Is it reasonable within industry standards, and in relationship to Argonne? The NPV share and number of kilograms per year are also tabulated in Figure 7.4. It turns out that a royalty of $0.0407 per kilogram, or less than 2 cents per pound, will make the two equal. This 2:1 ratio of Acme to Argonne is very close to the appropriate profit share between a technology inventor and a technology developer, and is shaded slightly in favor of Argonne.

Sensitivity to Market Size

A base template that works is far more useful than the problem immediately at hand, because a host of similar problems can be solved using the

FIGURE 7.4 Phenol Licensing Revenue Model (Millions)

Year	New Kg Produced	Total Annual Kg Produced	NPV of New Royalties	Pretax Royalty at Equivalent Rate	After-Tax Royalty
1	120	120	$52.38	$ 4.89	$ 3.03
2	125	245	$13.62	$ 9.98	$ 6.18
3	130	375	$14.16	$15.26	$ 9.46
4	135	510	$14.73	$20.76	$12.87
5	140	650	$15.32	$26.48	$16.42
6	146	796	$15.93	$32.43	$20.11
7	152	948	$16.57	$38.62	$23.95
8	158	110	$17.23	$45.06	$27.93
9	164	127	$17.92	$51.75	$32.08
10	171	144	$18.64	$58.71	$36.40
11	178	161	$19.38	$65.95	$40.89
12	185	180	$20.16	$73.47	$45.55
13	192	199	$20.96	$81.30	$50.41
14	200	219	$21.80	$89.44	$55.46
15	208	240	$22.67	$97.91	$60.71
Net Present Value			**$144.90**		**$144.90**

Running Royalty Equivalent

Royalty rate/kg	$0.0407
Royalty rate (AT)	$0.0253

same algorithms. Most importantly, it identifies the boundaries at which a project becomes economic. Sensitivity analysis looks at these boundaries one variable at a time, whereas a Monte Carlo analysis can compound several key uncertainties simultaneously.

A question that I have been asked in the course of my consulting business is: How big a market must there be in a commodity chemical to justify a process research project? Phenol is a potential test for that question. The Excel spreadsheet contains a feature called Goal Seek that allows a back calculation of a key parameter (here the market size) as a function of an output parameter, here the current value of the project as determined by DTRO. If the current value of the project (which nets out the cost and the risks of the R&D program from the NPV) is set to zero, the answer is 1.5 billion kilograms. Anything smaller is not worth doing unless the assumed advantages are greater than for phenol.

FIGURE 7.5   Phenol: Value Based on DTRO (Millions)

Licensor value first commercial year	$144.90
Cumulative probability of success	15.63%
Cumulative R&D cost (pretax)	$ 25.35
Cumulative R&D cost (after-tax)	$ 15.71
Value	
Current value as rifle shot	$ 0.75
Current value by DT	$ 7.42
Value added by DT	$ 6.67
Current value by DTRO	$ 7.64
Value added by RO	$ 0.23
Progression	
Current value by DTRO	$ 7.64
Value after Stage 1	$ 16.57
Value after Stage 2	$ 35.55
Value after Stage 3	$ 49.65
Value after Stage 4	$144.90

Other Sensitivities

Gina has used her best, most conservative judgment about the potential value of this project. But things could be better or worse. What if the line cannot be held on capital cost savings and only half of them are realized? What if the R&D program is twice as costly? Could both of these things occur at the same time, reflecting greater technical difficulty than anticipated? On the other hand, what if the variable cost savings are large? Would it be worthwhile to add back some capital to realize large variable cost savings?

First, a look at the downside scenarios. If only half the capital cost savings are realized, the value of the royalty stream and the current project are halved, but it is not a disaster (line 2, Figure 7.6). Likewise, a doubling of R&D costs decreases value by almost 40 percent (line 3)—again not a disaster if the promise is maintained. But the combination of these conditions (line 4) looks very dicey and, should this combination come into view, it may be time to pull the plug. The total analysis continues to support funding Stage 1.

Now let's look at the upsides. Wise planners seldom project the most optimistic case, and more usually present a case that is sufficient to gain approval. But history seems to suggest that most very successful ideas were, in hindsight, underestimated by their sponsors. The real contributions of new

FIGURE 7.6 Sensitivities of Phenol Case (Millions)

Case Parameters	NPV of Royalties	Current Value of Project
1 Base case	$144.90	$ 7.64
2 20 percent less fixed capital (vs. 40 percent)	$ 75.64	$ 3.45
3 Double the R&D cost (including pilot plant)	$144.90	$ 4.82
4 Double the R&D cost, 20 percent less fixed capital	$ 75.64	$ 0.48
5 20 percent lower variable cost (vs. 5 percent)	$240.52	$14.23
6 20 percent less fixed capital, 20 percent lower variable cost	$171.26	$ 9.48
7 Value capture 33 percent (vs. 25 percent)	$176.30	$ 9.78
8 Aggressive growth (150 percent of industry growth rate)	$434.69	$27.68

technology to shareholder value have often come from the options hidden in unanticipated upsides.

The first important upside would be material savings in variable costs. If these were 20 percent instead of the base case 5 percent (line 5), the value of the project doubles based on our assumptions. In fact, that condition could create even faster market penetration (see discussion of line 8) and might underestimate the value to be had.

If we have to give up some capital advantage to get a 20 percent variable cost advantage, line 6 suggests it is worth doing.

We might be being too conservative about our share of value capture. What if we get one-third (line 7)? This will improve the project economics by 28 percent—not really surprising.

The real surprise is in the aggressive rollout scenario; here we assume the new technology captures 6 percent of the market each year, instead of 2 percent. It grows faster than the market because the handwriting on the wall is perceived by producers operating inefficient plants. Line 8 suggests the NPV of the royalty stream under this circumstance rises to $434.69 million, and the current value of the project increases nearly fourfold to $27.68 million.

The perceptive reader will note that the happy circumstances are likely to be synergistic owing to technical simplicity; likewise, the unhappy circumstances will be additive owing to technical complexity. These relationships are difficult to model with confidence, but they do explain the tendency of projects to move away from the median expectation to the margin or to the sky.

DISCUSSION: PROCESS RESEARCH-BASED BUSINESS

Most process research today is carried out by large operating companies with a strategic interest in the result. It is still a major differentiator between American, European, and Japanese companies and their younger counterparts on the mainland of Asia. But the question can be raised whether process R&D could be a profitable business model by itself or for a division of an engineering service company.

Unfortunately, today there is no current model of a successful process research venture, although there have been very successful ones in the past, most notably Scientific Design. There have also been very successful licensing models, such as Unipol (Union Carbide) and UOP (refining processes). To quote Peter Spitz,[4] "Independent petrochemical research companies have almost vanished. Some, like Scientific Design, no longer exist. UOP and IFP were more successful in developing petroleum refining than petrochemical technology, and are not expected to provide a series of petrochemical 'breakthroughs.' The engineering contractors that made such major contributions in the design of petrochemical plants in the 1950–1970 period have almost all discontinued their research activities. Because of the current low level of construction work, these contractors can no longer support process development efforts. They will generally be unwilling to cooperate on development projects."

This climate virtually assures the need for internal financial support in the early project phases. When the technology is proven at bench scale, the choice will be whether to pilot it in a captive facility at an Acme's own cost, or, more remotely, by sharing costs at the site of a potential first licensee that would be granted favorable terms. (The latter strategy was employed by Scientific Design, which granted its first licensee exclusivity within the United Kingdom.)

In addition, a company like Acme will inevitably consider the option of restricting the new manufacturing process to itself, thus attempting to become a gorilla in a new commodity business based on large advantages in capital intensity and variable cost. Such a strategy could be successful, since the petrochemicals business favors consolidation: Witness the roll-up of large portions of the methanol industry by Methanex, which purchased old facilities from other petrochemical producers while building the world's largest and most modern facilities at sites with low feedstock costs. Arco similarly muscled its way to gorilla status in propylene oxide.

There are three factors that account for the demise of independent process engineering. Two are obvious: the slowing growth rate of commodity industries and the huge investment that must be risked to prove a major new process commercially. The third factor is diminishing technical returns; in field after field the low-hanging fruit has mostly been picked. The good news is that if the breakthroughs are technically compelling and the target markets are large enough (and many are growing very large), the rewards will still justify a strong development effort.

CHAPTER 8

Improved Products

The dream of most industrial scientists is the breakthrough discovery—the new-to-the-world product that forever changes the way we live. These achievements are comparatively rare, and the odds against commercial success are daunting.

The reality of industrial research is that most of the dollars are spent on incremental product improvements, where value creation is less dramatic, but the payoffs are also less uncertain. In many businesses, incremental R&D is the only kind of R&D that is performed. This situation is driven by the logic of competition: If there is not incremental R&D, the product line will soon fall behind competitors and relative market position will inexorably erode. So, a business must fund incremental R&D first. If more R&D is affordable, the business can then allocate additional funds to riskier, long-term ideas. For example, in the specialty chemicals business, R&D experts believe that 2 percent of revenues must be committed to R&D just to stay even,[1] and that only beyond this level can R&D address innovation and growth. Typically, specialty chemical companies spend 2 to 5 percent of revenues on R&D.

There are basically two approaches to product improvement R&D. *The first is to reduce cost. The second is to improve performance.* The happiest product improvements have both features.

WHAT IS MEANT BY A PRODUCT?

To understand product improvement research, it is also helpful, in this context, to recognize the broad meaning of the term *product*. A product is much more than a manufactured object or a physical substance; in fact, it can be a service.

Consider a simple product, aspirin. It is based on the compound acetosalicylic acid, a commodity that can be manufactured in plants around the world. The manufacturing process is important, since it affects impurity levels, and must be certified by regulatory authorities such as the FDA. Impurities can lead to side effects and also affect physical properties such as dissolution rates. Particle size is also an important physical attribute. One plant is not like another, and while the manufacturing processes are similar, they are slightly differentiated owing to learning processes and trade secrets. In particular, these plants will vary in their manufacturing costs.

After multiton batches of acetosalicylic acid have been produced and dried, it becomes necessary to convert the active pharmaceutical ingredient (API) to a finished dosage form. This step involves blending the API with starch and pressing it into tablets.

But the tablet is also not yet a product. It must be packaged and labeled. For relatively inexpensive materials, such as aspirin and flavored carbonated water (Coca-Cola), the cost of the package may be comparable to, or even exceed, the cost of the contents. The label must be approved by the FDA, and is a value-adding element.

Finally, the product takes on the aspect of a brand, such as Bayer aspirin, which represents in the minds of consumers a hundred or more years of quality or experience. Or it may be the house brand of a chain of drugstores or supermarkets, which would signify value pricing to consumers.

Hence, properties, costs, quality, packaging, branding, and price are all characteristics of a product. While this is a broad view, technologists too often forget the complete perspective and focus only on the front end. But the whole value chain must be considered to determine the value; parts of it are scientifically less glamorous, but they are important. For mature companies, the development of improved products takes up by far the largest portion of the R&D budget. In fact, the constant press of work in this area, plus the focus of operating managers on shorter-term results, often results in a crowding out of longer-term, breakthrough projects, an issue addressed at the end of this chapter.

This book has already outlined a quantitative approach to valuing breakthrough innovation; now it turns to some incremental cases. However, before digging deeper, a review of the value chain and pricing is in order.

THE VALUE CHAIN AND R&D

The use of the value chain concept has exploded in recent years, particularly because it has been embodied in sophisticated Enterprise Resource

Management (ERM) software packages supplied by SAP and others, and in analytical services hawked by a host of consultants.

The concept owes much to Professor Michael Porter,[2] and the core idea is that a firm creates value for its customers by performing both primary and support activities. The value created is measured by the amount buyers are willing to pay for the firm's products and services. In Porter's hierarchy, logistics, manufacturing, marketing and sales, and after-sale service are direct activities. Support activities are procurement, human resources management, finance, planning, and technology development.

Technology development is the focus of this book, with its impact, as I see it, being manifested directly in both manufacturing and marketing.

Firms create competitive advantage through innovation, which Porter defines broadly as both technological innovation (product and process changes) and new and better ways of performing other activities. Innovations shift competitive advantage when rivals are unable, unwilling, or slow to respond. Porter takes a holistic view of a firm's activities and sees the total value as more than the sum of the parts; there is a system of linkages between individual activities, such as manufacturing and after-sale service.

An obvious positive linkage of a technology advance is that a firm with a history of product innovation may become a preferred supplier (a value above that created by the advance itself).

Finally, Porter views the "value system" as a serial sequence.

1. Supplier value chain.
2. Firm value chain (internal issues).
3. Customer value chains.
4. Channel value chains (distributors and retailers).
5. Buyer value chains.

I have added item 3 because many industrial products pass through two or more industrial customers before they reach the distribution channels. For example, if the firm produces polyethylene (from supplied ethylene feedstock), it may sell pellets to a custom molder, who sells molded parts to a toy manufacturer (assembler), who then supplies the distribution network, with ultimate value being determined by the consumer. A key insight is that the firm needs to understand not only its customer (the custom molder), but the customer's customer (the assembler), who undoubtedly must approve any changes in specification.

Imagine a new polyethylene resin that has better flow properties, thus allowing the molder to make more parts per hour. This advance will always be meaningful to the customer, but of greatest value when the customer is capacity restrained. Getting used to the new resin will impose costs at the customer level (machine time, scrap). At the next level, the customer must negotiate with the assembler's purchasing agent, who, if she is shrewd, may ask for a price concession to expedite approving the change. Nor will she (the customer's customer) risk making a perceptible aesthetic or physical property change in the final toy. Understanding and managing the full picture is thus essential in marketing the advanced resin.

Some key observations:

- The value chain concept is essential for estimating the additional profit that can be gained from an incremental product improvement.
- The total calculation, including Porter's "linkages," can be very complex (business is complex). ERM and customer relationship management (CRM) software may eventually make the complexity manageable. For now, it may be better to attempt to isolate the technology improvement, and estimate any additional synergies or options.
- It is very important to analyze whether risk is being transferred.
- Value chain analysis by definition requires a deep understanding of the customer. In principle, this is a good thing. In some cases, however, deep understanding may not be worth the cost and effort.

PRICING MODELS

A key business question is always, "How do I get paid?" In this context it is, "How do I get paid for a product improvement?" (It is fully possible to manage not to get paid at all.) An analysis of pricing models is critical to the answer. There are several types of industrial pricing models that we will review only in passing, and we will focus on the one that is at the heart of this chapter. A full discussion of pricing is the subject of business school courses, and like value chain analysis, moves outside the scope of this book.

The first pricing model is *cost-based pricing*. In effect one earns one's profit by a markup above one's costs. Cost-based pricing is well accepted in certain industries, such as construction, defense contracting, and some areas of retailing, such as antiques shops. Buyers usually regard it as simple, transparent, and fair. Rightly so, since sellers using more advanced pricing models are likely to earn more! From the point of view of the seller, one gets paid, ironically, for incurring more cost—this may be from adding costly but desired features and add-ons, such as a Jacuzzi to a spec home. In addition, a superior product produced at equal cost and sold at equal price should win share from competition.

The second pricing model is *competition-based pricing*. This is a relatively unhappy circumstance that occurs when the seller has very little control of price, and must price in a narrow range or lose a great deal of volume. A gas station intuitively may be in this situation. It does not control wholesale prices, and its retail price is constrained to a small differential from neighboring stations, that differential being justified by location, brand, service, convenience, or aesthetic factors. Likewise, industrial firms that lack leadership in either technology or market position must follow on price. In this circumstance, the firm will not be paid for product improvements since it is merely trying to keep up with the technology leaders. But it must invest in product research just to ensure that it does not need to endure deeper price discounts! Product improvements do not create additional shareholder value, but they do protect against erosion of shareholder value. The appropriate baseline for justifying R&D expenditure becomes the "do nothing" or "harvest the business" cases.

A third pricing model is described as "value in exchange" and is typically contrasted to "value in use." The difference is that the customer does not directly use the product, but can exchange it for something more useful. An extreme case might be the production of glass beads, whiskey, or rifles for fur traders dealing with aboriginal hunters. While the fur trader will shop for the lowest price, he is more concerned about the rate at which he can exchange these goods for fur. Unlike value in use, value in exchange has limited applicability in the area of product improvements. In the broader technology marketplace, however, one of its applications is cross-licensing patented technology. When two firms have intellectual property positions that block each other's access to the marketplace, the value in exchange may far exceed value in use.

Value in Use

The fourth pricing model is called value in use. Sharing value in use down the value chain is the key to success in the product improvement game (assuming one is not constrained by cost-based or competition-based pricing). The term *sharing* is chosen deliberately, since there are two value drivers in play: How big is the pie, and how will it be shared? With a well-conceived innovation, there is a *range* of solutions that are win-win for both buyer and seller. Hence it is a combination of position, tradition, knowledge, and negotiation that determines the outcome. Analytically, the game is fascinating and rewarding, because it demands a firm understanding of customer economics, a sense for the sharing equation, and an estimate of the costs of introducing the proposed innovation.

Two keys to the calculation are to be sure to include all of the customer's costs in the calculation and to use the customer's cost of capital. Specifically, include as customer costs changeover costs and a risk premium.

In this chapter, we discuss two cases, the first a very simple one that illustrates the principle, and the second a more complex one involving technology that not only creates value but impacts demand.

Case 12: Value-in-Use Pricing for Engraving Equipment

This case is based on a template published on the Internet[3] for an engraving machine called the Abcor 2000. I will base this section on the original numbers, but develop a template (Figure 8.1) independently.

The template is a tool by which the inventor/manufacturer of a new and superior piece of engraving equipment can quickly assess the value it might have in a particular customer's hands, and tailor the pricing strategy to the customer's situation. But in addition, the inventor/manufacturer must understand its own costs!

The principal advantage of the new technology is lower variable

FIGURE 8.1 Engraving Plate Value Analysis

Initial Number of Plates	990		Abcor Machine Cost	$3,980
Customer Growth Rate	5.00%		Abcor Plate Cost	$0.60
Salvage Value—Old	$1,000		Proposed Machine Price	$12,000
Old Plate Price	$5.00		Proposed Plate Price	$2.00
Plate Price Escalator	3.00%		Salvage Value New	$3,000
Customer Cost of Capital	15.00%		Abcor Cost of Capital	15.00%

Year	Number of Plates	Old Price per Plate	New Price per Plate	Buyer Cash Flow	Buyer DCF	Seller Cash Flow	Seller DCF
1	990	$5.00	$2.00	−$ 8,030	−$ 8,030	$ 9,406	$ 9,406
2	1,040	$5.15	$2.06	$ 3,214	$ 2,794	$ 1,518	$ 1,320
3	1,092	$5.30	$2.12	$ 3,476	$ 2,628	$ 1,662	$ 1,257
4	1,147	$5.46	$2.19	$ 3,760	$ 2,472	$ 1,819	$ 1,196
5	1,204	$5.63	$2.25	$ 4,065	$ 2,324	$ 1,988	$ 1,137
6	1,264	$5.80	$2.32	$ 4,396	$ 2,186	$ 2,172	$ 1,080
7	1,327	$5.97	$2.39	$ 4,754	$ 2,055	$ 2,373	$ 1,026
8	1,393	$6.15	$2.46	$ 5,140	$ 1,932	$ 2,591	$ 974
9	1,463	$6.33	$2.53	$ 5,560	$ 1,818	$ 2,829	$ 925
10	1,536	$6.52	$2.61	$ 6,012	$ 1,709	$ 3,087	$ 877
Salvage				$ 3,000	$ 853		
			Total	$35,346	$12,741	$29,444	$19,197

Buyer NPV	$12,741
Buyer IRR	26.80%
Seller NPV	$19,197

costs for the customer—a compelling economic proposition. But, as so often happens, it requires a capital investment. How attractive is that investment?

Solution to Case 12

Abcor starts with its cost to produce an additional machine, $3,980, and its cost to produce an engraving plate, $0.60 per plate. No cost escalation is assumed. The customer, CustomCard, Inc., has an obsolescent machine (salvage value $1,000) and is paying $5 per plate. CustomCard is currently buying 990 plates per year, and anticipates its business will grow at 5 percent per annum. Price escalations in plates have averaged 3 percent over the past decade.

The method is a nonclassical version of breakeven analysis, where breakeven is defined not traditionally as zero profit in a given year, but as zero NPV over the life of the project. Also assume both Abcor and CustomCard have a 15 percent cost of capital, and that the new machine will be scrapped after 10 years with a salvage value of $3,000.

The cash flow picture for the buyer is negative in year 1 (Figure 8.1) CustomCard invests $12,000, less $1,000 for trading in the old machine. Based on a proposed new price of $2 per plate, it improves its operating profit by $3 per plate or $2,970, for a net cash flow of −$8,030. The following year, the cash flow is based on a difference of $3.09 per plate over a basis of 1,040 plates, or $3,214. Note that around year 4, CustomCard reaches the point where cumulative cash flow turns positive. This event defines what used to be called a four-year payback, which was considered satisfactory for investments of this type. Over the life of the project, the cumulative cash flow will be $35,346, giving an NPV of $12,741. The internal rate of return is also very attractive, 26.8 percent.

It turns out that at these prices the seller does even better, presumably because this is powerful new technology. In the first year, Abcor receives $12,000, less machine cost of $3,980, plus a profit of $1.40 each on 990 plates. The total is $9,406. In year 2 the entire profit is based on the margin earned on 1,040 plates, $1,518. (This margin begins to escalate with annual price increases of 3 percent.) Abcor's total cash flow will be $29,444, somewhat less than CustomCard's, so the pricing seems quite fair. The Abcor salesperson should play this card adroitly! But since Abcor's cash flow is front-end-loaded, its NPV is actually about 50 percent greater, $19,197, than the customer's—the time value of money is at play here.

We have established that the value in use of this technology at

CustomCard is $19,197 + $12,741, or more than $30,000. It will be different at other customers, but the template is well suited for this calculation.

Two comments: These calculations are simple and transparent—in a real business situation many other costs and value drivers must be considered: start-up costs, maintenance, warranties, taxes, inventory requirements, quality, security of supply, and so on. CustomCard's financial department can rework the analysis for a better estimate. In addition, it could be argued that the generous margins realized in this example might represent breakthrough rather than incremental technology. That may be, but the methods and template are well suited to narrower margins.

While this technology is a win-win situation for all, the trickier question is what is the optimum combination price proposal for Abcor. One way to begin is to understand the customer's breakeven point. We previously noted that Excel has a feature called Goal Seek, where buyer NPV can be set to zero (or some higher number), and a price can be varied to reach it. Figure 8.2 shows a small sample of possible results.

The buyer NPV at the proposed initial price is $12,741. How far can the plate price be raised before the value drops to breakeven? The answer is $3.67. Or if Abcor sticks with $2 per plate, what can it charge for the machine? $24,741. What about other combinations? Breakeven for an $18,000 machine comes at $2.88 per plate.

Suppose that the customer has told Abcor that its hurdle rate for this class of investment is 20 percent. Goal Seek can be applied to an internal rate of return of 20 percent. One solution is raising the plate price to $2.40, which will improve Abcor's NPV more than $3,000 to $22,215. The latter can be viewed as a potential profit that the original price proposal was leaving on the table.

Now look at the breakeven proposition from the seller's viewpoint. If we apply Goal Seek around seller NPV, we find breakeven at *negative* prices for either machines or plates. In other words, Abcor could sell the machine for $12,000 and give the plates away (NPV $3,938), or give the machine away and sell the plates at $2 (NPV $7,197). It is unlikely to do

FIGURE 8.2 Buyer Breakeven Analysis

Machine Price	Plate Price	Buyer NPV
$12,000	$2.00	$12,741
$12,000	$3.67	$ 0
$24,741	$2.00	$ 0
$18,000	$2.88	$ 0

either, but Abcor's enormous pricing flexibility is obvious, as is the range of win-win solutions. Its actual course will inevitably be determined by the spectrum of potential customers, by the threat of competitive response, and by its concern for fairness and reputation.

TANGIBLE VALUE IN USE: MATERIAL REDUCTION

A recurring theme in manufacturing productivity is the ability to do more with less using better materials. The theme is often "lighter and stronger." Plastic grocery bags are dramatically lighter and stronger today than products that might have been made with 1970s-era polymers. The plastic film industry refers to the results of this advance as "down-gauging," meaning that the thickness of film required to meet a physical specification has been steadily reduced. The equivalent in polyurethane or polystyrene foams has been density reduction. Very strong products can be made that are 97 percent air, as progress has yielded excellent products with densities below two pounds per cubic foot. Aluminum beverage cans and PET beverage bottles also are far lighter than their counterparts of 20 or 30 years ago. Every consumer has greatly benefited from these technologies. But the question we focus on here is whether the inventor has been rewarded. Selling less material, after all, means the market (at least in pounds) has shrunk!

Often, the inventor's motivation was only to provide an improved material with the hope that the customer would pay a premium for its virtues. But the customer will almost always explore the possibility of using the increase in a performance attribute (such as stiffness or strength) to make a technically equivalent product with less material, pocketing the difference in raw material costs. (Indeed, Busch and Tincher[4] have made a strong case that lower cost is a better strategy than higher performance when it comes to materials markets.) This strategy is far easier to implement than convincing the customer's customer of the virtues of a better-performing product using the tools of the market research trade. As another example, in the area of spandex or stretch fabrics, elastane fibers, such as Lycra, are added to conventional yarns. A better grade of elastane may allow less elastane to be used, thus lowering the mill's "cost of elastification."

But the inventor would be committing long-term economic suicide to give such improved products away for free; his firm must charge a premium, but at a level that the customer also makes an irresistible economic gain.

The following fictional case, adapted from a different textile application, explores the range in which the premium can be a win-win situation for both parties. It is based on the notion that one path toward material reduction in a fabric is to reduce the denier of the yarn (or "denier-down").[5]

Case 13: Lighter Sailcloth

The key attribute for sail performance is usually stiffness (or modulus), combined with the ability to resist stretch. Well-heeled racers have gone to great expense to rig their ships with expensive high-modulus sails made of Kevlar or similar aramid polymers. (High-performance sailcloths are usually identifiable because their color tends to be gold or brown.) For everyday sailors, however, modulus must be traded off for cost. If an increase in modulus is available in a yarn, the sail designer may choose between accepting the increased performance or "lightweighting" the sail to maintain equivalent performance. And, as every sailor who has wrestled a sail up a hatch and onto a halyard knows, there is a double advantage to the latter approach, making the sail not only less costly, but easier to store and handle.

Dacron fiber is the foundation of traditional woven sailcloth and has been the standard sail material since it replaced canvas in the 1950s. (Dacron is a DuPont trade name for its woven polyester yarn.) Polyester's properties include good ultraviolet and flex resistance (durability) as well as low cost. Its primary disadvantage is stretchiness. Dacron sails are typically white (the number of white sails at a marina pretty much measures Dacron's prevalence), although some colored sails may be made from dyed polyester yarns as well.[6]

Negotiating Scenario

Janice Woo is the product manager for polyester yarn at United Fiber Corporation, a supplier of commodity and specialty yarns to the textile industry. Her counterpart across the table is Tom Head, the technology manager for Performance Fabrics, Inc., a leading manufacturer of sailcloth and supplier to most of the major sailmakers.

United Fiber's research laboratories have learned that they can increase the modulus of polyester at negligible cost by changing the isomer ratio of one component of the polyester resin, and have filed for a patent on their discovery. Sailcloth has been identified as a possible application, and Janice has been assigned to determine the profit potential in this market segment. Clearly, a value chain is in play—from resin supplier to yarn producer to fabric producer to sailmaker to boat owner. Janice's basic concern is that her new product will cannibalize her existing products, and result in a net loss of poundage to the sail industry. If no price premium can be earned, the new technology will result in a loss of revenues and profit. Can a value-in-use pricing strategy be implemented to offset this danger and earn a financial reward?

Solution to Case 13

This solution explores both the quantitative and qualitative aspects of achieving a win-win result.

An Algorithm for Sharing Value

In preparation for her meeting with Ted, Janice develops a spreadsheet (Figure 8.3) to calculate the value proposition as seen by her customer under a variety of assumptions, while also looking at her own value proposition.

There are five key inputs. The first is the change in volume predicted. For the base case assume it is substantial, –25 percent. The second is the change in cost of goods sold (COGS) owing to a new resin. Assume it is small, 1 percent more. Third, Janice needs to reckon her current gross margin, which is calculated from her current ("old") selling price per unit less her ("old") incremental cost of goods sold (COGS). These are $1.50 per pound and $1.00 per pound respectively. There is also an input for

FIGURE 8.3   Value Sharing

Input	
Material change	–25%
Cost change	1%
Old COGS/unit	$1.00
Old selling price/unit	$1.50
Projected volume (units)	1,000,000
Seller's target share of value	50%
Output	
New volume (units)	750,000
New COGS/unit	$1.00
Required price premium	22.56%
New price/unit	$1.84
Value seller	$121,250
Value buyer	$121,250
Value total	$242,500

projected volume, although this input will not affect the new selling price. (Assume she chooses to discuss an arbitrary order for 1,000,000 pounds of yarn.) Finally, the key parameter is the proposed split of the total value created by the new technology. For the base case assume the seller seeks to retain 50 percent.

The key output is the selling price required to achieve that split. The algebra is straightforward though moderately complicated, and can be traced (use the "auditing" tool) in the spreadsheet. The logic is that the seller's additional profit is determined by the difference between her new volume and new margin and her old volume and old margin. The buyer's additional profit is the difference between his old price times his old volume and the new selling price times the new volume. The one unknown is the new selling price. For a 50–50 split, the buyer's and seller's sums are set equal, and the equation is solved for the new selling price.

$$\text{Value(Seller)} = Q_n(P_n - C_n) - Q_o(P_o - C_o) = P_oQ_o - P_nQ_n = \text{Value(Buyer)}$$

where P, C, and Q represent price, cost, and volume and n and o indicate new and old.

For other splits, buyer and seller values are related through an arithmetic ratio, and the solution is similar. This is simple and straightforward.

(This calculation for now ignores any possible give-back Tom's sailmaker customers may demand based on their view of his raw material costs, and also ignores the value-added aspects of lightweighting; these aspects will enter the discussion that surrounds the appropriate profit-sharing formula.)

The answer is given in the "Outputs" tier of Figure 8.3. The corresponding template is available on the CD-ROM. For a price premium of 22.56 percent and a new selling price of $1.84 per pound, buyer and seller each find $121,250 of value in a 750,000-pound order. The range of win-win values actually extends to a range of zero to $242,500 (total value) for each party. As in our previous case, it is a matter of business logic and negotiation skill where the actual outcome will be resolved. Janice does some sensitivity analysis to show the price she needs for a range of value-sharing outcomes. If she can negotiate a selling price of $1.92/pound, United Fiber will retain 75 percent of the value. At $1.76, it retains only 25 percent. This range would appear to be the box in which she can expect to negotiate.

How does the situation change if the technology improvement comes at considerable cost, say 10 percent more? The template can also be used to calculate this answer. There is less value to share, of course—$87,500 for each party assuming an even split. And the new selling price to achieve parity is $1.88 per pound, an increase of 25.56 percent rather than 22.56 percent.

Intangible Considerations

The merit of beginning with a calculation of tangible cost savings is that it creates a starting point for a negotiation. But the negotiation will still encompass many intangible factors, which may work in two ways: (1) in determining the fraction that divides the total reward, or (2) by affecting the total reward that is to be divided. Some possible examples are:

- *Other technical factors.* The down-denier strategy could expose a new technical weakness. For example, tenacity to break may be lower with a lighter fabric. If this issue cannot be overcome technically, the buyer must assess how important it is to the customer or to safety. Other technical factors may enhance value—for example, the convenience of a lighter sail.
- *Innovative technology.* Improved technology itself provides a platform for differentiation of product, and for advertising and promotion. These intangibles may be important in the technically conscious sailing community.
- *Patent strength.* The seller has a strong patent and could take the product to the competition. Can the buyer afford not to have access to this product?
- *Value chain precedents.* Precedents may be in place within the industry regarding the sharing of value created by improved technology. For example, in the patent licensing marketplace, a rule of thumb[7] is that the inventor receives only 25 percent of the value created. But United Fiber is more than just an inventor—it is manufacturing, distributing, and supporting the new product. How much more is it entitled to?
- *Start-up costs.* Performance Fabric will have a learning curve to climb in weaving the new fiber. It will likely involve setup time and the production of waste and substandard product until the mill adjusts to the new product. Similarly, the sales force will need to spend considerable effort educating the sailmakers about the virtues of the new cloth.
- *Assumption of risk.* Performance Fabric runs the risk that the sailmakers will resist the innovation. Will United Fiber take back unused fiber? What if skippers make claims regarding torn sails? Is this a significant liability?

These general issues, and undoubtedly some other elements in the historical relationship between the two firms (and even between Ted and Janice), will affect the final negotiation. The reader, from her own experience, may wish to weigh them as an exercise.

VALUE IN USE: CAPITAL PRODUCTIVITY

A very common element in value-in-use situations is to improve capital productivity in the customer's factory. This may have two effects. The customer may be able to increase the output of the factory, and in the process reduce the fixed costs per unit of the product by spreading them over more units. Hence margins improve. Secondly, the customer may be able to defer expanding the plant because of the new incremental capacity represented by vendor-supplied technology. These values may be additive. Obviously, the potential is greatest when the factory is in a position to sell every pound it makes. Firms that are struggling to sell their output are less likely to invest in capital productivity.

Case 14: Ethylene Cracking Furnaces

Ethylene is the mightiest of the petrochemicals, with worldwide capacity exceeding 225 billion pounds. It is produced in a unit called a thermal cracking furnace,[8] which rapidly heats the feedstock, typically ethane gas or naphtha (a gasoline-like liquid), to an extreme temperature, forming gaseous ethylene and a host of by-products. After it is cooled, the ethylene is separated from the by-products and unreacted feedstock in massive distillation towers. New crackers are big. For example, a report in *Chemical and Engineering News* on NOVA Chemicals and Dow's new world-scale unit at Joffre, Alberta, estimates a capacity of 2.8 billion pounds and a cost of $800 million.[9] It follows that the opportunities for capital productivity are also big.

A major operating problem for ethylene crackers is that the furnace tubes gradually build up coke (carbon). Coke has two detrimental effects. First, it limits heat exchange across the tube wall, and thus reduces cracking capacity, which depends on heat transfer. In other words, coke is a thermal insulator and prevents efficient heat transfer from the furnace firebox to the reacting gas within the tubes.

Second, coke buildup will reduce the interior diameter of the tube, permitting less feedstock to pass through. Either problem can limit capacity, and a point will be reached where shutdown for decoking is required.

The situation tends to be aggravated when producers faced with a high demand for product strive to run their plants hotter to boost output. This method works for a time, but the resulting higher temperatures mean that the inside of the tubes will build up coke even faster![10] The removal of the coke requires frequent decokes of the furnace tubes, each a nonproductive downtime for the furnace, as well as a maintenance expense. What value can be created by reducing coke formation?

Solution to Case 14

ChemSystems[11] has estimated the difference in cost between operating 85 and 100 percent of the time is 1.7 cents per pound. Now there are other reasons for furnace downtime besides decoking, and each plant will have its own baseline operating rate and supply/demand balance. Another consideration is that the downstream units of the plant may have insufficient capacity to handle increased furnace output (this is unlikely since the plant will likely be designed to have all furnaces operating simultaneously). But under optimal circumstances, there is clearly a potential to save one cent per pound, corresponding approximately to a 10 percent increase in operating time. As an example of an improved furnace-tube product, NOVA Chemicals has developed coating technology, now marketed commercially in furnace tubes supplied by Kubota,[12] which in some cases increases run life between decokes by a factor of five—often a year or more, versus typical run lives of a few months. Other coking inhibitor technologies exist in the marketplace, some based on coatings, and others on feedstock additives.

What is the value of this technology based on cost savings? As a reference point, one cent per pound on a billion-pound cracker is $10 million annually, less the premium paid to the technology vendor. The amount of this total value that will be captured by the inventor and the furnace tube supplier may be limited by competition-based pricing, discussed earlier in this chapter, since the plant manager will be charged with determining which of several alternative technologies he may employ. Chemical businesses are typically valued at six to seven times EBITDA, so the total value of this innovation could be $60 million to $70 million per billion pounds of plant capacity.

The second source of value is in terms of capital deferred. Based on the NOVA/Dow benchmark, a billion pounds of modern ethylene capacity is worth approximately $300 million. Increasing that capacity by 10 percent is worth $30 million.

EVOLUTION/REVOLUTION CONTROVERSY

Earlier in the chapter, allusion is made to the trend for incremental research to crowd out more fundamental research in large industrial laboratories. (Note that none of the innovative product improvements cited earlier have the potential to transform the industries in which they are deployed.) The causes may be varied. Economic factors, such as heightened global competition and a higher cost of capital, have put pressure on long-term research. This was a huge problem in the 1980s, but more recently it has abated. Some management philosophies, especially the trends to decentralize business operations into strategic business units (SBUs) have come at the expense of large central R&D laboratories. SBUs breed parochial views, particularly when combined with strong near-term incentive programs.

The alternative popular business philosophy of focus on core competencies is also apt to constrain R&D creativity. Per its champions, Hamel and Prahaladad, "The goal . . . is to focus senior management's attention on those competencies that lie at the center, rather than the periphery, of long-term competitive success."[13] This approach not only limits the scope for creativity, but may ignore the widely observed phenomenon of the most serious competitive threats coming from unforeseen directions.

Finally, the trend to incrementalism may be driven by diminishing returns on fundamental research, as the low-hanging fruit (in discovery terms) is harvested in field after field. Could incremental research drive the search for scientific breakthroughs completely off the playing field?

Here is the case for incrementalism:

Repeated incremental improvements are a process that Ralph Gomory and Roland Schmitt[14] have described in Science *magazine as "always doing a little better than the other guy." Gomory and Schmitt pointed out that "incremental improvement has given us better resolution and quieter and better quality printers each year. It has given us jet engines with double the thrust per unit weight of three decades ago." There are many examples that can be added to this list—for example, consumer electronics, automobiles, and civilian aircraft. All are characterized not by breakthroughs but by improving the design of products and the way they are made. Sony's co-founder Akio Morita put it this way: "Look at the case of the Walkman. Many have called it an innovation marvel, but where is the technology? Frankly it did not contain any breakthrough technology. Its success was built on product planning and marketing." In recent years, many American firms have learned to become good at frequent incremental improvements of their products and more efficient production—factors in the remarkable resurgence of the American economy.[15]*

The Gomory/Schmitt viewpoint is controversial, even within IBM (which did not thrive in the decade following Gomory's espousal of incremental research). Other observers believe that if there is a collapse in the U.S. capacity for breakthrough innovation, the "remarkable resurgence" will be short-lived. Alan Fowler, also of IBM, has aptly summarized this view:

> *What effect has all this had on the research stemming from these laboratories? For those who desire more than anecdotal evidence, publication records are perhaps a better measure than counting the number of people doing industrial research. The number of papers submitted for publication in* Physical Review *and* Physical Review Letters *by AT&T/Bell Telephone Laboratories, by IBM, and [by] a group of other larger industrial laboratories, for the years 1984, 1989, and 1994 have been tabulated. IBM saw a precipitous drop in that time period. Bell declined by a factor of 2, IBM by 2.5, and other labs queried declined by a factor of 1.5. Xerox and Exxon were basically stable. There was a corresponding decline in the number of invited papers at the annual American Physical Society March Meeting.*
>
> *Many of the reasons commonly cited for shortening the attention span of industrial research should not be accepted in their entirety. For example, there is the argument that we are overloaded with technologies and most work should be incremental to contend with market competition and 18-month product cycles. Many companies can afford to do little more. They can point to extremely successful companies like Intel, as well as [companies in] European and Asian countries, who support no long-term research, but are generally horizontally integrated companies with very narrow interests. (The recent AT&T split-up is a move towards less vertical integration.)*
>
> *No matter how successful incremental improvements are in the short term, if pursued exclusively they lead to disaster in the long term. [Emphasis added.] There is a danger that if something does not fill the role of the great industrial laboratories, not only the companies themselves, but the entire American economy will be made obsolete by developments from overseas. As much as some companies, many politicians, and many ordinary citizens would welcome a chance to catch their breath after increasingly rapid changes, we have a tiger by the tail.*[16]

As heated as this philosophical controversy can become, most businesspeople will want to make their decisions by the numbers. That is the spirit of this book. There is ample anecdotal evidence supporting great wealth creation via technology breakthroughs. Many are reasonably recent. We have seen there are even larger numbers of examples of wealth creation through a stream of ever-better new products. To some extent, the right balance is industry-specific. The car industry lives off constant improvement, although it dabbles in radical innovation. But incremental innovation may be too expensive (!) in some cases such as health care, owing to the cost of incremental changes imposed by FDA regulations. As a result, the pharmaceutical industry is in increasing measure wedded to blockbuster innovations. At the end of the day, the CEO and the CTO must seek the optimum mix of the two alternatives for their business, blending the analytical tools at hand with informed instinct.

CHAPTER 9

Balanced R&D Portfolios

Portfolio theory as applied to financial investments is a highly developed craft. Nobel Prizes have been granted to economists such as Harry Markowitz who have developed the foundations. Optimization software is widely available and is widely used. For a fee, investors can subscribe to services such as Morningstar that combine proprietary software with enormous financial data bases to allow them to construct stock portfolios precisely suited to their investment goals. Most major financial firms rigorously test their investment portfolios on a value-at-risk basis.

The importance of managing R&D portfolios is just as widely recognized, but the state of the theory is frankly a mess. Experienced R&D chiefs are uniform in their assertion that a balanced R&D portfolio is the key to R&D effectiveness. But what they mean by balance may differ. There is a substantial amount of literature on this subject, yet the authors typically address only part of the picture and seem to be talking past one another. A pithy article[1] based on a survey of R&D practitioners indicates the level of satisfaction with the common methods of portfolio analysis is low.

Why? The short answer is that the components of an R&D portfolio (the projects) are not liquid. This fact enormously complicates the analysis. To attempt a comprehensive solution remains foolhardy, but a review of what is known is worthwhile.

The present chapter focuses on developing an understanding of the opportunities and constraints imposed by the linkage of R&D to a real-world corporation. The following chapter (Chapter 10), on "optimum portfolios," will explore the narrower subject of applying conventional financial tools to R&D portfolios, and how they can inform R&D strategy. This is in the spirit of all of my books: For R&D executives to communicate with business and financial executives, they must learn to speak financial language, for the language of the laboratory will never suffice. Because there are important nonfinancial considerations in a balanced R&D portfolio, it follows that a well-balanced portfolio in the real world is not the same as one developed on the basis of financial theory alone.

STRUCTURAL REALITIES

When an R&D executive first gets her job, she gains more than an R&D portfolio. She now controls (1) a specialized staff, (2) equipment and buildings, (3) intellectual property, (4) a budget, and (5) a host of inherited relationships with different units and functions of the company. Some of the individual assets are enormously valuable; others will prove no more than liabilities. While the pace of change can be accelerated and new strategies adopted, the realities of dealing with people ensure that the change process will be primarily evolutionary.

A change in the portfolio may require hiring, purchasing, and integrating new assets, while leaving other assets stranded. Both are problems that will take time and effort to address.

Liquidity is again the underlying problem because transaction costs affecting R&D people and equipment are very high. Recruiting, training, and orienting a staff scientist may take the better part of a year. Laying off staff will involve significant severance costs. New equipment may require months and dollars for installation and validation. Yet used laboratory equipment may be worth no more than 10 percent of the purchase price.

In the meantime, the R&D executive must make the best possible use of the assets she has in place, or write off those assets that no longer fit. A software engineer cannot be reassigned to organic synthesis, nor can a big Pfaudler reactor be adapted to mammalian cell fermentation. A skilled R&D chief will therefore seek to effectively deploy her most valuable resources—skilled scientists and engineers, plus specialized equipment—to the best available project. This consideration may distort the optimum portfolio as seen from the risk/reward viewpoint. But there *is* lower cost and risk in deploying proven assets versus acquiring and engaging new ones. Generally, the optimum course is to adjust the skill base to new business and technical trends rather than radically restructure it to fit a "paper" strategy. (Of course, technological progress is relentless and an overly gradual approach can trap the firm in a technical cul de sac.) In summary, the current R&D project mix must be consistent with the R&D asset base, but the latter must evolve as quickly as possible to fit the R&D strategy of the future.

The second structural reality is that the portfolio must be balanced in the time dimension. An R&D portfolio becomes seriously imbalanced when all its projects are early stage and cash flow generation is many years away. It is equally imbalanced when all projects are short-term (and highly vulnerable to adverse developments) and late stage. Because failure rates occur at each stage and subsequent stages are increasingly costly, an optimum time-balanced portfolio has a larger number of small early-stage projects and a smaller number of well-thought-out developmental projects approaching commercialization. The asset base will be constrained in a time dimension as well, since different skills and facilities are required for exploratory research as opposed to advanced development. The right ratio of early-stage to late-stage projects will be industry-specific.

The selection and initiation of early-stage projects is critical to portfolio balance and R&D strategy for the seemingly obvious reason that only those projects can be advanced to commercialization that have passed through the earlier stages. The research pipeline must contain attractive early-stage opportunities for the organization to have worthy developmental opportunities. R&D experts bemoan the problems of managing "the fuzzy front end" and the risks of making bad decisions based on weak or premature data, *but the effort must be attempted*, for this point presents the best single opportunity to forge an optimum portfolio. (A central purpose of this book is to make that analytical process less onerous than it might be.)

Also, from a liquidity viewpoint, projects generally need to be completed before most of their value is realized. During their lifetimes, they are dependent on the illiquid assets enumerated earlier. In this way they are unlike financial securities, which can be bought and sold efficiently at the market price. The decision boils down to "go/no go." True, various forms of technology acquisition and technology salvage are available, but because of the high cost of technology transfer these transactions are usually inefficient as well.

In summary, we shall see that while a financial profile can be determined for an R&D portfolio, changing that profile is limited by liquidity and structural constraints.

Case 15: Evolution of a Portfolio

This five-part case is a personal account of my experiences in analyzing and managing an R&D portfolio over a 14-year time frame at W. R. Grace and Company. At any point in time, that portfolio consisted of 60 to 80 projects. Mine is necessarily a partial account: The topics are chosen to illustrate issues and principles, rather than to attempt to paint an accurate history of a very complex and fluid series of events, often driven by factors far outside the scope of this book.

One point should be made about Grace's corporate culture: The firm was much more financially oriented than any other with which I have been associated, where decision making has tended to be primarily strategic. Rather than proving to be a drawback (R&D managers are instinctively, but often unjustifiably, mistrustful of the bean counters), this circumstance proved to be the opposite. Grace business reviews provided a wealth of financial and market data and a deep insight into the business models of very different industries, from energy to health care. Participating in them improved both my understanding of my "customers" and my financial skills. This combination in turn broadened my own perspectives of R&D's role in a way that a strategic perspective alone could not provide. This is not to say strategy had no role in guiding the company. Strategy was critical, but it was thoroughly illuminated by financial analysis.

Getting Started

I was new to the company, so my initial steps were basic. People first. In my first meeting with my direct reports, I took pains to get every name and role right the first time. I soon had met the entire staff by lunching with 5 to 10 employees at a time in the cafeteria, and invited them to express their ideas and concerns. I scheduled meetings with all the business unit presidents and preceded each discussion with a brief review of the projects in the portfolio that pertained to those units.

A few surprises were discovered. While all the business units had their own internal R&D functions, they relied to very different degrees on the Corporate Research Center. The Polyfibron and Construction Products Divisions had built much of their business on Research Division inventions, and were skilled in managing the interface. The Davison Chemical catalysis business had also benefited in very important ways from the Research Division, but had built a strong internal group (in the same building yet), and the working relationships had become "siloed." The Cryovac Packaging business in South Carolina was even more fiercely independent, and there were initially no shared projects. This attitude particularly disturbed me, since I had some expertise in packaging, having just worked for a competitor, and I was well aware of opportunities and also weaknesses in the packaging portfolio.

The Organic Chemicals business was anxious to work with Research, and with strong corporate backing was sponsoring a very broad and expensive initiative into amino acids, based on biotechnology. There were several other important divisions with which we interacted, but they would needlessly complicate this story. Corporate management wanted some home runs, and at the same time encouraged Research to exploit strategic opportunities afforded by acquisitions in membranes, ceramics, and later health care.

Another philosophical problem was difficult to overcome. The group executive for Chemicals, with whom I always enjoyed a good personal relationship, felt that R&D should focus on fixing his weaker operations, such as Organic Chemicals, while the stronger units like Davison and Cryovac could be left on their own. In contrast, I believed that Research's report card would be based on its track record, and sensed that dollars spent in areas of real strength would be more productive than with weak units. This conviction grew stronger with time as I analyzed the annual results from the portfolio.

How did these relationships evolve with time? Relationships with Polyfibron and Construction Products remained strong and productive. For Construction Products alone, the Research team developed a new superplasticizer, a new strength enhancer, a new quality improver, a new (nailable) roofing membrane, and asbestos abatement technology that won *Industrial Research* magazine's IR100 award.

I was able in time to smooth relationships with Davison at the top, but the silo mentality could never be entirely overcome. Even so, we created the technical foundation that put Davison into the metallocene catalyst business. A working relationship was established with Cryovac, mostly by putting very good young scientists on packaging projects. This program grew year by year and had a very high percentage of successes. As for the Organic Chemicals people, surely they were disappointed as I shifted resources to more promising projects.

Finally, aside from the projects directly aligned with business units, the Research Division assisted in creating a number of new business initiatives, such as a gas separation membrane company, a company specializing in natural pesticides, and three different catalyst businesses. Overall, our scorecard showed a steady, productive contribution to the company.[2]

Success and Failure

Research is a business of managing risk, reward, and cost. The experience over these years suggested good results could be obtained without being exceptionally lucky. We kept records of our success rates and reported them annually to management. In all cases, the decision to terminate projects was made by the Research Division itself. Over the period described, the division's level of competence was improved by strengthening infrastructure, especially engineering and analytical chemistry; by attracting very bright new people; and by pruning resources that were unable to contribute value. Bread-and-butter projects were coming through. We had identified perhaps five potential home runs: The biggest (the artificial pancreas) failed to achieve its technical goals. Our cloning project put calves on the ground at the University of Wisconsin, but the method was not yet efficient enough to revolutionize milk production. Phenylalanine and selective catalytic reduction met their technical objectives, but the market evolved in ways that had not been anticipated, and we properly cut our losses when our annual business reviews showed the forecast markets were receding from view. Our scouting effort in genetic engineering of crops created a very valuable intellectual property position, but at the time it was sold (at a handsome profit), Grace had realized only a fraction of its potential value. Even so, working on some big, exciting projects invigorated our organization, and our reliance on objective analysis earned respect.

Case 15, Part One: Creating a Workable Analytical Foundation

The analytical capabilities I inherited were impressive. The division had on its staff five "commercial planners," most of whom had a higher technical degree plus an MBA. Their job was to assist researchers with planning, develop market information, and handle the first phases of market development for projects that were not directly tied to an operating division. Each was responsible for a group of 10 to 20 projects. Their presence reflected the fact that Grace fully recognized the need to put commercial savvy behind its projects. I was somewhat surprised to see this number of indirect professional head count in the organization. Very likely, my former employer, Dow Chemical, would have regarded it as excess overhead, but at no time was it questioned at Grace.

Still, there was a big problem. Much of the commercial planners' time was committed to what I regarded as an unproductive task. They were writing proposal documents called requests for project authorization (RPAs) that contained as much project detail as Grace's standard "Request for Capital Authorization." These documents could run to 50 or 100 pages replete with detailed charts. The problem was that a commercial planner would need weeks or months to issue such a report, so that many projects had no documentation, and those that did were mostly out of date.

Solution to Case 15, Part One

The New Fact Sheets

I needed something faster, and an existing document known locally as a "fact sheet" was streamlined (limited to a two-page of summary of the project), and focused toward business issues. Technical detail would be discussed at regular project reviews and in technical reports. The heart of the fact sheet was (1) identification of the objective, including a quantification of the market target; (2) the budget; and (3) the milestones. Each project was assigned a stage—conceptual, feasibility, development, or early commercialization—and criteria were developed to define stages. Small exploratory projects were excluded from the system—research directors were given exploratory budgets to handle projects of less than three months' duration, after which they must choose between formalizing the project in a fact sheet or quietly shutting it down. Exploratory budgets also served to cushion the impact on researchers of project termination. In financial terms, they reduced transaction costs.

The milestone system was extremely useful for tracking progress and training managers. *A missed milestone meant either flawed execution or flawed planning, usually the latter.* While there was generally an excuse or a change in circumstances to explain the deviation, the discipline of milestone reporting provided the project leader with feedback. A pattern of missed milestones would put in question the premises of the project. At the same time, we did not expect or desire a high success rate, since easy milestones meant the researchers were not stretching. At too slow a pace, the project economics would turn sour. In hindsight, I think an overall 50 to 80 percent success rate was healthy, but some milestones were much more important than others.

Other information in the fact sheet would describe the technical approach, relevant market statistics, the project's history, and patent strategy and status, and give a qualitative assessment of strengths, weaknesses, and open issues. The format was sufficiently simple that a revision could be made whenever the project leader or commercial planner desired it. A new fact sheet book was issued semiannually, and ran to only about 150 pages. Obviously there was a concern about the security of this document, so distribution was carefully controlled, but it proved extremely useful for planning and for answering questions raised elsewhere in the company.

The system was quickly up and running and it endured. It has been emulated at other companies. It also freed up the commercial planners to focus on the real value drivers such as markets and competition.

Pro Forma Analysis

With the fact sheets in hand, I still lacked a tool, other than my own instincts, as to which projects were best and which were marginal. Certainly, I had a sense that some were in trouble, and some had market targets that were too small to justify the level of effort. I strongly felt, just as for the fact sheets, a "quick and dirty" system for identifying value would be far better than no system at all. If a project were to fare poorly in the initial analysis, the project champions would be given a full chance to demonstrate analytically why its merits were misunderstood.

At an early project stage, researchers typically have a rough idea of the size of the potential market and their raw material costs. Of the other components of the financial statement, they have little clue. The innovation we developed was the notion that variable margins (revenues less cost of goods sold/revenues) and capital intensity (ratio of total capital employed to revenues) in a business over the years stayed in a fairly narrow range. The evidence was clear in the detailed charts of Grace business reviews, which included at least a five-year financial history for every product line. However, these numbers were unique for each business—Packaging was different from Davison.

Why worry now about how much the new plant will cost before it has been designed? Assume it will be in line with the business's previous capital investments. If facts subsequently show otherwise, the profit can be recalculated. Similarly, one can work off either price or cost estimates (choose the one in which you have more confidence) but keep your margin in line with what the business has historically earned. Most of our customers were industrial and it was a good bet they would allow us margins we traditionally enjoyed, but expanding margins based on better technology would always be a difficult sell. One of the commercial planners undertook to write a small spreadsheet program based on these and other plausible assumptions.[3] His work allowed a series of simple charts to be drawn that allowed the calculation of NPV based on three values: market size, gross margin, and capital intensity. The method is described in my book *The Valuation of Technology*.[4] Figure 9.1 shows a sample. (The chart assumes a standard market target of $100 million. The NPV was then adjusted by the ratio of the target market to this standard.)

The value of the project NPV could then be compared to the cost of the project to give an initial measure of relative project attractiveness. (Big projects with big NPVs would not necessarily rank highest.) This simple risk-versus-reward approach became the prototype for the more complex spreadsheets described in Chapters 2 through 4, and is perfectly usable today. It lacks the features of decision trees and real options, as thinking about probabilities of success would come later. The portfolio could then be put in better balance by weeding out less attractive projects, while adding resources to those that were more attractive.

Tracking the Portfolio

Over the next decade my staff and I added two other methods for tracking the portfolio. The Research Division had long kept a list of projects that

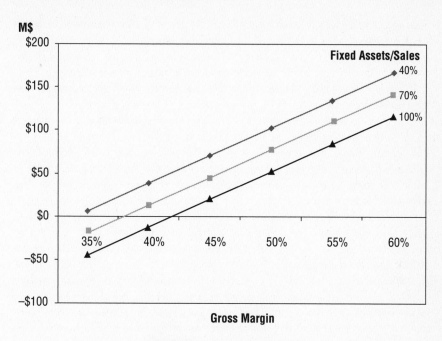

FIGURE 9.1   Net Present Value

were successfully commercialized, and added about three to seven projects per year, representing the tangible value created by the Research Division in the current year.

The metric of success was the five-year revenue forecast, as provided by the business unit. This number, divided by the cost of the research program as a whole, gave us a measure of the productivity of the research effort.[5] It was assumed that the value created would result from a higher growth rate for the company, that discipline would be maintained by ensuring that research productivity was sufficient to more than offset costs, and that capital investments would earn the hurdle rate for capital. This metric has since been adopted by other firms.

The next step came with the realization that we were developing some significant information about rates of project success through the discipline of the staging system. We knew each year, by stage, how many projects were started, how many were terminated, and how many had advanced to the next stage. (Our previous metric of projects commercialized was just the final step in this entire process.) This new method gave a transparency to the full portfolio of the Research Division, and a real sense for the distribution of risk. It was shared with the corporation at annual reviews, and often provoked questions like, "What happened to the lithium battery project?" Figure 9.2 shows some simulated data in this format. The obvious focus of attention in the business review would be on the current year (1990), with the historical results allowing a comparison to past performance.

The second type of chart (Figure 9.3) tracked the project inventory of the portfolio by stage. In this format, the first line shows that 23 new conceptual projects were started in the current year and 15 were terminated. However, 8 projects were advanced to the feasibility stage, indicating a success rate of 8/23 or 34.8 percent. Not counted in the success rate are the 24 projects that are continuing for another year without being advanced. Clearly a pipeline that starts 20 new conceptual projects per year and enjoys a 10 percent overall rate of success can expect to commercialize two projects a year. The portfolio in Figure 9.3 may do slightly better than this.

An important feature of this type of chart is that it provides management a tool to ensure enough projects are started, and also that not too many projects are advanced. The latter is important because advanced projects demand increasingly larger resources, giving management only two choices: ask for a larger budget or sacrifice the new projects. If management does not have the discipline to cancel weaker projects and advances too many, the portfolio will soon get hopelessly out of balance.

Finally, we were able to use the inventory of projects and the calculated success rates to project future sales of new products to be expected from the portfolio. The methods were now sound enough that I felt we could use them in a presentation chart at annual business reviews. The

FIGURE 9.2 Representative Rates of Project Advancement (Percent Advancing)

Year	Concept to Feasibility	Feasibility to Development	Development to Early Commercialization	Early Commercialization to Commercial
Historic				
1985	30.0%	54.5%	80.0%	71.4%
1986	36.4%	40.0%	81.8%	100.0%
1987	21.8%	42.1%	72.7%	83.3%
1988	33.3%	63.2%	75.0%	50.0%
1989	40.9%	52.2%	58.3%	100.0%
Five-year average	32.5%	50.4%	73.6%	81.0%
Current				
1990	33.9%	47.4%	72.7%	85.7%

FIGURE 9.3 Percent of Projects Advancing in Portfolio

Stage	New	Continued	Total Continuing	Advanced	Stopped	Prior Total	Percent Advancing	Cumulative Percent
Conceptual	23	24	47	8	15	47	34.8%	13.0%
Feasibility	8	9	17	4	4	17	50.0%	37.5%
Development	4	3	7	3	1	7	75.0%	75.0%
Early commercial	3	2	5	2	0	4	100.0%	100.0%
Commercial	2							
Total projects			76			75		

calculation is somewhat complicated owing to the different time periods to reach commercialization dates, and the dependence of probability of success on project stage, but the results are quite useful in projecting what new revenues the company can expect to get from the portfolio, and when these results can reasonably be expected. A sample of such a forward-looking chart (a 10-year projection) and a detailed explanation of the calculation are published in my book *The Valuation of Technology*.[6] Like all business projections, it is subject to very considerable uncertainty, but the exercise at least provides a likely outcome and a sense for the upside potential.

Tackling Portfolio Issues

While it is necessary to run the numbers from time to time to check the health of the overall portfolio, the real work of portfolio management must be done on a project-by-project, and person-to-person, basis. The five project histories (a small fraction of the projects pursued from 1982 to 1996) that follow illustrate how projects are initiated and shaped, and the considerations that lead to their abandonment. As an author, it is more fun to write about successes, such as ion chromatography, but the case histories of failures or partial successes are at least as illuminating.

Case 15, Part Two: Amino Acids

The amino acid project was a prominent part of the Grace research portfolio when I joined the company in 1982.

The strategic rationale for the project, as I understood it, was that the emerging field of biotechnology would revolutionize specialty chemicals, and that Grace was well positioned to participate. (The first premise proved mostly untrue, but a scouting project in this field was probably a wise investment, both defensively and because it would create options for using biotechnology down the road.) The initial target of amino acids was chosen, because the Organic Chemicals Division already produced one, glycine, and possessed some technology applicable to a few others. Furthermore, the three prominent producers of parenteral (intravenous) nutrition supplements[7] for hospitalized patients had encouraged Grace to enter this business, since they were almost totally dependent on two Japanese sources, Ajinomoto and Kyowa Hakko. Given technical success, we could expect perhaps $100 million in revenues.

A word about the technology. Proteins are synthesized in the body from 17 naturally occurring amino acids, using the genetic code. All but glycine occur naturally only as left-handed molecules, which generally require a biologically based synthesis. The Japanese had become experts in producing amino acids based on fermentation, an older biological process akin to brewing beer and which did not require modern biotechnology. The hope was that the new inventions could be used to make them more cheaply (this premise, at least in part, proved true).

Solution to Case 15, Part Two

To me, the obvious problem was that Grace was funding projects, both externally and internally, that addressed fewer than half of the amino acids. These projects were expensive, and some were in technical difficulty. Justifying 16 risky projects aimed at a $100 million market certainly did not stand up to financial analysis, and faced daunting odds of technical success. We briefly explored purchasing and purifying some of the compounds from other sources, but this avenue held limited promise. Could something be done to salvage the program?

One amino acid, L-phenylalanine, was in the news since it was the major component of Searle's recently approved sweetener, aspartame.[8] Searle was building a new fermentation plant while temporarily buying phenylalanine from Japanese sources. Aspartame was destined to be a billion-dollar business (Searle sold the Nutrasweet business to Monsanto shortly thereafter for almost $2 billion). The basic aspartame patent would expire in five years. The timing seemed right for a better process, and we had a head start. The initial decision was to focus on phenylalanine and defer parenterals.

The basic technical idea was to use an intermediate[9] that Grace could readily produce in its New Hampshire plant, and design a biological catalyst that would transform it to L-phenylalanine via an enzyme reaction. (In hindsight, this was a good idea.)

Where to get the biocatalyst? Grace had negotiated a contract with the preeminent biotechnology firm Genentech to produce one using its recombinant DNA expertise. Soon I faced writing a large check for a milestone payment, and the contract got my attention. One feature stood out: The royalty rate was more typical for a new drug than for a specialty chemical. Pro forma financial analysis was put to work, and the conclusion was that the net present value of a successful project was positive in total, but it was negative for Grace (and highly positive for Genentech). A Grace team journeyed to South San Francisco and discussed the numbers. Initially, Genentech thought Grace was just bargaining, but the analysis was rigorous enough and withstood scrutiny. While there were still some twists and turns, this was the beginning of the end of the Genentech phase. Genentech felt they had too many better opportunities in pharmaceuticals to dedicate effort to earn the seemingly mundane royalties characteristic of the chemical business. In time, quite possibly because of this experience, they abandoned their proposed thrust into biological synthesis of chemicals entirely. They were right to do so.

This experience, probably more than any other, made me a believer in running the numbers—using financial analysis to inform R&D strategy.

But the Grace phenylalanine project was hardly finished. Our biotechnology research director suggested screening various natural enzymes that might act as a biocatalyst. Before a year had gone we had found a good one, had immobilized it on a column, and were pouring Organic's intermediate in at one end and collecting phenylalanine at the other. A preliminary economic analysis suggested we could beat Monsanto's expected cost by its fermentation route by 40 percent. Feasibility had been shown, and the engineers were beginning to design a process. Enthusiasm was never higher.

It was time to call on the soft drink companies, since they were the major consumers of aspartame, and we now had something to offer. Internally, we debated whether we could risk building the plant on speculation or we should first require a "take-or-pay" contract. Visits to Atlanta and Valhalla headquarters of Coca-Cola and PepsiCo revealed great interest in a cheaper source (big money was on the table), but also a clear hesitation to take the risk of incurring Nutrasweet's wrath. The new diet drinks were extremely popular, and it was clear that any risk to these products was unacceptable. As long as the majors were buying Nutrasweet on similar terms, a cheaper source did not provide competitive advantage.

At the next budget review, I suggested terminating the project. My commercial counterparts were of the view it should go another year, but did not object strenuously when I took it out of the budget. In hindsight, I expect that, had we built the plant, it would have been severely underutilized for several years, leading to a negative NPV. Nutrasweet was a ruthless competitor; we remembered it had destroyed Genex a few years earlier. It was also not well liked at Coca-Cola or PepsiCo, in part because of its demand that the Nutrasweet logo be printed on every can. In time, as Nutrasweet's patent position expired, Holland Sweetener's aspartame and Hoechst's acesulfame-K began to erode a once-impregnable position, and the swirl is no longer visible on the can. But this process took time.

The postmortem suggests there was a lot right about this project. It was business driven at heart, not a laboratory orphan looking for a home. It was based in part on a core competency and proprietary technology. It was cost driven, rather than performance driven. There was little risk at the end user (consumer) level. The fatal flaw was not understanding the risk element at the customer level. We were focused only on the cost element of the value chain. How could we have done better? Possibly some consultant could have given us that crucial insight (or possibly not, because the situation was unique and quite fluid). Possibly we might have visited with the customers earlier. But we were not credible until we had demonstrated the process and estimated our economic advantage.

Case 15, Part Three: Environmental Catalysis

While commercial failure in the phenylalanine case hinged on a nonobvious detail, the failure of environmental catalysis is linked with an adverse major market trend. As such, it is a good case study for real options.

The project's origins were top-down. At its inception in the mid-1980s, Friedrich Flick, said to be the richest man in Germany, owned 26 percent of W. R. Grace and sat on its board. His relationship with Peter Grace was cordial, and usually he was a passive investor. But possibly for tax reasons in Germany, he wanted to create a joint venture (subsequently called Noxeram) with one of his group of German operating companies. His suggestion was that the venture be in clean air catalysts with his firm Feldmuehle. The idea was that Feldmuehle would position Noxeram in the marketplace, and Grace would bring the technology.

Solution to Case 15, Part Three

Given its heavyweight corporate sponsors, I probably had no choice about this project, but the more I learned about it, the more I came to like it. The technology was called selective catalytic reduction (SCR),[10] and it was specifically deployed to eliminate nitrogen oxides (NO_x) from stack gases, especially from coal-burning utilities. It had been first deployed in Japan and had done a wonderful job cleaning the air there. Now the Germans were becoming very concerned about their dying forests, and had mandated SCR as well. While Germany was a large market, we would be a late entry. Therefore, our strategy was to learn the technology and develop a foothold in the German marketplace, and then to use the experience to build a leading position for the U.S. market, where concerns were rapidly building about acid rain. About half of acid rain pollution was NO_x. NO_x also contributed significantly to photochemical smog, and to unhealthy ozone levels in many communities. My ace in the hole was a renowned catalyst expert, who happened to be a fluent German speaker.

We traveled to Japan and licensed state-of-the-art technology from Sakai Chemical. This technology quickly became the basis for the new Noxeram plant that went up in the German town of Bergisch Gladbach. The licensed technology was successfully implemented, and catalysts were made and some sold. But our expert's main contribution was an idea for a better and cheaper catalyst. Instead of using titanium dioxide in bulk, we proposed to coat it on silica, a Davison product. Synox, as the new product was called, would be a cheaper product based on its high silica content, and better because of its higher surface area per unit of volume. Hence the power plants could build smaller, cheaper reactors and still achieve the mandated NO_x reduction. There were technical problems in extruding Synox, but they were gradually overcome. Synox entered pilot tests, sometimes side by side with conventional Noxeram, at major American utilities such as the Southern Company. There remained one element of unique risk, a possibility that Mitsubishi would claim we infringed one of its patents. Our lawyers expected Synox would prevail, but this uncertainty weighed on the go/no-go decision.

The strategy failed at both ends. Noxeram won only a few commercial orders, because of the integrated links between German catalyst suppliers and engineering companies, and sometimes the utilities themselves. Engineering companies, which designed the SCR units, were in a strong position to specify the catalysts. Siemens, the vast German electrical conglomerate, in particular thwarted Noxeram's market launch, and our partner, Feldmuehle, proved to be a weak reed. However, the German setback would have mattered little if the U.S. market had developed as forecast and Synox had been commercialized.

The U.S. market potential was regularly estimated by our commercial planning staff based on the number and types of existing power plants and the published deadlines for their coming into compliance. In fact, I had given testimony on the economics (which were far better than opponents of the legislation depicted) at the U.S. Senate.[11] We reasoned we would be a major supplier, as the only U.S. source and a reliable supplier of catalysts. We had established good working relationships with a few major utilities and with the Department of Energy.

The problems were twofold: The utility industry and its allies convinced legislators that SCR would be an intolerable economic burden,[12] quite a remarkable assertion given that Japan was at the height of its economic game at the time. But the sad fact was that each successive year our forecasts for the market were lowered and extended in time—what has been depicted as an "ever-receding mirage." Secondly, with the allowance in the United States of cross-trading SO_x and NO_x emissions,[13] the combination of a scrubber and low-NO_x burners proved more attractive than originally estimated. Such cross-trading was not allowed in Germany and Japan. Today, the SCR market in the United States is still tiny, and dominated by Japanese suppliers. In time, the economic forecast for the program slipped into the range of marginal returns and the project was terminated.

I have since concluded that the demise of this project was due mainly to market risk. We had worked on a number of other advanced environmental technologies at Grace, including the NOXSO process for simultaneously eliminating SO_x and NO_x, and the Camet electrically heated catalytic converter[14] giving near-zero tailpipe emissions. All the technologies worked well, sometimes spectacularly, but none was widely adopted. In a conversation with a senior executive in quite a different area of advanced environmental technology, he recounted very similar experiences. I put that together with the fact that venture capitalists now shun environmental start-ups like the plague.

Simply put, customers do not want to pay for environmental technology, and only force can make it happen. It is especially risky to invest in technology your customers don't want. This market has universally disappointed investors, and despite the glamorous story lines written by environmentally conscious reporters, it has been a financial disaster. The story continues today with even less likely technology breakthroughs such as CO_2 sequestration, electric cars, and the hydrogen economy, while the environmentalists have shifted their focus from acid rain to global warming. Perhaps the option value of having scouting projects in this sector is justified, but history suggests the investor's best defense is a diversified portfolio, and that was what saved us at Grace.

Case 15, Part Four: Cloning Cattle

Since the publicity surrounding Dolly, the cloned sheep born in 1997, it is harder to remember that the first cloned cattle were produced by Granada Genetics and W. R. Grace in 1986. The Grace project leader was Professor Neal First at the University of Wisconsin. (The difference between Dolly and the first cows was that the 1986 work cloned embryos, while Dolly was cloned from an adult.)

The driving force for this project[15] was milk production, a business whose economics we understood. W. R. Grace had a unit called American Breeders Service (ABS), which was the largest marketer of bull semen in North America. (Almost all dairy cattle are sired by artificial insemination.) The value proposition was based on the milk production records of a bull's progeny. That took years to determine because a bull and a significant number of daughters had to come to maturity, but top bulls created wonderful profits. ABS's legendary Valiant sired some 100,000 daughters (the semen could be significantly diluted) at premium prices. Unfortunately, the natural lifetime of a bull allowed for very few profitable years. One thought was that a cloned embryo could be stored in a refrigerator and implanted in a surrogate mother many years later, thus extending the economic lifetime of its successful twin.

Solution to Case 15, Part Four

However, Grace soon realized cloning offered the possibility of virtually eliminating the bull! The notion was to create multiple identical embryos of a cow (then nonroutine), and bring one or more to life by implanting embryos in surrogate mothers (routine). The remaining embryo cells would be frozen. If excellent milk production were to be found in the first batch of cows, the frozen embryos would be recloned and many thousands of identical supercows would be generated.

Based on typical milk production statistics, a supercow might produce 10,000 or more pounds of milk per year above the industry average, a big incentive for a dairy farmer.

With traditional artificial insemination, there is uncertainty whether the prize bull's best genes would be expressed. Also, there is a very limited number of ova from top cows (obtainable by flushing). Breeding was still a game of chance. With the new technology, genetic chance would be virtually eliminated.

The key invention that gave this project hope was the demonstration of *recloning*. Let me first give a perfect example. If an embryo could be grown to the 16-cell stage, each of the 16 nuclei could be removed and inserted in other one-cell embryos whose original nuclei were removed. Each of these 16 could be grown to the 16-cell stage and the process repeated. Now there are 256 copies. A few more cycles and there are many thousands of copies, all of which can be implanted in surrogate mothers—leading to quite a herd of supercows.

Grace-sponsored researchers had demonstrated recloning through at least five generations. Unfortunately, there were significant losses in every step of the process and the cloning efficiency was not 100 percent, but only 1 or 2 percent. Worse, it dropped off after each successive round of recloning. This level of efficiency fell far short of what was required to support a viable business model. After a few unsuccessful efforts to make material technical improvements, the project was dropped. Nonetheless, it is widely accepted that technology is improving and the business model will one day work. In addition, cattle cloning is being explored for other business applications, such as mass production of antibodies to combat bioterror agents.[16]

The commercial purposes of this project were serious, the vehicles for commercial introduction (embryo transplant services) were available, and the business strategy was plausible. However, the technical preconditions for mounting a successful enterprise have yet to be attained, and all indications are that, absent a new insight at the fundamental level of embryo science, progress will be slow.

A retrospective look suggests the primary planning error was insufficient understanding of basic embryo science. We had a great run, but it was a bridge too far.

Case 15, Part Five: Agracetus

The Agracetus name was an ingenious composite that included the name of the founding company, a leading biotechnology firm named Cetus Corporation; the connotation of agriculture (the target market); and the letters "grace" representing my firm, W. R. Grace and Company. In many ways it was a typical business history, with some very uncertain moments, but a generally good outcome.

A major biotech industry, with publicly traded stocks, was created in the late 1970s to exploit the now-apparent potential of genetic engineering to create new products for health care, agriculture, and specialty chemicals. The leading companies at that time were Genentech (described earlier); Cetus (subsequently acquired by Chiron, but the largest of the four); Biogen; and Genex. Genex was not a survivor (thanks to its fatal involvement with Nutrasweet), but Genentech and Biogen continue in the industry as leading players, to be joined by Amgen and many others.

These companies started with no meaningful operating revenues, huge R&D budgets, and some great people and ideas. To survive, they needed continuing infusions of cash from investors or support from strategic partners with deep pockets. All planned to transform themselves into independent operating companies before their cash ran out. None of the first group fully succeeded in meeting their founders' goals, though Amgen did, and Genentech came close. The situation was in many ways an early parallel to the Internet stock situation two decades later.

Cetus created a subsidiary in 1981, originally called Cetus Madison, in Madison, Wisconsin, to exploit the potential of its genetic engineering technology in agriculture. A distinguished scientist recruited from the University of Wisconsin, Dr. Winston Brill, headed it, and a small but very talented scientific staff was assembled.

In need of financing, Cetus approached W. R. Grace in 1983 with a proposal to create a joint venture in the field of agriculture. To summarize the heart of the deal: in return for Grace financing the R&D costs of the operation for five years, Cetus would donate to the joint venture the results of Cetus Madison research, full access to all Cetus technology, and exclusive rights to that technology in the field of agriculture. In option terms, Grace was asked to purchase a five-year call, at a cost of five years of research support, to enjoy half the income generated by the venture.

Grace had strategic reasons for being interested: It was enjoying peak cyclic earnings in agricultural chemicals at the time, based primarily on its commodity fertilizer business. Grace Agricultural Chemicals had only minimal R&D programs in agriculture, but an extensive distribution network and a feeling for the agricultural market. Opportunities to invest its cash in more fertilizer assets were unattractive at the time, so other alternatives were sought to improve the future of the business. Also developing a corporate window on biotechnology was seen as a good long-term investment for the company as a whole.

As I recall the initial meeting of these firms, two things stand out. The first was a presentation by a very articulate young Cetus executive of a business plan whereby Agracetus would create five or six high-margin businesses, mostly in genetically modified crops (now called GM crops). The revenues of these hypothetical businesses were projected to exceed $100 million in a few years, and growth thereafter would be powerful. The presenter had no operating experience, and the Grace executives there, including myself, were profoundly skeptical that the plan could be executed, if from a timing standpoint alone. And about that we were right.

The second memorable event was a presentation by Cetus scientist Kary Mullis showing a new way to amplify small gene segments called polymerase chain reaction (PCR). Mullis was awarded the 1993 Nobel Prize for this work, which became arguably the most valuable intellectual property owned by Cetus. Under the terms of the deal, Agracetus was to own exclusive rights to PCR in agriculture.

Before long, the deal was done.

During the next five years, Agracetus worked diligently to commercialize new products based on the nitrogen-fixing bacteria called *rhizobia*, which were in the field of Winston Brill's expertise. These products ultimately failed. But two other important things happened. First, the scientific staff made substantial progress in learning how to genetically engineer plants, and began to accumulate a portfolio of potentially valuable patents. The best of these concerned cotton.

Second, Agracetus acquired rights to radical new technology, originally called Biolistics (as in ballistics) and later trademarked by Agracetus as Accell. It had been invented at Cornell University. The idea was to coat small strands of DNA onto tiny gold particles and shoot these particles into living cells using a "gene gun"—a mechanical device. The tiny bullet holes made by the gold were repaired quickly by the target cells, and the DNA that was delivered could be taken up by the cells to produce proteins not normally made by the target organism. While the method was neither efficient nor predictable, it had the advantage of not involving any viruses. This advantage could be useful not only in plants, but in human applications such as gene therapy and genetic vaccines.

Agracetus had some new options, although they would be expensive to exercise.

According to the deal, when five years were up, Grace and Cetus would split subsequent expenses. But as that date approached it was clear that Cetus was having serious financial difficulty and could not afford the cash drain of supporting its Madison subsidiary. It was also now clear that PCR was going to be of high value and Cetus would seek to monetize that asset. But Grace's partial ownership of PCR for agriculture might encumber that value from Cetus' viewpoint. Thus, a new deal was engineered: Grace would acquire Cetus' share of Agracetus in exchange for Grace's rights to PCR and a small amount of cash.

In view of changing circumstances, the strategic alliance no longer made sense—Grace now had Accell, the plant program, and the plant patents, and Cetus had PCR and the ability to move on. Cetus was soon acquired by Chiron, which sold the PCR patent to Hoffman–La Roche for $300 million.

But Grace also had a financial crisis on its hands: A major shareholder (Herr Flick) decided to sell his 26 percent ownership of the company. To avoid a potential takeover, CEO J. Peter Grace used his line of credit to buy those shares. Cash had to be raised quickly, and it was decided to monetize the commodity agricultural chemicals business. The eventual buyers were financial investors who had no interest in Agracetus. What were we to do with Agracetus?

Solution to Case 15, Part Five

So, to Grace, Agracetus was no longer much of a strategic asset. Some securities analysts began to question top management as to why Grace was continuing to support it. Internally we realized that the negative cash flow of more than $5 million per year for the Agracetus program could be a sizable negative for analysts attempting to value Grace based on its cash flow. However, I remember one analyst adding an arbitrary 75 cents per share to his valuation of Grace for its Agracetus holding. In general, top management was divided as to whether to continue to invest based on continuing technological promise and a sunk R&D investment of over $30 million, or to cut the cord because of the absence of short-term commercial opportunities.

At the same time, the marketplace was changing. While Grace had once held aspirations of challenging Monsanto and DuPont in the life sciences marketplace, it was apparent Agracetus was now far behind these giants in overall competitive capabilities. Its patents, though, particularly in cotton and soybeans, could still give it a niche position. We used a number of techniques, including a pro forma DCF valuation of a genetically engineered cotton business, to attempt to value the agricultural piece of Agracetus. The values were in the $40 million to $70 million range. Options methods were not used.

Subsequently, the plant assets were put up for sale. Monsanto was very interested both in the technical capabilities of the research group and in acquiring the critical cotton patents. But another giant, Hoechst-Celanese, was also interested because of the intriguing possibilities of genetically engineering new forms of cotton fiber—and fibers were an important business for that company. Both Monsanto and Hoechst held strategic options well beyond what Grace could effect by itself. The agricultural assets were sold to Monsanto for about $150 million in 1996.

Grace was still left with Accell and the options in medicine (gene therapy and genetic vaccines), veterinary medicine, and improved livestock. Among the genetic vaccine programs were one for HIV, which was under evaluation in chimpanzees, and other potentials for hepatitis B, influenza, malaria, measles, dengue, and rheumatoid arthritis. This research, also no longer strategic to Grace, was continued for a time under the name Auragen Inc. In 1996, it was combined with a stronger partner—privately held Oxford BioSciences Ltd. (U.K.)—to form a new joint venture, Geniva, Inc.

As a result of these transactions, Grace recovered substantially more than its initial investment from the Monsanto sale alone—and was left with a stake in Geniva of indeterminate, but potentially very high, value.

THE IMPLANTABLE ARTIFICIAL PANCREAS (CASE 7)—OUTCOME

A fictionalized version of the artificial pancreas project was presented in Chapter 4 as Case 7. The fundamental problem was technical, namely that there were many experimental failures in preclinical trials owing to blood clots forming in the device. However, some animals thrived on the device for extended periods of time. At least eight generations of devices were designed to solve this problem, but none did so completely. It took considerable time and money to evaluate each improvement, which slowed the project considerably. At several points, a limited human trial was considered on the basis that the human system clots less aggressively than the animal model, but the risk was always daunting and the required paperwork was not submitted. The project was eventually terminated.

The program nonetheless salvaged considerable value. A small parallel program by the same research group pioneered an artificial liver (a membrane-based extracorporeal device containing porcine liver cells that maintains patients awaiting a liver transplant). It proved very successful in human trials, occasionally allowing a damaged liver to recover spontaneously. Many lives have been saved. But this worthy achievement is not in the home run category in economic terms.

SUMMARY OF FIVE CASE HISTORIES

The five Grace case histories represent some of the most radical big projects in the R&D portfolio of a reasonably conservative company. All five engaged the calculated risk of partnering with other firms. Close to 200 other projects were in the portfolio over the same period, and many succeeded (only a minority involved partnering). Four of the risky five were failures. Two failed because of technical (unique) risk, one failed due to a commercial issue (unique risk), and one failed owing to market risk.

More than $30 million was spent on the implantable artificial pancreas (not unusual for a health care project) and a similar amount on Agracetus. There were no home runs, but with a 10 percent overall success rate for risky new concepts, hitting a single (liver assist) and a double (Agracetus) was more than respectable. In fact, Agracetus alone recouped its costs *plus the costs of all the others*. Grace shareholders were not badly served, and they might have been far luckier.

In broader terms, the ideas and people involved in these efforts continue to create value, albeit in spin-off projects (such as the liver assist device) or as part of promising new organizations (such as Hematech). Some of the failures will eventually be viewed as efforts that were ahead of their time (cattle cloning and improved SCR).

CONCENTRATION VERSUS DIVERSIFICATION IN R&D PORTFOLIOS

Several projects can often be created off a single discovery, patent, or lead program. The virtue of so doing is focus, scale, and shared expertise, which translate financially into lower cost, higher efficiency, higher probability of success, and higher return on R&D investment. The apex of this strategy is the "platform" concept where a single technical platform feeds multiple product opportunities. The primary drawback is that focus and synergy run counter to risk mitigation via diversification (unique risk), and this exposes the firm to greater market risk. A single adverse development can significantly impact portfolio value. A secondary drawback is human nature: Once an organization is convinced its platform ensures its future, its ability to perceive opportunities and threats outside a narrow frame of reference can be significantly impaired.

PLATFORMS

The platform concept was initially popularized with the introduction of the K-car by Chrysler in 1981: a common drive train for the Plymouth Reliant, Dodge Aries, Chrysler LeBaron, Chrysler New Yorker, and (partially) the Dodge Daytona.[17] Chrysler continued to advance this concept with the introduction of platform teams in its technology centers. Black & Decker had singular success with the platform concept in hand tools, learning to make a large variety of electric motors on a single manufacturing line.[18] It did so by fixing the diameters of motors, while varying the length. IBM recently championed platforms,[19] initially in an attempt to reduce the complexity of its parts inventory, but also claims very large savings in new product development costs. Fundamental organizational transformation was required, and IBM concluded that the chief technical officer must lead it. An important economic finding was that in a platform environment, a single hurdle rate test for the introduction of a new product is no longer appropriate.

All of the preceding examples involve *assembled* products.

Equally evidently, software makes extensive use of platforms. The common menu features and object compatibility in the Microsoft Office suite is such an example. Computer game makers develop common "game engines" that drive a series of new games, each with different plots and characters, but all sharing a common user interface.

The general belief is that process industries, such as chemicals, metals, and paper, lag the assembly industries in appreciating the value of a process platform. My experience is otherwise; the problem may be that the term *platform* is not commonly employed there. For example, there are at least three fundamentally different ways to make polyethylene: in gas phase reactors, solution reactors, and slurry reactors. In addition, there are obsolete technologies such as autoclaves. Each of these is a platform, and often the best technology resides with a different industry leader. Each platform has strengths and weaknesses. An individual company may operate three or more different platforms to round off its product line so it can compete in more markets. In any case, the introduction of a new platform is a relatively rare event in the industry. What is not rare is a continuing stream of new products being built off the existing platforms.

It should be recognized that there are risks in developing new platforms that put many eggs in a single basket. Two conspicuous platform flops come to mind. The first was IBM's failed attempt to develop the OS2 operating system, which older techies will remember as the intended successor to DOS. This failure broke IBM's dominance of the PC, and created the window of opportunity for Microsoft Windows. The second was Motorola's noble attempt to revolutionize worldwide cellular telecommunications with its satellite-based Iridium system, which was too costly for the marketplace and collapsed in a sea of red ink.

Platform Obsolescence and Renewal

Platform economics involve a large up-front investment (essentially a fixed cost), but offer very low cost introductions of derivative products. A competitive platform is a very valuable asset, making it imperative to know how and when to abandon it or renew it. There is a temptation to ride the platform, but software platforms have a life cycle of only three or four years, while in industrial or medical equipment the cycle seems to be 10 years.[20] Major chemical processes may last 15 to 25 years. Continuous renewal of the existing platform must be an important part of the R&D portfolio, as is the search for the conceptual breakthrough that signals it is time to initiate work on the next new platform.

DISCUSSION: FINANCIAL VERSUS OTHER VIEWS OF R&D PORTFOLIOS

What is the best way to manage an R&D portfolio? In a provocative article on this subject Cooper, Edgett, and Kleinschmidt[21] discuss five methods of portfolio analysis: (1) financial analysis, (2) strategic analysis, (3) bubble diagrams (portfolio maps), (4) scoring models, and (5) checklists. Financial analysis involves profitability metrics such as NPV, return on investment (ROI), or payback period. Strategic analysis involves allocating resources into categories (or "buckets") and then rating or ranking projects within each category.[22] Typical categories include markets, product lines, strategic thrusts, or project type (exploratory research, product development, process research, and so on).

The most commonly used method is financial analysis, followed by strategic analysis. But interestingly, the authors conclude that practitioners of strategic portfolio management are much more satisfied than those using financial methods.[23] Why might this be? (The other three techniques are less widely used, but will be briefly discussed at the end of this section.)

Financial Models

Those who have purchased and read this book share with the author an interest in financial models. It is timely to look at the heart of the criticism of such models.

Here are two views of the subject:

1. The NPV method is fine in theory . . . but it ignores probabilities and risk; it assumes that financial projections are accurate (they usually are not!); it assumes that only financial goals are important (e.g., that strategic considerations are irrelevant); and it fails to deal with constrained resources—the desire to maximize the value for a limited resource commitment, (getting the most bang for the limited buck). A final objection is more subtle: the fact that NPV assumes an all-or-nothing investment decision, whereas in new product projects, the decision process is an incremental one—more like buying a series of options on a project.[24]
2. Unreliable financial estimates are a significant cause of poor resource allocation decisions for projects in the concept and prototype stages.[25]

Let us briefly look at the merits of these arguments, of which there are basically only four:

1. Financial methods do not take into account probabilities and risk. This is true if NPV alone is used, but in fact financial methods can be used to illuminate risk.
2. Early-stage financial estimates are unreliable. This is true, but they are better than nothing! Pondering the uncertainties is a valuable exercise in itself. Furthermore, the uncertainty can be quantified by sensitivity analysis or Monte Carlo. Ignoring project economics is akin to flying by the seat of one's pants and not checking the instrument panel.
3. NPV fails to deal with constrained resources. This is absolutely true, and was covered in an earlier section. But the constraints are so obvious that it is not an argument against financial methods. The decision makers' issue is to maximize value within the constraints.
4. NPV ignores option values. In fact, this book advocates the use of options analysis in R&D strategy. Intuition is not particularly good for estimating the value of options; financial tools are better. For that we need NPV as a first step.

In brief, it is easily possible to use financial models stupidly. The same holds for any other system. But the argument should not be directed against financial modeling, but against stupidity. The key to success is to develop models that are not time-consuming to build and that do instantly reflect how a project looks under a variety of assumptions. The debate can thereafter be focused on the fertile territory of assumptions and uncertainties, rather than on the model itself.

Strategic Models

The principal arguments for strategic models are:

- Strategic approaches align projects with the business's strategic direction.
- Spending reflects the business's strategic priorities.
- The method is user-friendly.
- Projects tend to be done on time—no gridlock.[26]

All of these arguments are valid, but they risk abdication of informed analysis to a view that the business unit manager knows best. There are some brilliant general managers. But as often, the business unit manager may have little knowledge of the development process, and the pressures and incentives may be short-term.

A strategic plan may be no more than a collection of real options;[27] therefore it is imperative that the decision makers understand what options they actually have available. In most companies, the view prevails that the decision that will be made is the one that creates the most value, and that determination should be made by a group of experts. Financial methods are well suited to this situation. Mine is not an argument that R&D can ignore the business's strategy. That approach is doomed to failure. It is an argument that R&D can and should influence business strategy.

Bubble Diagrams

Since it was popularized by the Boston Consulting Group (BCG) in the 1970s, the bubble diagram has been beloved of professional consulting firms. The BCG model projects business units into four quadrants along two axes: market attractiveness and business position. The term *bubble* refers to the practice of drawing circles representing the size of the opportunity on the chart. The BCG quadrants were labeled "star, cash cow, dog, and wildcat." It was an important insight. But other axes can be chosen. Arthur D. Little (ADL)[28] looked at competitive position versus technological uncertainty. Its division of technologies into the categories "base, key, pacing, and embryonic" was a very useful advance, as was the characterization of business position as "weak, tenable, favorable, strong, or dominant."

(These scales were used to good effect for technology assessment at W. R. Grace, but we went beyond this level of analysis.) The Decision Resources Group[29] employs a bubble diagram to rate probability of technical success versus potential commercial value, and enlists another menagerie, "white elephants, oysters, pearls, and bread and butter."

The Product Development Institute[30] prefers, quite logically, risk/reward axes. They rely not only on bubble diagrams, but on scoring models. They are skeptical of NPV because it is viewed as not taking into account probabilities and risk as noted earlier, such skepticism is overdone; this book makes clear that a risk-adjusted NPV can be developed that takes into account unique risk, market risk, the costs of R&D, and the time value of money. As we shall argue in the next section, scoring models have serious pitfalls, and do not rest on financial bedrock.

Another interesting variant[31] is a plot of probability of success (as Y) versus NPV (as X), where the bubbles represent the *uncertainty* in the estimate. This is essentially financial in approach, but it risks a bias against early-stage projects, where the probability of success is still low.

Bubble diagrams have enormous utility and versatility in summarizing a portfolio and spotting strategic problems or analytic inconsistencies. They are more a visualization tool than an analytical method, and their value will be as good as, and no better than, the data on which they are based.

Scoring Models

A method for using a scoring model was published by Arthur D. Little[32] in the early 1990s. Scores were assigned to projects on a 1 to 5 scale, using as criteria inventive merit (including platform merit), durability of advantage, reward, probability of technical success, probability of commercial success, R&D costs, time to completion, and capital and/or marketing. The criteria were then weighted to come up with a composite score for each project. A number of bubble diagrams were produced to put the project into strategic perspective.

As for direct financial analysis, ADL's view was that, "although some companies try to impose net present value (NPV) or discounted cash flow (DCF) calculations, the range of uncertainty for research reaching out more than a year or two is so substantial that the rigor implied by NPV or DCF considerations becomes not only meaningless but possibly harmful." I have addressed these concerns. There is a major concern, too, about scoring models. Their weakness is the absence of supporting data showing that they offer better results. This is an experiment without a control. In addition, experience teaches that there is nothing linear about R&D—a single nonobvious flaw can sink a project that is outstanding in every other respect. A weighted scoring model will inevitably overlook this circumstance.

A more sophisticated scoring model has been offered by the Product Development Institute,[33] but similar considerations apply.

The methods used in this book have some overlap with the aforementioned criteria. Reward, probability of success,[34] R&D costs, and time to completion are explicit in our financial model. The more qualitative criteria, such as inventive merit and durability of advantage, would be built into the revenue model. In particular, my own experience has been (regrettably) that inventive merit has not been a guarantor of project success.

I agree that the uncertainty in an NPV model is large, and it is important to make that point clear at the outset. Uncertainty can be readily quantified, though, using either Monte Carlo or "10/50/90" (Decision and Risk Analysis) methodology.[35] Beyond that reasonable concern, the reader will surely discover that looking at how the sensitive parameters interact with project attractiveness is invaluable, and the business information incorporated in a quantitative model is an excellent tool in discussions with business unit and corporate decision makers.

Checklists and Questionnaires

As a former pilot, I am rather fond of the discipline imposed by checklists. In the enthusiasm of embarking on a voyage, an easily overlooked item can lead to a fatal crash. The checklist is extremely useful in ensuring this does not happen. Less dramatically, it can raise important issues that had hitherto been ignored. Robert Cooper has published useful checklists and questionnaires for new product development,[36] and has noted that their principal weakness is the arbitrariness of the questions (mitigated by the fact that the questions are developed by experts). I have found checklists to be very useful in technology transfer processes such as scaling up raw chemical entities in the pharmaceutical business, where the originating party may not fully recognize the problems of the receiving group. All this being said, checklists and questionnaires are only tools; decision making will require methods that can provide an integrated assessment of risk and reward.

CHAPTER 10

Optimum Portfolios and the Efficient Frontier

This chapter explores the intriguing question of whether a diversified portfolio can be worth more than the sum of its parts. We have seen that diversification reduces risk and, therefore, makes sense for investors. But does it also make sense for the firm? Is a diversified firm more attractive to investors than an undiversified one? If it is, we have an *extremely* disturbing result. If diversification is an appropriate corporate objective, each project has to be analyzed as a potential addition to the firm's portfolio of assets. The value of the diversified package would be greater than the sum of the parts. So present values would no longer add.[1]

OPTIMUM R&D PORTFOLIO

There are four important considerations in developing an optimum R&D portfolio.

1. *Structural balance.* This important constraint was discussed in the prior chapter. Positive structural synergies add to R&D efficiency.
2. *Diversification of market risk.* Markowitz portfolio theory teaches that an optimum portfolio of stocks can be developed that gives a desired return at minimum risk, or a maximum return for a stipulated level of risk. This algorithm can be applied to an R&D portfolio containing projects that address different markets. For securities, it can be argued that no premium will be paid for market diversification because the investor can do it himself. This is not true for R&D portfolios, which contain utterly illiquid properties.
3. *Diversification of unique risk.* Unique risk is in principle diversifiable through the law of large numbers. The larger the number of technically

independent projects in the portfolio, the more predictable will be the number of technical successes.

4. *Economies of scale.* R&D is scale sensitive, with important implications for R&D productivity.

Each of the last three subjects will be covered in the remainder of this chapter.

MARKET RISK

The financial theory of efficient portfolios is a theory about market risk, which is in principle undiversifiable. Investors in liquid securities can diversify just about everything except the stock market itself. Companies cannot. It is held that investors will not knowingly pay a premium for diversification, since they can diversify their portfolios on the stock market. Indeed, there has been a trend to apply a "holding company discount" to firms that attempt to diversify. The central idea is that senior executives of holding companies are insufficiently focused on understanding the component businesses, and thus are at a competitive disadvantage. The 1960s, which watched the collapse of Litton Industries and the struggles of ITT, led credence to the argument that conglomeration was a poor business model. Nonetheless, I question this hypothesis because Wall Street is notorious for being wedded to predictability of earnings, and has richly rewarded successful conglomerates such as General Electric, although that firm understandably does not associate itself with the label. Since diversification reduces volatility, and volatility, according to the prevailing capital asset pricing model, increases cost of capital, a successfully diversified company should enjoy a higher stock price. In any case, the investor does not have the option of diversifying a project portfolio, so it can be reasoned that he may pay a premium for one that is artfully crafted.

My own experience at W. R. Grace may bias my thinking. J. Peter Grace saved his company by diversifying a shipping line with a focus on Latin America into agricultural and specialty chemicals, and later energy. The company thrived until the mid-1980s and in one year, 1982, when agricultural chemical and energy earnings soared, had net income that exceeded either Dow or DuPont. However, the cash flow was unwisely (in hindsight) invested into further diversification in restaurant and retail businesses, and a wiser diversification into health care. The holding company stigma was applied. But when CEO Al Costello restructured the business in 1996, selling off some prime assets, the stock more than doubled. The discount was premature.

What is true from an operating business perspective is that an operating business cannot escape the business it is in, at least not for some time. The events of 1993 demonstrated that a pharmaceutical company is subject to the political climate in Washington, D.C. When Pfizer's stock dropped, Merck's was likely to follow, absent specific unique favorable events. In fact, the value of every R&D project in drug company portfolios was negatively affected. Few drug companies could escape the carnage. The same will hold true in other business sectors. If energy prices fall, the value of sophisticated new energy technologies will fall with them. Petroleum companies are at present more or less bound to the petroleum business.

So, diversification is a limited option at the business unit level, but it is still an important option that must be under constant review. If diversification is to be successfully achieved, it must be through the R&D portfolio and strategic, digestible acquisitions. In 20 years, an astute company can achieve a major transformation. Lockheed and Allied Chemical did this very effectively, changing even their corporate names. And in 20 years a company in an unattractive sector without diversification options can see itself trapped in a vortex of continuing value destruction. This list is quite long.

Case 16: The New Ventures Manager

Dr. Morgan Walters has been given a new and exciting assignment. She has established a stellar record in R&D at General Enterprises, and the new CEO has expressed a desire for more radical innovation in the research department. He has observed a trend for developmental projects to cannibalize resources earmarked for exploratory work, because the research managers are very anxious to bring their established projects to commercial fruition. Their commitment to succeed is laudable, but in his view will not significantly differentiate the firm from its competitors. A new platform for growth is needed. He proposes that a CEO's special fund be established under Morgan's leadership.

Morgan knows that many companies enjoying strong cash flow have attempted to invest it in new ventures, and most have not succeeded. Exxon Enterprises was a classic case of this type. She knows taking this assignment is a career risk. But she is tempted because she knows there are two very promising project ideas in the laboratory that have barely been able to get off the ground for lack of resources. Each could be a home run, and one may be a bases-loaded home run. She judges both projects to have a similar degree of technical risk. But the market risk is dissimilar—one is involved with food packaging, a market with limited volatility, while the other is tied to the highly cyclic defense market. Almost inevitably, the bases-loaded home run is in the riskier market. With a clean slate and an adequate budget, should she support the home run (project A) or the bases-loaded home run (project B), or both? If both, should she divide her resources equally?

Solution to Case 16

Using the methods described in Chapter 5, Morgan determines that project A offers a 30 percent return on investment, while project B offers a fantastic 40 percent. How can she measure the risk? A search of a stock market database indicates that food-packaging companies have had an average standard deviation of 18.6 percent in stock price over the past decade, slightly less than the 21.2 percent characteristic of the market as a whole. Comparable companies in the defense business have had a risk level of 28 percent. Morgan has been studying at night for an MBA, and she decides this would be a fine elementary case for portfolio analysis.

The new ventures budget allows her to employ 20 scientists. Her first step is to construct a table of possible returns with various combinations of investment in each project, at 5 percent increments (see the first two columns of Figure 10.1). The results in column 3 vary linearly from 30 percent (all project A) to 40 percent (the maximum possible return, all project B).

She knows from business school that the risks will not vary linearly, unless the two investments are perfectly correlated and the market values move in lockstep with each other. Indeed, there is a possibility of having less risk with two investments than with an investment in the less risky project alone. How much less will depend on the correlation between the two markets.

Correlation is a dimensionless parameter that varies from plus 1 to minus 1. The next section will demonstrate how to calculate it from a time series of data. For now, note that plus 1 means perfect correlation (lockstep), zero means complete independence, and minus 1 represents complete counterdependence. (The fortunes of a stockholder and a short seller in the same stock will be almost perfectly counterdependent.) Stocks tend for the most part to be mildly positively correlated with coefficients of about 0.2, with their fortunes rising and falling with the general market, but with some sectors more in favor and others less in favor at any point in time.

The formula[2] for calculating the standard deviation for two securities with correlation coefficient C_{AB} is:

$$S = \text{sqrt}\{w_A^2 \times S_A^2 + w_B^2 \times S_B^2 + 2C_{AB}w_Aw_BS_AS_B\}$$

Morgan begins this exercise by calculating her minimum risk portfolio, assuming for the moment $C_{AB} = 0.2$ (see column 7 of Figure 10.1). That risk is 16.8 percent, and occurs for a portfolio of about 75 percent A and 25 percent of B. The whole risk/return plot is shown as Figure

FIGURE 10.1 Risk and Return for a Two-Project Portfolio

r(A)	30.0%	r(B)	40.0%						
SD(A)	18.6%	SD(B)	28.0%						

			Covariance			Covariance		
			0.2	0.5	−0.2	0.2	0.5	−0.2
				Portfolio			Portfolio	
w(A)	w(B)	r(E)1		Variance			Standard Deviation	
0%	100%	40.0%	0.0784	0.0784	0.0784	28.0%	28.0%	28.0%
5%	95%	39.5%	0.0718	0.0733	0.0699	26.8%	27.1%	26.4%
10%	90%	39.0%	0.0657	0.0685	0.0620	25.6%	26.2%	24.9%
15%	85%	38.5%	0.0601	0.0641	0.0548	24.5%	25.3%	23.4%
20%	80%	38.0%	0.0549	0.0599	0.0482	23.4%	24.5%	22.0%
25%	75%	37.5%	0.0502	0.0560	0.0424	22.4%	23.7%	20.6%
30%	70%	37.0%	0.0459	0.0525	0.0372	21.4%	22.9%	19.3%
35%	65%	36.5%	0.0421	0.0492	0.0326	20.5%	22.2%	18.1%
40%	60%	36.0%	0.0388	0.0463	0.0288	19.7%	21.5%	17.0%
45%	55%	35.5%	0.0359	0.0436	0.0256	18.9%	20.9%	16.0%
50%	50%	35.0%	0.0335	0.0413	0.0230	18.3%	20.3%	15.2%
55%	45%	34.5%	0.0315	0.0392	0.0212	17.7%	19.8%	14.6%
60%	40%	34.0%	0.0300	0.0375	0.0200	17.3%	19.4%	14.1%
65%	35%	33.5%	0.0290	0.0361	0.0195	17.0%	19.0%	14.0%
70%	30%	33.0%	0.0284	0.0349	0.0196	16.8%	18.7%	14.0%
75%	25%	32.5%	0.0283	0.0341	0.0205	16.8%	18.5%	14.3%
80%	20%	32.0%	0.0286	0.0336	0.0219	16.9%	18.3%	14.8%
85%	15%	31.5%	0.0294	0.0334	0.0241	17.2%	18.3%	15.5%
90%	10%	31.0%	0.0307	0.0335	0.0269	17.5%	18.3%	16.4%
95%	5%	30.5%	0.0324	0.0339	0.0304	18.0%	18.4%	17.4%
100%	0%	30.0%	0.0346	0.0346	0.0346	18.6%	18.6%	18.6%

10.1a. This is considerably less risk than 18.6 percent for A alone, and it offers a higher return, 32.5 percent. This result illustrates the power of diversification.

Morgan considers another option as well. What return could she expect with a combination that has risk equivalent to project A (the less risky project), or 18.6 percent? A distribution of effort of 50 percent on each project gives a return of 35 percent but with a risk of only 18.3 percent. The benefits of distributing market risk are very considerable.

Figures 10.1 and 10.1b demonstrate that the gains would be less dramatic if the markets were more closely correlated. The risk level for $C_{AB} = 0.5$ never drops below 18.3 percent, providing a much smaller benefit from diversification.

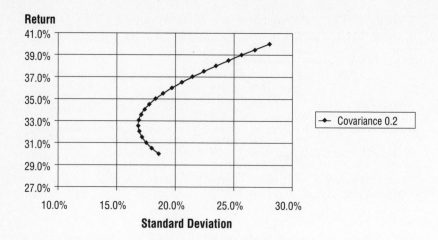

FIGURE 10.1a   Low Correlation

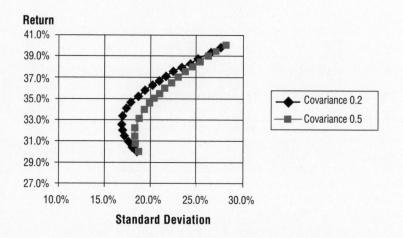

FIGURE 10.1b   Low versus Medium Correlation

Next consider what the possibilities might be if the two markets were anticorrelated—that is, war versus peace. Using $C_{AB} = -0.2$, the curve looks like Figure 10.1c.

In this case, the risk can be lowered to 14.0 percent for a mix of 65 percent A and 35 percent B. And a portfolio of 35 percent A and 65 percent B would have a risk of 18.1 percent (last column of Figure 10.1), still

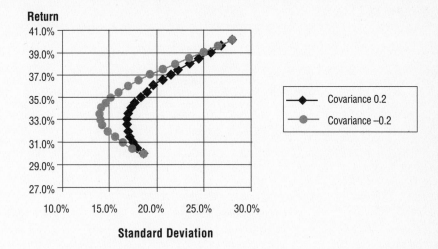

FIGURE 10.1c   Low Correlation versus Anticorrelation

below that of A alone, while yielding an outstanding 36.5 percent return. In general, very low (market) risk portfolios can be created when strongly anticorrelated securities are available.

Variance, Covariance, and Correlation

Having satisfied herself that correlation may be important to her future, Morgan's next step is to figure out how to calculate it. The process is simple, and the procedure is worked out in detail in Figure 10.2. This figure is also intended to be a template for the user to calculate the correlation between any two time series of interest. In the present case, instead of using a series of stock prices, Morgan chooses return on sales in two different businesses over a 10-year time frame.

Business X has been reasonably stable with returns varying from 6 percent to 12 percent. The mean is 8.70 percent ±1.79 percent. The standard deviation is calculated by taking the difference between each data point and the mean (X – MX), squaring it, and summing the squares. That sum divided by 10 is the variance. Below it is VARP, an Excel function whose argument is the array of returns on X. The result is identical. (I find it very useful to reproduce Excel functions, since they occasionally contain surprises.) The standard deviation is just the square root of the variance.

Business Y has much greater fluctuations and its mean return is 7.10 percent ±11.10 percent. In many years it is deep in the red. Superficially the curve looks very different from X.

FIGURE 10.2 Highly Correlated Businesses

Period	Return Business X	X – MX	(X – MX) ^ 2	Return Business Y	Y – MY	(Y – MY) ^ 2	(X – MX) × (Y – MY)
1	10.00%	1.30%	0.0169%	15.00%	7.90%	0.6241%	0.1027%
2	12.00%	3.30%	0.1089%	17.00%	9.90%	0.9801%	0.3267%
3	8.00%	–0.70%	0.0049%	4.00%	–3.10%	0.0961%	0.0217%
4	7.00%	–1.70%	0.0289%	–8.00%	–15.10%	2.2801%	0.2567%
5	9.00%	0.30%	0.0009%	15.00%	7.90%	0.6241%	0.0237%
6	7.00%	–1.70%	0.0289%	22.00%	14.90%	2.2201%	–0.2533%
7	8.00%	–0.70%	0.0049%	3.00%	–4.10%	0.1681%	0.0287%
8	6.00%	–2.70%	0.0729%	–14.00%	–21.10%	4.4521%	0.5697%
9	9.00%	0.30%	0.0009%	2.00%	–5.10%	0.2601%	–0.0153%
10	11.00%	2.30%	0.0529%	15.00%	7.90%	0.6241%	0.1817%

	Business X			Business Y			
Mean	8.70%			7.10%		Sum/10	0.1243%
Variance	0.000321			0.012329		COVAR	0.001243
Standard						Correlation	0.6248
deviation	0.01792	1.79%	0.11104	11.10%			

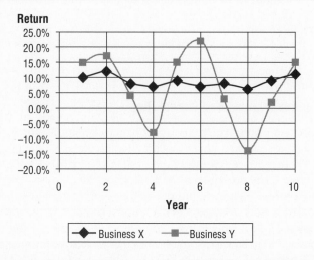

Next Morgan calculates the covariance and the correlation. The first step is to multiply together the individual deviations from the mean of X and Y for each of the 10 periods. This calculation is shown in the last column. They are summed and divided by 10 (because the weight of each point is one-tenth). Alternatively and identically, the Excel function CO-VAR is used to calculate it from the 20 data points in the X and Y arrays. Variances and covariances have very little physical meaning; standard deviations and correlation coefficients are much more intuitive. The correlation coefficient C_{XY} is readily calculated from the COVAR(X,Y) and the standard deviations of X and Y, the relationship being:

$$C_{XY} = COVAR(X,Y)/S_X \times S_Y$$

Surprisingly, these two business are very highly correlated, $C_{XY} = 0.625$. A closer examination of the curves shows they move up and down nearly in lockstep, although the swings have considerably different amplitudes.

Remember the objective is to obtain a correlation coefficient between economic conditions in two markets. In principle, any data that fairly reflect market conditions over a period of time can be used. Stock prices, stocks indexes, commodity prices, cash margins, profits, return on capital, or return on sales (Morgan's choice) are possible proxies.

Obviously, each choice will give a somewhat different answer. The answer will also be affected by the time period selected. There can be no absolute answer. The issues for the analyst are which proxy is most relevant to the calculation, and which data are most readily available.

Negative Covariance

Figure 10.3 shows the guns or butter case.

Here business X represents the firm's packaging business, while Y again represents the wildly cyclic defense business. The mean return on sales for packaging is 6.90 percent ±2.26 percent. Packaging business returns have a mildly positive response to peacetime conditions, while defense is the opposite. The correlation coefficient is about –0.2, which is very close to one of the parameters tested in Morgan's original exercise. From the point of view of her personal risk and the risk to the company, this is a happy circumstance.

Based on the analysis laid out in Figure 10.1, she elects to go with a 50–50 distribution of resources with a risk factor of 15.2 percent, not quite the minimum of 14.0 percent, but affording a 35 percent return and significant resources to each project. *Along the way, she has demonstrated why a diversified R&D portfolio is worth more than the sum of its parts. It is because market risk is reduced, implicitly lowering the cost of R&D investment.*

Case 17: The Efficient Frontier

Five years have gone by. Morgan's new ventures department has made a fine name for itself, and both of her key projects have now been transferred to operating groups, while a number of new initiatives are under way. Her skills as a planner are widely recognized in the company, and she is promoted to the job of director of R&D planning and widely considered as a future candidate

FIGURE 10.3   Anticorrelated Businesses

Period	Return Business X	X – MX	(X – MX) ^2	Return Business Y	Y – MY	(Y – MY) ^2	(X – MX) × (Y – MY)
1	5.00%	–1.90%	0.0361%	15.00%	7.90%	0.6241%	0.1501%
2	8.00%	1.10%	0.0121%	17.00%	9.90%	0.9801%	0.1089%
3	10.00%	3.10%	0.0961%	4.00%	–3.10%	0.0961%	–0.0961%
4	9.00%	2.10%	0.0441%	–8.00%	–15.10%	2.2801%	–0.3171%
5	5.00%	–1.90%	0.0361%	15.00%	7.90%	0.6241%	–0.1501%
6	4.00%	–2.90%	0.0841%	22.00%	14.90%	2.2201%	–0.4321%
7	4.00%	–2.90%	0.0841%	3.00%	–4.10%	0.1681%	0.1189%
8	6.00%	–0.90%	0.0081%	–14.00%	–21.10%	4.4521%	0.1899%
9	8.00%	1.10%	0.0121%	2.00%	–5.10%	0.2601%	–0.0561%
10	10.00%	3.10%	0.0961%	15.00%	7.90%	0.6241%	0.2449%

	Business X		*Business Y*				
Mean	6.90%		7.10%			Sum/10	–0.0539%
Variance	0.000509		0.012329			COVAR	–0.000539
Standard deviation	0.02256	2.26%	0.11104	11.10%		Correlation	–0.2152

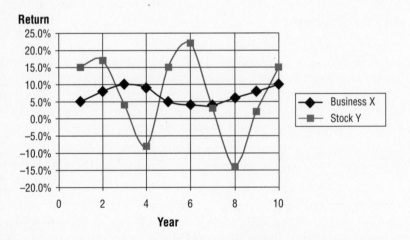

to become chief technical officer (CTO). But first, she has a difficult new task. The CEO is concerned that the allocation of R&D resources among the operating groups is not optimal. In the current environment, those business groups who request R&D resources and are willing to fund their requests get served, but business results have not always been forthcoming. Often, the dialogue has revolved about R&D spending as a percentage of sales, rather than about value creation, and there remains a telltale preponderance of effort on incremental projects. Is a better method available?

Solution to Case 17

First, Morgan groups the R&D portfolio into five business thrusts. Defense, we have seen, is highly cyclical. The construction business is also cyclic, but not as much as defense, and typically lags the economy as a whole. The packaging and biomedical businesses have relatively stable margins. Organic chemicals is intermediate—somewhat more volatile than packaging and bio- medical but far less so than defense and construction (see Figure 10.4).

She needs one other type of data: the expected returns from each group of R&D projects. These can be obtained from the individual projects in the portfolio using the methods of Chapter 5 for calculating R&D returns. As- sume the returns (with standard deviations in parentheses) are packaging, 20.0 percent (1.6 percent); biomedical, 21.5 percent (1.9 percent); organic chemicals, 23.0 percent (2.8 percent); construction, 26.0 percent (7.2 per- cent); and defense, 35.0 percent (10.8 percent). The standard deviations represent the market risk in these returns; they are identical to those calcu- lated from the business returns in Figure 10.5. Note also that the riskier projects are associated with the higher-return projects. This condition is normal, but it is not necessarily the case.

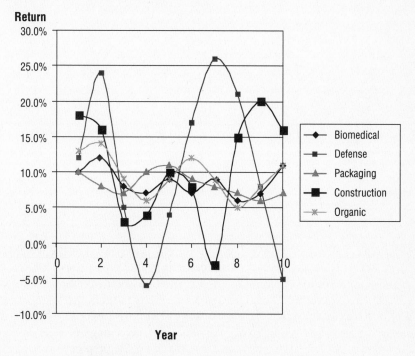

FIGURE 10.4 Historic Returns for Five Businesses

FIGURE 10.5   Analysis of Historic Performance of Five Businesses

Historical Data (Returns) on Businesses

Period	Biomedical	Defense	Packaging	Construction	Organic
1	10.00%	12.00%	10.00%	18.00%	13.00%
2	12.00%	24.00%	8.00%	16.00%	14.00%
3	8.00%	5.00%	7.00%	3.00%	9.00%
4	7.00%	−6.00%	10.00%	4.00%	6.00%
5	9.00%	4.00%	11.00%	10.00%	9.00%
6	7.00%	17.00%	9.00%	8.00%	12.00%
7	9.00%	26.00%	8.00%	−3.00%	9.00%
8	6.00%	21.00%	7.00%	15.00%	5.00%
9	7.00%	8.00%	6.00%	20.00%	8.00%
10	11.00%	−5.00%	7.00%	16.00%	11.00%

Variance/Covariance Matrix

	Biomedical	Defense	Packaging	Construction	Organic
Biomedical	0.034%	0.010%	0.003%	0.029%	0.039%
Defense	0.010%	1.168%	−0.028%	−0.050%	0.071%
Packaging	0.003%	−0.028%	0.024%	−0.024%	0.007%
Construction	0.029%	−0.050%	−0.024%	0.514%	0.052%
Organic	0.039%	0.071%	0.007%	0.052%	0.076%
Variance	0.000344	0.011684	0.000241	0.005141	0.000764
Standard Deviation	1.855%	10.809%	1.552%	7.170%	2.764%
Mean	8.60%	10.60%	8.30%	10.70%	9.60%

Correlation Matrix

	Biomedical	Defense	Packaging	Construction	Organic
Biomedical	1.000	0.052	0.111	0.217	0.166
Defense	0.052	1.000	−0.166	−0.065	0.239
Packaging	0.111	−0.166	1.000	−0.217	0.168
Construction	0.217	0.166	−0.217	1.000	0.261
Organic	0.166	0.239	0.168	0.261	1.000

Now she is ready to do the heavy lifting: calculating the "efficient portfolio" that minimizes market risk. Market risk is measured by the weighted sum of the variances of each portfolio component. The analysis requires an exercise in quadratic programming,[3] a variant of linear programming. Fortunately, Excel contains an add-in called the Solver that performs this task, and it is not hard to use.[4] The steps are:

1. Be sure the Solver is installed.
2. Specify the parameters sought, in this case the percent of each component of the portfolio.

3. Specify the parameter to be minimized, in this case the weighted sum of the variances.
4. Specify two additional constraints: that the portfolio percentages are positive numbers and that they add up to 1.
5. Most importantly, specify the desired rate of return.

By running the program over the range of possible returns, one can calculate the efficient portfolio for each individual point, and the corresponding risk for that point!

Figure 10.6 shows the calculation for one sample point on the efficient frontier representing a desired return of 25 percent. The key outputs are the portfolio percentages on the first line and the variance they imply (on the right), from which the standard deviation (2.79 percent) of that portfolio is calculated. The efficient frontier itself is shown as Figure 10.7.

This data, also summarized as Figures 10.8 and 10.9, has some very interesting features. The minimum standard deviation for the portfolio of 1.19 percent occurs at a return of 21.11 percent. As expected, the standard deviation is lower than for any single element (1.552 percent). See the box in Figure 10.8. The lowest-risk portfolio basically consists of the two most conservative elements, biomedical and packaging, a very limited amount of defense and construction, and zero organic chemicals.

As the portfolio is pressed for higher returns, defense and construction gradually increase, and organic chemicals enters the portfolio at 24 percent. At 28 percent it becomes the largest portfolio element, while biomedical and packaging disappear; they cannot offer the returns being sought. Organic chemicals disappears, too, at 31 percent. It is interesting that it has no role in either the most conservative or the most risky portfolios, but is very useful for a balanced strategy.

From 31 percent to 34 percent the portfolio is down to its two most profitable elements, construction and defense. Note that the portfolio standard deviation of 6.6 percent at 31 percent is less than that for either construction (7.2 percent) or defense (10.8 percent). Diversification is still doing its work. Finally, at 35 percent only defense remains and obviously the portfolio standard deviation is the same as its only component.

Morgan's issue is what to recommend to her boss. She elects the 25 percent return portfolio, which has a substantially improved return over very conservative portfolios, while retaining a position with very low market risk (2.8 percent). But her reasoning contains another element; this portfolio includes significant contributions for all five research programs, thus allowing several projects in each group. With more projects she also obtains more diversification of her unique risk! (See next section.)

FIGURE 10.6 Portfolio Optimization—Markowitz Method

	Biomedical	Defense	Packaging	Construction	Organic	Total		
Portfolio%	22.28%	20.83%	24.34%	18.84%	13.72%	100.00%		
Expected return	21.50%	35.00%	20.00%	26.00%	23.00%			
Variance	0.000344	0.011684	0.000241	0.005141	0.000764			
Standard deviation	1.855%	10.809%	1.552%	7.170%	2.764%			
Mean	8.600%	10.600%	8.300%	10.700%	9.600%			
Variance terms	0.005%	0.050%	-0.001%	0.018%	0.006%	Variance		0.0779%
						Standard deviation		2.79%
Return terms	4.789%	7.290%	4.869%	4.898%	3.155%	Return		25.00%

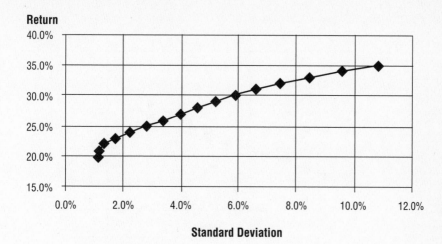

FIGURE 10.7   Portfolio Risk versus Return

FIGURE 10.8   Efficient Portfolios

Return Sought	Standard Deviation	Percent in Portfolio				
		Biomedical	Defense	Packaging	Construction	Organic
20.00%	1.19%	31.3%	2.6%	62.0%	4.2%	0.0%
21.00%	1.19%	31.3%	2.6%	62.0%	4.2%	0.0%
21.11%	1.19%	31.3%	2.6%	62.0%	4.2%	0.0%
22.00%	1.33%	32.1%	7.0%	53.2%	7.7%	0.0%
23.00%	1.71%	33.0%	12.0%	43.3%	11.8%	0.0%
24.00%	2.23%	29.7%	16.6%	33.7%	15.5%	4.6%
25.00%	2.79%	22.3%	20.8%	24.3%	18.8%	13.7%
26.00%	3.38%	14.9%	25.1%	15.0%	22.2%	22.8%
27.00%	3.98%	7.5%	29.3%	5.7%	25.6%	31.9%
28.00%	4.59%	0.0%	34.3%	0.0%	29.5%	36.2%
29.00%	5.24%	0.0%	41.3%	0.0%	34.7%	24.0%
30.00%	5.91%	0.0%	48.4%	0.0%	39.8%	11.8%
31.00%	6.61%	0.0%	55.6%	0.0%	44.4%	0.0%
32.00%	7.44%	0.0%	66.7%	0.0%	33.3%	0.0%
33.00%	8.45%	0.0%	77.8%	0.0%	22.2%	0.0%
34.00%	9.59%	0.0%	88.9%	0.0%	11.1%	0.0%
35.00%	10.81%	0.0%	100.0%	0.0%	0.0%	0.0%

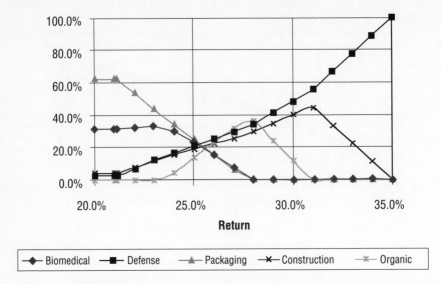

FIGURE 10.9　　Percent in Portfolio versus Desired Return

UNIQUE RISK

Unique risk is, in principle, diversifiable. Consider how to diversify unique risk in a situation where unique risk is very high. Assume drug companies all have similar productivity in drug discovery; that is, their hit rates in the discovery of new drugs are 9 ± 3 hits per 100,000 molecules synthesized, where "hit" means a drug sufficiently promising to enter clinical trials. Statistically, the standard deviations are known to vary as the inverse square root of the number of trials. Figure 10.10 shows this effect.

For a drug company synthesizing 100,000 molecules per year, the year-to-year variation in hits is 33.3 percent, quite a high level of risk. A small drug company, say one that synthesizes only 20,000 molecules per year, can expect only 1.8 hits per year, and it will have a standard deviation of ±1.34 or 74.5 percent. At this rate, it is bound to experience quite a few hitless years, which may be an intolerable level of risk for its owners. Certainly, investors should think twice before investing in a tiny company capable of synthesizing only 1,000 compounds a year (at this level of productivity). In contrast, a large drug company synthesizing 400,000 molecules per year will experience a standard deviation of only 16.7 percent, in line with the standard deviation of a typical S&P 500 stock. Its research output will be reasonably predictable.

In an industry where value is largely driven by drug discovery, diversification in part explains the forces driving industry mergers. If two companies, each synthesizing 100,000 molecules per year, merge their R&D

FIGURE 10.10 Diversifying Risk over Large Portfolios

Probability of Hit: 0.009%

Trials	Hits	Standard Deviation	Standard Deviation as % of Hits
11,110	1.0	1.00	100.0
20,000	1.8	1.34	74.5
50,000	4.5	2.12	47.1
100,000	9.0	3.00	33.3
200,000	18.0	4.24	23.6
400,000	36.0	6.00	16.7
1,000,000	90.0	9.49	10.5

portfolios, their standard deviations of 33.3 percent would drop to 23.6 percent—an enormous risk reduction. The economic power of large numbers also explains the rising popularity of combinatorial chemistry, where robots synthesize enormous numbers of new molecules (each in tiny quantities) and other robots screen them for desirable biological properties.

R&D-driven companies also face systematic risk. For example, a drug company may have a significant percentage of its R&D portfolio committed to blood pressure reducing drugs. If a competitor discovers, patents, and markets an outstanding drug in this field, it will have a negative effect on the entire portion of the portfolio related to drug pressure reduction. In other words, all blood pressure projects have a degree of correlation, and the entire risk cannot be diversified away. But this risk can be substantially diversified by a portfolio that addresses a variety of indications and is not overly concentrated in the cardiovascular area.

But other risks remain undiversifiable within the context of being a pharmaceutical company. The entire drug discovery portfolio may be subject to systematic risks relating to changes in health care reimbursement, regulatory trends at the FDA, changing demographics, global competition, and a host of factors large and small. These, too, are undiversifiable within the context of being a pharmaceutical company.

SCALE ECONOMIES

The concept of scale economies in research is widely acknowledged. It comes in two forms: relative economies and absolute ones.

If one accepts the notion that R&D as a percent of revenues is an important metric, and R&D productivity is more or less even across the industry (a point that is about to be examined), it follows that a company with more revenues can spend more on R&D than its smaller rivals. It will thus increase its technological competitiveness. If the number one firm's market share is overwhelming, so will be its long-term technology advantage. As an example, consider three firms each spending 2 percent of sales annually in R&D in a $5 billion market. Firm A with 80 percent share spends $80 million. Firms B and C with 10 percent each spend $10 million each. With such an overwhelming relative advantage, Firm A can reduce R&D spending, thus increasing its return on capital, with no apparent need to fear its rivals. Whether it will do so will likely depend on its view of the technology opportunities available.

The arguments for absolute advantage are equally powerful. First, consider the general theory of the experience curve:

Cost of value added declines approximately 20–30 percent each time accumulated experience is doubled. This is an observable phenomenon. Whatever the reason, it happens. Explanations are rationalizations. The whole history of increased productivity and industrialization is based on specialization of effort and investment in tools. So is the experience curve. It is a measure of the potential effect of specialization and investment.

Workers learn. If they learn to do a task better, they can do it in less time. This is equivalent to producing more in the same time. Characteristically, output can increase 10–15 percent each time total output is doubled. This is the well-known learning curve measure of man-hour productivity increase.

Based on the learning curve, labor costs only should decline 10–15 percent each time accumulated experience doubles. When scale of activity increases so that numbers of people are involved, then it becomes possible to specialize. If two people are doing the same thing, it becomes possible to break the task into two parts. One person does all of one half. The other person does all of the other half. Each will therefore do his respective task twice as often for a given total output.

The learning curve described above predicts that with twice the experience the labor time should be reduced 10–15 percent. Increase in scale permits such specialization. Consequently, each worker will approach a total experience at any point in time which would be twice as much as he could have achieved without specialization. Doing half as much but twice as often equals the same amount of effort but twice the experience with the task. Consequently, specialization permits 10–15 percent less time per unit or 10–15 percent more output in a given time.

If the scale doubles simultaneously with total experience, then these two effects should occur simultaneously. Costs decline 10–15 percent because of learning plus 10–15 percent because of specialization. The sum of 20–30 percent cost decline is alone an approximation of the total experience curve effect.[5]

This argument was developed for manufacturing industries, but there is no reason it cannot be applied to R&D. Aboody and Lev have developed strong financial evidence[6] that larger chemical companies (DuPont, Dow) enjoy a significantly higher level of R&D productivity than their smaller peers. The amount does not appear to be inconsistent with what one might expect based on experience curve theory. They invest in specialization. Specialization in R&D means that the corporate analytical laboratory will have more instruments, the library will have better resources, the engineering department a broader variety of specialized talents, and so on. Cumulative experience includes more technical reports in the archives, more issued patents, more contacts in the technical community, and above all a scientific staff with a knowledge of more case histories—knowing what has worked before and what has not.

All is not lost for smaller firms. They have a strong incentive to be more astute in investing their limited resources. They will seek strategies of mitigating risk by being fast followers, or of partnering with firms inside and outside the industry.[7] They may even be more receptive to innovative ideas. But the laws of large numbers seem to be working against them.

DISCUSSION

Several authors have used portfolio theory to illuminate R&D issues. Carter and Edwards[8] have constructed an efficient portfolio curve for the balance of research versus development in federal R&D programs, assuming they have different returns and only a mildly positive correlation. This may be valid for some sectors of government that do not see projects through to commercial fruition, and where research results are made available to the world via publication or licensing (and costs are possibly recouped by taxation or royalties). Their approach is quite different from that taken in this book, which assumes successful research progresses into development as part of an ordered industrial process. In my model, research that does not progress into development has a negative economic return.

A somewhat different algorithm than used here has been published by Graves, Ringuest, and Case[9] and applied to questionnaire-based data from several companies. One difference in methodology is that these authors do not distinguish unique from market risk, but commingle the two in an estimate of upside and downside cases.

Two of their observations are especially interesting, and I comment on them.

1. "To use our model, the R&D manager needs only to compute a risk-adjusted return for each R&D project."

This step is clearly enabled by the methodology and software described in this book.

2. "One problem that arises when we attempt to apply this technique to an R&D portfolio is that there are no historical market data from which to estimate the probability distribution of portfolio returns. To circumvent this obstacle, we used a simple Monte Carlo simulation to generate the appropriate probability distributions."

There is another way to circumvent this problem: to estimate market risk from proxy time series economic data (returns, margins, stock prices, and so on). Judgment must be exercised in choosing the right (most relevant) economic data.

Almost all of the templates provided with this book are amenable to Monte Carlo analysis,[10] giving an excellent estimate for the uncertainty of any given calculation. (I have used the method, but am excluding it from the scope of this book because it requires the purchase of proprietary software.) For example, very sensitive parameters that can be varied are probability of success, variable margin, and capital intensity. The Decision and Risk Analysis "10/50/90" approach of using experts to define the bounds and the bounds to define a normal distribution can also be very helpful. Similarly, the Monte Carlo method requires judgment to be exercised in choosing the parameters subject to uncertainty and in setting probability distributions for those parameters.

The key question boils down to whether Markowitz-type R&D portfolio analysis is worth the trouble. Candidly, I have mixed feelings. On the positive side, the calculations are not difficult, and provide useful insight and guidance. They can nudge the strategy in the right direction. Basing the analysis on historical data is sound. Most importantly, they prove diversification adds value. My principal concern is that the optimum distribution of portfolio elements is overly sensitive to the input assumptions, especially projected rates of return. Since these rates are uncertain and possibly controversial, there is a peril of drawing important conclusions on flimsy evidence. For the CTO, it is a useful input, but no panacea.

About the CD-ROM

INTRODUCTION

Purposes

The software has two basic purposes.

First, it allows the reader to trace the calculations used in creating the figures. The particular formulas underlying each cell can thus be viewed, and the sequence of the calculations traced, either manually or using the Excel auditing toolbar. The latter feature is extremely helpful in identifying the sources of data used in the calculations, or in tracing where this data will be subsequently used. The reader is especially encouraged to change a few key inputs to determine the sensitivity of the calculations, for example NPV as a function of cost of capital.

Second, the software is meant to be useful to start the reader off on his own calculations. Many of the figures are themselves useful for this purpose, but the FSDTRO.xls spreadsheet is meant to allow the analysis of complex R&D projects leading to a capital investment and a business model. It is extensively commented for ease of navigation. Smaller algorithms are the BLACKSCHOLES.xls option calculator, the WACC.xls calculator for cost of capital, and the GROWTH.xls calculator for growth rates, which calculates the annual growth rate between any two parameters or applies a growth rate to a single parameter over a specified time duration.

The software, based on Excel, is semiautomatic. That is, if the reader wants the same number of years or the same line items in a financial projection, or the same number of stages in a project, the numbers can be readily inserted in FSDTRO. If not, the reader must insert the appropriate new rows, columns, and input parameters, and take the necessary quality control measures (usually best checked by running examples with known answers).

Conventions, Features, and Hints

Generally, input parameters are highlighted in yellow, and outputs (key results) in green. Some critical intermediate numbers are identified in red or by comment. The comments can be activated by scanning the cursor over the appropriate cell if the cell has a small red triangle in the upper right corner. Occasionally a variable is named, particularly to facilitate relationships between different worksheets in the same workbook. Hence I tend to prefer replacing IO!B12, representing the cost of capital as a cell in the IO worksheet, by the more obvious term WACC.

The more complex spreadsheets such as FSDTRO are organized so that the key input parameters and the key outputs are available on the same screen, allowing instantaneous viewing of the effect of any change in the inputs.

Some Excel functions, especially NPV, IRR, NORMSDIST, CORREL, COVAR, and VARP, are used, and the add-in, the Solver, is used to tackle quadratic equations in Chapter 10. The Solver takes a little time to get used to, but I suggest just trying it with sample data. It will be rewarding. Otherwise, Billo[1] gives detailed instructions. Indeed, I find Excel to be a very sophisticated program with great features for power users, but the help menus and the documentation are hard to access and often very disappointing. Billo and other books about modeling[2] give many useful hints about its capabilities.

Finally, most of my spreadsheets are compatible with Crystal Ball Monte Carlo software from Decisioneering, Inc. If one wants to cumulate the uncertainty in different input parameters using normal distributions or the like, one needs only to purchase this software (free demos are available) and identify the parameters one seeks to vary (that is, revenues or costs) and the outputs (that is, NPV and IRR) in which one is interested. Beyond this suggestion, I have excluded Monte Carlo from the scope of this book.

Basically, this is a case study book, and I have included in the CD-ROM mostly software that supports the cases. But it is my hope that the reader will build his own models based on some of these software templates, as I have time and again when confronted with a new problem with its own special circumstances.

CD-ROM TABLE OF CONTENTS

Figure 2.4 Case 3 Project Values by Five Methods.xls
Figure 3.2 Incentive Stock Options.xls
Figure 4.1 Revenue Model for IAP Business.xls
Figure 4.2 Calculation of Cash Flows Based on IAP Business.xls
Figure 4.3 NPV and Decision Tree for IAP Business Plan.xls
Figure 5.1 Polyarothene Fixed Capital Investment versus Volume.xls
Figures 5.2, 5.3, and 5.4 Case 8 Polyarothene FSDTRO.xls
Figure 6.1 MiracleCure Capitalization Model.xls
Figures 6.2 and 6.3 IC Case.xls
Figures 7.2, 7.3, 7.4, and 7.5 Phenol Case.xls
Figures 8.1 and 8.2 Engraving Case.xls
Figure 8.3 Value Sharing.xls
Figure 9.2 Success Rates.xls
Figure 9.3 Percent of Projects Advancing in Portfolio.xls
Figure 10.1 a, b, and c Risk and Return for 2 Project Portfolio.xls
Figures 10.2 and 10.3 Correlated and Anticorrelated Businesses.xls
Figures 10.4 through 10.9 Markowitz Theory.xls
Figure 10.10 Diversifying Risk over Large Portfolios.xls
FSDTRO.xls
GROWTH.xls
MarkIBS.xls
Medical.xls
MedicalPatentCaseBS.xls
WACC.xls

MINIMUM SYSTEM REQUIREMENTS

Make sure that your computer meets the minimum system requirements listed in this section. If your computer doesn't match up to most of these requirements, you may have a problem using the contents of the CD.

For Windows 9*x*, Windows 2000, Windows NT4 (with SP 4 or later), Windows Me, or Windows XP:

- PC with a Pentium processor running at 120 Mhz or faster.
- At least 32 MB of total RAM installed on your computer; for best performance, we recommend at least 64 MB.
- Ethernet network interface card (NIC) or modem with a speed of at least 28,800 bps.
- A CD-ROM drive.

For Macintosh:

■ Mac OS computer with a 68040 or faster processor running OS 7.6 or later.
■ At least 32 MB of total RAM installed on your computer; for best performance, we recommend at least 64 MB.

USING THE CD WITH WINDOWS

To install the items from the CD to your hard drive, follow these steps:

1. Insert the CD into your computer's CD-ROM drive.
2. A window appears with the following options: Install, Explore, Links and Exit.
   Install: Gives you the option to install the supplied software and/or the author-created samples on the CD-ROM.
   Explore: Enables you to view the contents of the CD-ROM in its directory structure.
   Exit: Closes the autorun window.

If you do not have autorun enabled, or if the autorun window does not appear, follow these steps to access the CD:

1. Click Start @> Run.
2. In the dialog box that appears, type **d:\setup.exe**, where *d* is the letter of your CD-ROM drive. This brings up the autorun window described in the preceding set of steps.
3. Choose the Install, Explore, or Exit option from the menu. (See Step 2 in the preceding list for a description of these options.)

USING THE CD WITH THE MAC OS

To install the items from the CD to your hard drive, follow these steps:

1. Insert the CD into your CD-ROM drive.
2. Double-click the icon for the CD after it appears on the desktop.
3. Most programs come with installers; for those, simply open the program's folder on the CD and double-click the Install or Installer icon.
   Note: To install some programs, just drag the program's folder from the CD window and drop it on your hard drive icon.

TROUBLESHOOTING

If you have difficulty installing or using any of the materials on the companion CD, try the following solutions:

- **Turn off any anti-virus software that you may have running.** Installers sometimes mimic virus activity and can make your computer incorrectly believe that it is being infected by a virus. (Be sure to turn the antivirus software back on later.)
- **Close all running programs.** The more programs you're running, the less memory is available to other programs. Installers also typically update files and programs; if you keep other programs running, installation may not work properly.
- **Reference the ReadMe.** Please refer to the ReadMe file located at the root of the CD-ROM for the latest product information at the time of publication.

CUSTOMER CARE

If you have trouble with the CD-ROM, please call the Wiley Product Technical Support phone number at 800-762-2974. Outside the United States, call 317-572-3994. You can also contact Wiley Product Technical Support at http://www.wiley.com/techsupport. John Wiley & Sons will provide technical support only for installation and other general quality control items. For technical support on the applications themselves, consult the program's vendor or author.

To place additional orders or to request information about other Wiley products, please call 877-762-2974.

CUSTOMER NOTE

PLEASE READ THE FOLLOWING
This software contains files to help you utilize the models described in the accompanying book. By opening the package, you are agreeing to be bound by the following agreement:

This software product is protected by copyright and all rights are reserved by the author, John Wiley & Sons, Inc., or their licensors. You are licensed to use this software on a single computer. Copying the software to another medium or format for use on a single computer does not violate the U.S. Copyright Law. Copying the software for any other purpose is a violation of the U.S. Copyright Law.

This software product is sold as is without warranty of any kind, either express or implied, including but not limited to the implied warranty of merchantability and fitness for a particular purpose. Neither Wiley nor its dealers or distributors assumes any liability for any alleged or actual damages arising from the use of or the inability to use this software. (Some states do not allow the exclusion of implied warranties, so the exclusion may not apply to you.)

Notes

Preface

1. An exception: Lowell W. Steele, *Managing Technology: The Strategic View* (New York: McGraw-Hill, 1989).
2. Laurence J. Lau, "The Sources of Long-Term Economic Growth," in *The Mosaic of Economic Growth*, ed. R. Landau (Stanford, CA: Stanford University Press, 1996), 63–91.
3. Greg A. Stevens and James Burley, "3,000 Raw Ideas = 1 Commercial Success," *Research·Technology Management* (May–June 1997): 16–27.
4. Philip A. Roussel, Kamal N. Saad, and Tamara J. Erickson, *Third Generation R&D* (Boston: Harvard Business School Press, 1991), 97.
5. F. Peter Boer, *The Valuation of Technology: Business and Financial Issues in R&D* (New York: John Wiley & Sons, 1999).
6. F. Peter Boer, "Financial Management of R&D 2002," *Research·Technology Management* (July–August 2002): 23–35.
7. Robert G. Cooper, *Winning at New Products* (New York: Addison Wesley, 1993), 102–106.
8. F. Peter Boer, "Real Options: The IT Investment Risk-Buster," *Optimize* (July 2002): 64.
9. Books on real options include L. Trigeorgis, *Real Options: Managerial Flexibility and Strategy in Resource Allocation* (Cambridge, MA: MIT Press, 1998); M. Amram and N. Kulatilaka, *Real Options: Managing Strategic Investment in an Uncertain World* (Boston: Harvard Business School Press, 1999); T. Copeland and V. Antikarov, *Real Options: A Practitioner's Guide* (New York: Texere LLC, 2001); D. Newton, D. Paxson, S. Howell, M. Cavus, and A. Stack, *Real Options: Principles and Practice* (New York: Financial Times/Prentice Hall, 2001); J. Mun, *Real Options Analysis: Tools and Techniques for Valuing Strategic Investments and Decisions* (New York: John Wiley & Sons, 2002).

Chapter 1 "I'll Teach You the Value of Money"

1. Richard A. Brealey and Stewart C. Myers, *Principles of Corporate Finance*, 5th ed. (New York: McGraw-Hill, 1996), 34–50.

2. Ralph Landau, "Lessons from the Chemical Industry," in *The Mosaic of Economic Growth*, ed. R. Landau (Stanford, CA: Stanford University Press, 1996), 398–399.
3. Brealey and Myers, *Principles of Corporate Finance*, 180–188.
4. Ibid., 180.
5. With either form of royalty arrangement, BMX's payments will be tax deductible, making its investment even more attractive.
6. Tom Copeland, Tim Koller, and Jack Murrin, *Valuation: Measuring and Managing the Value of Companies*, 3rd ed. (New York: John Wiley & Sons, 2000), 221. This premium is significantly lower than that used by Brealey and Myers for reasons discussed in this text.
7. The data from A. Damodaran is from a web site referenced in Figure 1.3.

Chapter 2   Horizon Value by Five Methods

1. This term is also called "terminal value" or "residual value."
2. This approach differs from, but gives the same result as, the power series method presented in F. Peter Boer, *The Valuation of Technology: Business and Financial Issues in R&D* (New York: John Wiley & Sons, 1999), pp. 118–120.
3. The symbol ^ is used as in Excel to signify exponentiation.
4. Tom Copeland, Tim Koller, and Jack Murrin, *Valuation: Measuring and Managing the Value of Companies*, 3rd ed. (New York: John Wiley & Sons, 2000), 221.

Chapter 3   Factoring in the Risk

1. Books on real options include L. Trigeorgis, *Real Options: Managerial Flexibility and Strategy in Resource Allocation* (Cambridge, MA: MIT Press, 1998); M. Amram, and N. Kulatilaka, *Real Options: Managing Strategic Investment in an Uncertain World* (Boston: Harvard Business School Press, 1999); T. Copeland, and V. Antikarov, *Real Options: A Practitioner's Guide* (New York: Texere LLC, 2001); D. Newton, D. Paxson, S. Howell, M. Cavus, and A. Stack, *Real Options: Principles and Practice* (New York: Financial Times/Prentice Hall, 2001); J. Mun, *Real Options Analysis: Tools and Techniques for Valuing Strategic Investments and Decisions* (New York: John Wiley & Sons, 2002).
2. F. Peter Boer, *The Valuation of Technology: Financial Issues in R&D* (New York: John Wiley & Sons, 1999), 290–297.
3. Robert G. Cooper, *Winning at New Products: Accelerating the Process from Idea to Launch*, 2nd ed. (Reading, MA: Addison Wesley, 1993). A

recent brochure from Stage-Gate, Inc., claims that 70 percent of U.S. companies have adopted this method.

4. F. Peter Boer, *The Real Options Solution: Finding Total Value in a High-Risk World* (New York: John Wiley & Sons, 2002), 137–163.

5. R. Balachandra and Klaus Brockhoff, "Are R&D Project Termination Factors Universal?" *Research·Technology Management* (July–August 1995): 31.

6. Richard A. Brealey and Stewart C. Myers, *Principles of Corporate Finance*, 5th ed. (New York: McGraw-Hill, 1996), 255–264.

7. Ibid., 578.

8. Sheldon Natenberg, *Option Volatility and Pricing* (New York: McGraw-Hill, 1994), Appendix B.

9. Brealey and Myers, *Principles of Corporate Finance*.

10. Ibid., 590–591.

11. Brealey and Myers, apparently inadvertently, used a risk-free rate of 10 percent in their calculation, although the text refers to a 5 percent interest rate. I will use the 10 percent rate for consistency.

12. Although this number may at first seem astronomical, it must be viewed in the context of an option to invest nearly $5 billion. Even valuations "turbocharged" by optionality have sensible business limits.

13. Recall the gross cost of R&D Stage 2 was $1 million, which was discounted at the cost of capital (12 percent) to –$0.399 + –$0.356 = –$0.754. But this is the *net present value* of the strike price. The strike price is related to its net present value in the Black-Scholes algorithm by the risk-free rate (5 percent) over the two-year duration of this stage, yielding for the strike price –$0.754 × –1.050^2 = –$0.792. This treatment of the R&D strike price is essential to ensuring the identity of decision tree with decision tree/real options methods.

Chapter 4   Medical Device Case Study: A New Product for a New Application

1. Compliant with the Food and Drug Administration's Good Manufacturing Practices.

2. If it were not for the timing effect of the tax deduction for depreciation, discounted cash flow analysis would be independent of depreciation schedules. Generally the resulting NPV is not significantly affected, but will be slightly higher for faster depreciation schedules. This can be tested easily in the accompanying spreadsheets.

3. The Excel workbook Medical.xls includes a decision tree/real options (DTRO) valuation of this project. However, because the economics are

very much in-the-money, real options add very little value to the decision tree result.

4. Greg A. Stevens and James Burley, "3,000 Raw Ideas = 1 Commercial Success," *Research•Technology Management* (May–June 1997): 16–27.

Chapter 5   A New Product for an Existing Application

1. Crystal Ball, Decisioneering, Inc., Boulder, Colorado.
2. Using prices of $0.25 and $0.70 per pound for steel and aluminum respectively.
3. OEM is common parlance for automobile companies.
4. See worksheet "DTROCalcs" of Figures 5.2, 5.3, and 5.4 Case 8 Polyarothene FSDTRO.xls for the after-tax, time-discounted figures. Note also that all times are relative to the middle of year 0. Hence the conceptual stage expense is discounted 1.5 years, as its midpoint occurs at the end of year 1. The feasibility stage is discounted 3.5 years, and so on. The NPV is discounted 8 years, as year 0 of the commercial phase corresponds to year 8 of R&D.
5. David Aboody and Baruch Lev, "R&D Productivity in the Chemical Industry," in *Measuring Up: Research & Development Counts for the Chemical Industry* (Washington, DC: Council for Chemical Research, 2001), 26.
6. Robert Carter and David Edwards, "Financial Analysis Extends Management of R&D," *Research•Technology Management* (September–October 2001): 47–57.
7. John R. Gibbons, Keynote Address, ONR Investing in the Future 1946–1996: A Symposium (Washington, DC: National Academy of Sciences, 1996), 5–8.

Chapter 6   Start-Ups

1. John L. Nesheim, *High Tech Start-Up: The Complete How-to Handbook for Creating Successful New High Tech Companies* (Saratoga, CA: John Nesheim, 1997).
2. Richard A. Brealey and Stewart C. Myers, *Principles of Corporate Finance*, 5th ed. (New York: McGraw-Hill, 1996), 173–188.
3. Robert Kunze, *Nothing Ventured* (New York: HarperCollins, 1990).
4. William D. Bygrave and Jeffry A. Timmons, *Venture Capital at the Crossroads* (Boston: Harvard Business School Press, 1992), 16–21.
5. Ibid., 67–93.
6. Ibid., 20.
7. Contact Recombinant Capital, San Francisco, California, Mark Edwards, managing director.

8. Bygrave and Timmons, *Venture Capital*, 165.
9. Nesheim, *High Tech Start-Up.*
10. In 1982–1983, the author was negotiating for W. R. Grace with Genentech on development of novel technology for the production of phenylalanine (the principal market was aspartame). Pro forma financial statements and an analysis of development costs played a major role in Grace's negotiating position, but the tools described here had yet to be fully developed.

Chapter 7 Process Breakthrough!

1. June 15, 2001—Qatar Petroleum and ExxonMobil Corporation announced today that they have signed a letter of intent (LOI) to conduct a technical feasibility study for a world-scale gas-to-liquids (GTL) plant in Qatar. (From press release.)
2. Posted at www.cmt.anl.gov/science-technology/basicsci/one-step-phenol.shtml.
3. This is consistent with the 0.6 power-scaling algorithm.
4. Peter Spitz, *Petrochemicals: The Rise of an Industry* (New York: John Wiley & Sons, 1988), 543.

Chapter 8 Improved Products

1. Nigel Palmer, private communication.
2. Michael E. Porter, *The Competitive Advantage of Nations* (New York: Free Press, 1990), 40–44.
3. See http://fisher.osu.edu/~allenby_1/value.pdf.
4. John Busch and Gabe Tincher, "Winning in Industrial Markets," *Research•Technology Management* (July–August 1998): 48–54.
5. Denier is the weight in grams of 9,000 meters of yarn. A lower denier signifies a lighter fiber.
6. Maine Sailing Partners, www.mesailing.com.
7. Richard A. Razgaitis, *Early Stage Technologies, Valuation and Pricing* (New York: John Wiley & Sons, 1999), 98.
8. Globally, there is a host of cracking furnace designs, reflecting type of feedstock, plant size, and engineering design.
9. Michael McCoy, "New Cracker Highlights Optimism," *Chemical and Engineering News* 78, no. 50, (December 11, 2000): 22–23.
10. ChemSystems Reports, "PERP Program—New Report Alert" (August 2003), www.chemsystems.com.
11. Ibid.

12. ERTC Petrochemical 2002 Conference, February 20–22, 2002, Hilton Hotel, Amsterdam, Netherlands.
13. Gary Hamel and C. J. Prahaladad, *Competing for the Future* (Boston: Harvard Business School Press, 1994), 203–204.
14. Ralph Gomory and Roland Schmitt are former CTOs of IBM and General Electric, respectively.
15. Frank Press, "Research Universities and the New Era," speech presented at North Carolina State University, Raleigh, North Carolina, April 17, 1999.
16. Alan B. Fowler is an IBM Fellow Emeritus at IBM in Yorktown Heights, New York. Copyright © 1995, American Physical Society, www.aps.org/apsnews/1295/129513.cfm.

Chapter 9   Balanced R&D Portfolios

1. Robert G. Cooper, Scott J. Edgett, and Elko J. Kleinschmidt, "New Problems, New Solutions: Making Portfolio Management More Effective," *Research·Technology Management* (March–April 2000): 18–33.
2. F. P. Boer, "The Culture Called Specialty Chemicals," *CHEMTEC* (1989): 75–78.
3. David Seifert did this work on an early vintage IBM PC.
4. F. Peter Boer, *The Valuation of Technology: Business and Financial Issues in R&D* (New York: John Wiley & Sons, 1999), 239.
5. F. Peter Boer, "Linking R&D to Growth and Shareholder Value," *Research·Technology Management* (May–June, 1994): 16.
6. Boer, *Valuation of Technology*, 348–350.
7. Ray E. Clouse, "Parenteral Nutrition," in *Cecil Textbook of Medicine*, ed. J. B. WynGaarden and L. H. Smith, vol. 2 (Philadelphia: W. B. Saunders Company, 1985), 1215–1218.
8. Produced from aspartic acid (also an amino acid), phenylalanine, and methanol.
9. This would be 2-benzylhydantoin, based on Grace's expertise in cyanide chemistry.
10. F. P. Boer, L. L. Hegedus, T. R. Gouker and K. P. Zak, "Controlling Power Plant NO_x Emissions," *CHEMTEC* (1990): 312–319.
11. F. Peter Boer, "Acid Rain Control Technologies," Hearings before Committee on Environment and Public Works, United States Senate re Clean Air Standards Attainment Act of 1987, S. 1894, March 4, 1987.
12. The *Portsmouth Herald* (New Hampshire) editorialized (October 6, 1987) that SCR would cost 862,000 jobs by the year 2000 and reduce gross domestic product (GDP) by $223 billion.
13. The abbreviations stand for sulfur oxides and nitrogen oxides.

14. This business was sold to Engelhard Corporation.

15. The author made it a condition for research support that human cloning was not an objective and would not be explored, nor would researchers publicly speculate about it. We also recognized a possible ethical issue and technical risk in reducing the biodiversity of the herd, but considered this problem manageable.

16. See www.hematech.com.

17. Lee Iacocca, *Iacocca* (New York: Bantam Books, 1984), 251–263.

18. James M. Utterback, *Mastering the Dynamics of Innovation* (Boston: Harvard Business School Press, 1994), 142–143.

19. Marc H. Meyer and Paul C. Mugge, "Make Platform Innovation Drive Enterprise Growth," *Research·Technology Management* (January–February 2001): 25–40.

20. Ibid., 39.

21. Robert G. Cooper, Scott J. Edgett and Elko J. Kleinschmidt, "Best Practices for Managing R&D Portfolios," *Research·Technology Management* (July–August 1998): 20–33.

22. An example of this approach is outlined by Ian C. MacMillan and Rita Gunther McGrath, "Crafting R&D Project Portfolios," *Research·Technology Management* (September–October 2002): 48–59.

23. Cooper, Edgett, and Kleinschmidt, "Best Practices," 29. The authors find that "top performers" rely much less on financial models, while average performers use them more extensively. However, top performance is defined by degree of user satisfaction on a questionnaire, a criterion less convincing than top *financial* performance.

24. Robert G. Cooper, Scott J. Edgett, and Elko J. Kleinschmidt, *Portfolio Management—Fundamental to New Product Success*, Working Paper 12, July 2001, Ancaster, Ontario, Canada, 5.

25. Gary L. Tritle, Eric F. V. Scriven, and Alan R. Fusfeld, "Resolving Uncertainty in R&D Portfolios," *Research·Technology Management* (November–December 2000): 47.

26. Cooper, Edgett, and Kleinschmidt, "Best Practices," 29.

27. Timothy Luehrman, "Strategy as a Portfolio of Real Options," *Harvard Business Review* (September–October 1998): 89–99; F. Peter Boer, *The Real Options Solution* (New York: John Wiley & Sons, 2002), Chapter 6.

28. Philip A. Roussel, Kamal N. Saad, and Tamara J. Erickson, *Third Generation R&D* (Boston: Harvard Business School Press, 1991), 93–112.

29. James E. Matheson and Michael M. Menke, "Using Decision Quality Principles to Balance Your R&D Portfolio," *Research·Technology Management* (May–June 1994): 38–43.

30. Cooper, Edgett, and Kleinschmidt, *Portfolio Management*, 10.
31. Tritle, Scriven, and Fusfeld, "Resolving Uncertainty," 51.
32. Ibid., 93–121.
33. Cooper, Edgett, and Kleinschmidt, *Portfolio Management*, 6.
34. Probability of success is defined in this book as the probability of moving to the next gate, based on both technical and commercial factors. It measures unique (diversifiable) risk. Market (undiversifiable) risk is handled differently using the real options tool, which recognizes its ability to increase value.
35. In addition to a best (50 percent probability) value, experts estimate a range where a parameter has only a 10 percent probability of being achieved, and another where there is a 90 percent probability.
36. Robert G. Cooper, *Winning at New Products* (New York: Addison Wesley, 1993), Appendixes A, B, and C, 177–178.

Chapter 10 Optimum Portfolios and the Efficient Frontier

1. Richard A. Brealey and Stewart C. Myers, *Principles of Corporate Finance*, 5th Edition (New York: McGraw-Hill, 1996), 165.
2. Ibid., 158.
3. This template is adapted from one developed by Edwin Straver, Frontline Systems, Inc.
4. A good description is included in the chapter "Non-linear Regression Using the Solver" in Joseph E. Billo, *Excel for Chemists* (New York: Wiley VCH, 1997).
5. Bruce D. Henderson, Boston Consulting Group, Inc., 1974.
6. David Aboody and Baruch Lev, "R&D Productivity in the Chemical Industry," in *Measuring Up: Research & Development Counts for the Chemical Industry*, (Washington, DC: Council for Chemical Research, 2001), 26.
7. "Alliances bring together different knowledge and resource capabilities and create a much more powerful entity than you have in a stand-alone organization," says Darryl Harrison, leader of research and development for NOVA Chemicals. "It's a very astute way of doing R and D." (*Plastics Progress*, Winter 2000).
8. Robert Carter and David Edwards, "Financial Analysis Extends Management of R&D," *Research·Technology Management* (September-October 2001): 47–57.
9. Samuel B. Graves, Jeffrey L. Ringuest, and Randolph H. Case, "Formulating Optimal R&D Portfolios," *Research·Technology Management* (May–June 2000): 47–51; Jeffrey L. Ringuest, Samuel B. Graves,

and Randolph H. Case, "Formulating R&D Portfolios That Account for Risk," *Research•Technology Management* (November–December 1999): 40–43.
10. Using the Crystal Ball add-on from Decisioneering, Inc.

About the CD-ROM

1. See the chapter "Non-linear Regression Using the Solver" in Joseph E. Billo, *Excel for Chemists* (New York: Wiley VCH, 1997).
2. Stephen G. Powell and Kenneth R. Baker, *The Art of Modeling with Spreadsheets* (Hoboken, NJ: John Wiley & Sons, 2004).

About the Author

Dr. F. Peter Boer is the author of *The Valuation of Technology* and *The Real Options Solution* (both published by John Wiley & Sons), as well as nearly one hundred articles in the scientific and business literature. Some of his more recent articles may be downloaded at his web site (www.boer.org).

Dr. F. Peter Boer has extensive practical experience in the valuation of R&D projects and portfolios, from the differing perspectives of an R&D practitioner, a senior R&D executive, a senior business executive, and a member of the board of directors. In recent years he has focused on issues in R&D finance, including the development of business models for early-stage projects, decision and risk analysis, and real options.

Dr. Boer is also president and CEO of Tiger Scientific Inc., a firm providing consulting and investment services in the technology arena. Current or recent clients include DuPont, Medtronic, UOP, Crompton Corporation, Atofina, Air Products and Chemicals, United Technologies, Purdue Pharmaceutical, W. R. Grace & Company, and Hydro-Quebec.

He has served as the John J. Lee Adjunct Professor in the School of Engineering at Yale University (where he taught environmental engineering) and in addition taught technology valuation at the Yale School of Management

He has had extensive operating and technical experience with three Fortune 100 companies: Dow Chemical Company, American Can Company, and W. R. Grace & Company. He was executive vice president and chief technical officer of W. R. Grace & Company with responsibilities for R&D, engineering, business development, environment, health, and safety. At Dow, he had profit-and-loss responsibilities for eight individual operating businesses with revenues exceeding $350 million (1978 dollars). At American Can, his responsibilities included the entire R&D organization and the lignin chemicals business.

He has served on the board of directors of two multibillion-dollar corporations, W. R. Grace and NOVA Chemical, and dealt directly with critical issues such as CEO succession, management compensation and incentives, corporate finance, capital planning, and R&D planning. He is also a board member of ENSCO, Inc., which specializes in signal processing and sensor-based systems; Rhodes Technologies, Inc., and Scientific Protein Laboratories, manufacturers of bulk active pharmaceutical ingredients; and LaureatePharma, a manufacturer of biopharmaceuticals.

Dr. Boer is a former president of the Industrial Research Institute, an organization of 280 technically based companies in the United States and Canada, whose members perform approximately 85 percent of the industrial R&D in the United States. He has been twice appointed as chairman of the National Medal of Technology Evaluation Committee (under Presidents Bush and Clinton, who presented the awards). His government-related service includes advisory bodies for the Los Alamos National Laboratory, the Sandia National Laboratory, the Environmental Protection Agency, the Department of Commerce, the Board on Manufacturing and Engineering Design (National Research Council), and the National Technology Transfer Center. Dr. Boer was elected in 1993 to the National Academy of Engineering.

He has served, or is serving, on advisory committees of Harvard University, Princeton University, the University of Chicago, Johns Hopkins University, the Georgia Institute of Technology, and Texas A&M University. He holds an AB degree in physics from Princeton University and a PhD in chemical physics from Harvard University, where he did research in boron hydride chemistry that contributed to Professor W. N. Lipscomb's 1976 Nobel Prize in Chemistry.

Index